# Masters

# Masters

## The Invisible War of the Powerful Against their Subjects

MARCO D'ERAMO

Translated by Alice Kilgarriff

polity

Originally published in Italian as *Dominio: La guerra invisibile dei potenti contro i suddti* © Giangiacomo Feltrinelli Editore Milano, October 2020

This English edition © Polity Press, 2024

This work has been translated with the contribution of the Centre for Books and Reading of the Italian Ministry of Culture.

The translation of this work has been funded by SEPS
Segretariato Europeo per le Pubblicazioni Scientifiche

Via Val d'Aposa 7 – 40123 Bologna – Italy
seps@seps.it – www.seps.it

Polity Press
65 Bridge Street
Cambridge CB2 1UR, UK

Polity Press
111 River Street
Hoboken, NJ 07030, USA

ISBN-13: 978-1-5095-5743-1 – hardback
ISBN-13: 978-1-5095-5744-8 – paperback

A catalogue record for this book is available from the British Library.

Library of Congress Control Number: 2023936984

Typeset in 11 on 14pt Warnock Pro
by Cheshire Typesetting Ltd, Cuddington, Cheshire
Printed and bound in Great Britain by TJ Books Ltd, Padstow, Cornwall

The publisher has used its best endeavours to ensure that the URLs for external websites referred to in this book are correct and active at the time of going to press. However, the publisher has no responsibility for the websites and can make no guarantee that a site will remain live or that the content is or will remain appropriate.

Every effort has been made to trace all copyright holders, but if any have been overlooked the publisher will be pleased to include any necessary credits in any subsequent reprint or edition.

For further information on Polity, visit our website:
politybooks.com

# Contents

*Prologue*                                                    vii

1. Counterintelligentsia                                        1
2. Ideas Are Weapons                                           23
3. The Justice Market                                          50
4. Trigger-Happy Parents                                       66
5. The Tyranny of Benevolence                                  76
6. *Capitale sive Natura*                                      88
7. The Politics Pricelist                                     112
8. Arsenic and Witchcraft I: The Remote-Control
   Society                                                    126
9. Arsenic and Witchcraft II: Do Not Forgive Us Our
   Debts as We Do Not Forgive Those Indebted to Us            136
10. And They All Lived Antily Ever After                      159
11. Social Pornography                                        183
12. The Circular Thought of the Economic Circuit              193
13. The Game is Rigged. However . . .                         212
14. Time to Learn from Your Enemies                           222

Postscript: In the Name of the Father, the Son and the Bank
Account                                                      234

*Bibliography*                                               254
*Index*                                                      266

# Prologue

When we hear the word *revolution*, we invariably think of the oppressed rising up against their oppressors, of subjects overthrowing the powerful, the dominated rebelling against those dominating them. We imagine the Levellers who decapitated King Charles I in London in 1649; the *sans-culottes* of Paris who stormed the Bastille in 1789 and condemned King Louis XVI to the guillotine in 1793; the black slaves in Haiti who in 1791 set fire to their masters' plantations and declared independence for the nation in 1801; the Bolsheviks who took the Winter Palace in St Petersburg in 1917 and shot Tzar Nicholas II in Ekaterinburg in 1918; the Cuban *barbudos* who attacked the Moncada barracks in 1953 and chased out dictator Fulgencio Batista in 1959.

But in reality, there is not just one kind of revolution; there are two and they are opposites, as Aristotle observed some 2,400 years ago in a splendid (and inexplicably ignored) passage of *Politics*: 'The universal and chief cause of this revolutionary feeling has been already mentioned; viz. the desire of equality, when men think that they are equal to others who have more than themselves; or, again, the desire of inequality and superiority, when conceiving themselves to be superior they think that they have not more but the same or less than their inferiors; pretensions which may and may not be just. *Inferiors revolt in order that they may be equal, and equals that they may be superior.*[1] Those who are dominated rebel because they are not equal enough; those who dominate revolt because they are too equal. 'For the weaker are always asking for equality and justice, but the stronger care for none of these things.'[2]

Seeing this is both shocking and enlightening. It opens up the horizon of a revolution from those above against those below. Aristotle makes a further point: 'Now, in oligarchies the masses make revolution under the idea that they are unjustly treated, because, as I said before, they are equals, and have not an equal share, and in democracies the notables revolt, because they are not equals, and yet have only an equal share.'[3] This suggests that when confronted with what they perceive as too strong a push for democracy, the dominant react and revolt against the dominated.

My thesis here is that the last fifty years have seen the enactment of a colossal revolution of the rich against the poor, masters against servants, the dominant against the dominated. This revolution has been invisible, a 'stealth' revolution, as US philosopher Wendy Brown calls it,[4] using language borrowed from military aviation. Stealth bombers do not show up on radar. The military metaphor is appropriate because it has been a real war, even if it has been fought without us noticing. However, none other than Warren Buffett, one of the wealthiest men in the world, acknowledged it fourteen years ago, candidly telling a *New York Times* reporter that: 'There's class warfare

---

[1] Aristotle, *Politics*, Book V (trans. Benjamin Jowett). Oxford: Clarendon Press, 1885. Available at: https://www.files.ethz.ch/isn/125519/5013_Aristotle_Politics.pdf, p. 137

[2] Ibid., Book V, p. 157.

[3] Ibid., Book V, p. 139.

[4] Wendy Brown, *Undoing the Demos: Neoliberalism's Stealth Revolution*. New York: Zone Books, 2015.

all right, but it's my class, the rich class, that's making war, and we're winning.'[5] Five years later, in 2011, Buffett doubled down and stated that the rich were no longer just winning the war: 'Actually, there's been class warfare going on for the last 20 years, and my class has won. [...] If there's class warfare, the rich class has won.' The *Washington Post* columnist goes on to comment: 'if there's been any class warfare in this country, it has been waged from the top down for decades, and the rich have won'.[6] This is not some fanatic talking about class warfare from the top down, but a protagonist of that very war: their victory is so total that they can talk about it openly. We, on the other hand, are too ashamed to mention it, not least because we risk being suspected immediately of extremism.

This all-out ideological warfare is the story I want to relate here. Like any war, it has required planning, strategies, choices of battlefield and the careful use of crises. As Barack Obama's former Chief of Staff Rahm Emanuel said: 'You never want a serious crisis to go to waste.'[7] Never waste a shortage, an insolvency, an attack; definitely don't waste a financial crisis or pandemic.

The story of this war begins with the United States, because it is the empire of our age and all other countries are its variously docile or unruly subjects. What's more, one of the effects the victory of the dominant has delivered is that it renders us oblivious to our own subjugation and clouds our perception of power relations. Thank goodness Donald Trump arrived to

---

[5] Ben Stein, 'In Class Warfare, Guess Which Class Is Winning', *The New York Times*, 26 November 2006, https://www.nytimes.com/2006/11/26/business/yourmoney/26every.html.

[6] Greg Sargent, 'There's been class warfare for the last 20 years, and my class has won', *The Washington Post*, 30 September 2011, https://www.washingtonpost.com/blogs/plum-line/post/theres-been-class-warfare-for-the-last-20-years-and-my-class-has-won/2011/03/03/gIQApaFbAL_blog.html.

[7] He said this in 2008 during the most acute stage of the financial crisis, inspiring Philip Mirowski's book, *Never Let a Serious Crisis Go to Waste: How Neoliberalism Survived the Financial Meltdown*. London: Verso, 2013.

remind us of the tyranny, arrogance and callousness of every imperial domination. Still, not even his breath-taking vulgarity could rouse us from our intellectual torpor. If we want proof, we need merely observe the Western left: what remains of it is now entirely Thatcherite, having adopted the slogan T.I.N.A. – there is no alternative – made famous by the Iron Lady and internalized by global financial capitalism as the only possible future for the planet. As Mark Fisher, who is sadly missed, put it in *Capitalism Realism*, 'It's easier to imagine the end of the world than the end of capitalism.'[8] There is an abyss separating us from the 1960s, when the economist John Kenneth Galbraith wrote that 'With regard to the designation "liberal", almost everyone now so describes himself' (1964).[9] Fifty years later, the word liberal has become an insult.

How did this reversal happen? We tend to attribute it to megatrends, from globalization and the new digital revolution to long-term objective and statistical phenomena, not least because this interpretation consoles the Marxist who still lives within us. In fact, it happened because one side waged a war that the other side didn't notice. And why didn't we notice? Because of the tendency that prevails in so-called progressive opinion: we underestimate adversaries, dismissing the right's victories as 'belly aching', 'exasperation', 'resentment' or 'ignorance' without recognizing the long-term trends. We have been unable to see the wood for the trees.

---

[8] Mark Fisher, *Capitalist Realism: Is There No Alternative?* Winchester: Zero Books, 2009, p. 1.
[9] Cited by Lewis H. Lapham in his wonderful essay 'Tentacles of Rage: The Republican Propaganda Mill, A Brief History', *Harper's Magazine*, September 2004, pp. 31–41, p. 31.

*The terms of the social compact between these two estates of men may be summed up in a few words. 'You have need of me, because I am rich and you are poor. We will therefore come to an agreement. I will permit you to have the honour of serving me, on condition that you bestow on me the little you have left, in return for the pains I shall take to command you.'*

Jean-Jacques Rousseau,
*Discourse on Political Economy* (1755)*

* Jean-Jacques Rousseau, *Discourse on Political Economy*, available at: https://www.files.ethz.ch/isn/125495/5020_Rousseau_A_Discourse_on_Political_Economy.pdf (my italics), p. 19.

# 1

# Counterintelligentsia

The ideological defeat is so absolute that the left has arrived at the point where it is ashamed of its own ideology. We have been so thoroughly convinced that 'ideology' is a dirty word that we no longer dare use it, when instead ideology's critical importance is recognized even by the Pentagon.

## The Marines Study Ideology

This is a direct quote from the official US Army/Marine Corps Counterinsurgency Field Manual, written by Generals David H. Petraeus and James Ames (2007):

> Ideas are a motivating factor [. . .]. Insurgencies gather recruits and amass popular support through ideological appeal. [. . .] The movement's ideology explains its followers' tribulations and provides a course of action to remedy those ills. The most powerful ideologies tap latent, emotive concerns of the populace, such as the desire for justice, religious beliefs, or liberation from foreign occupation. Ideology provides a prism, including a vocabulary and analytical categories, through which

the situation is assessed. As such, ideology can shape the movement's organization and operational methods [. . .] The central mechanism through which ideologies are expressed and absorbed is the narrative. A narrative is an organizational scheme expressed in story form. Narratives are central to the representation of identity [. . .] (1-65–1-66).

The manual returns repeatedly to the *narrative*, particularly in the chapter on Intelligence:

> The most important cultural form for COIN [Counter Insurgency] forces to understand is the narrative. A cultural narrative is a story recounted in the form of a causally linked set of events that explains an event in a group's history and expresses the values, character, or self-identity of the group. Narratives are the means through which ideologies are expressed and absorbed by individuals in a society. [. . .] By listening to narratives, COIN forces can identify the basic core values of the society (3-51).[1]

What is most interesting (and disconcerting) is how, in their use of the language and jargon of the US human sciences, they draw on two fundamental theses expressed by French Marxist philosopher Louis Althusser 50 years ago: (a) 'Ideology is a "Representation" of the Imaginary Relationship of Individuals to their Real Conditions of Existence'; (b) 'all ideology has the function (which defines it) of "constituting" concrete individuals as subjects'[2] (referred to in the Manual as 'subjects of insurgence').

---

[1] D.H. Petraeus and James Ames, *FM-324 Counterinsurgency*, can be downloaded here: https://fas.org/irp/doddir/army/fm3-24fd.pdf. In hard copy, *The U.S. Army/Marine Corps Counterinsurgency Field Manual*. Chicago, IL: University of Chicago Press, 2007.

[2] Louis Althusser, 'Ideology and Ideological State Apparatuses (Notes Towards an Investigation)', in *On Ideology*. London: Verso, 2008, pp. 1–60, citations are from pp. 36 and 45.

The upshot is that we always have an ideology, whether we want it or not, hence why no one can say 'I am not ideological'. When you do not adhere voluntarily to an ideology (such as a religion), you adhere to one involuntarily. We 'breathe' ideology, and usually one ideology that denies itself as such. Indeed, it thrives precisely by denying itself to be one while labelling all other 'representations' as ideologisms. So, while even the marines have to learn how important ideology is, the Western left clutches its pearls, accusing its own cultural and political legacy of ideologism!

In some ways, we might view the ideological war unleashed against the left, fought and resoundingly won over the last 50 years, to have been precisely a form of counter-insurgency, a reaction to the movements in the 1960s. This war was fought and won first and foremost in the United States.

What follows is not the umpteenth history of the crushing advance of the reactionary right in the US, a story that has been told a million times over. These tales are often decentred, focusing more on the alliances rather than the battlefield, more on the armies than on the potential spoils of war. Instead, we will concentrate on the ideological side of the conflict and on everything that has happened in the United States, yes, but which is of planetary significance.

Notice of the conflict was first given by John Merrill Olin (1892–1982), owner of the corporation bearing his name that specialized in chemical and military industries (caustic soda, defoliants for the army and, most importantly, the Winchester weapons and munitions brand), founded in Illinois and eventually relocated to Missouri.

Created in 1953, Olin's foundation remained pretty much inactive until 1969, the year when the magnate was appalled to see a photo of black militants carrying rifles with bandoliers of bullets strapped across their chests as they occupied the Dean's office at Cornell University, where he had studied as a young man. Let's remind ourselves of how America must have seemed to a capitalist at that time: universities in turmoil, black ghettos in revolt, the war in Vietnam hurtling towards a dishonourable defeat, and Robert Kennedy and Martin Luther King killed the year before. It is understandable, then, that the photo from Cornell shook John Olin and led him to provide his foundation with renewed means and a new objective: that of bringing order back to the universities.

Unlike other foundations, which were built to last, John Olin wanted his resources to be spent within a generation from his death, and so the foundation was officially dissolved in 2005, but not before distributing more than $370 million to promote causes favoured by the extreme right. To take up such political positions was new in the world of foundations, which until then had been devoted to charitable donations, such as buying new works of art, building hospitals, financing study grants or shoring up the actions of the American government (and its secret services) at home and abroad, but always maintaining a semblance of political neutrality, as in the case of the Rockefeller and Ford foundations.

## *That Fatal Memorandum of 1971*

The actions of the Olin Foundation remained isolated, however, at least until 1971; or more precisely, 23 August 1971, the date cited by official history as the starting point for the great conservative counter-offensive. That day, Lewis F. Powell Jr. wrote a confidential memorandum to the US Chamber of Commerce titled *Attack on American Free Enterprise System.*[3]

---

[3] The pdf of the Memorandum can be downloaded from many sites, such as https://www.historyisaweapon.com/defcon1/powellmemo.html or https://www.greenpeace.org/usa/democracy/the-lewis-powell-memo-a-corporate-blueprint-to-dominate-democracy/. All citations that follow are taken from the Memorandum unless directly specified.

Powell (1907–1998) was a Virginia lawyer who specialized in defending the tobacco industries (he was a member of the board for Philip Morris between 1962 and 1971) and, as such, he had made an archenemy of Ralph Nader's consumer defence movement. Two months after writing his Memorandum, Powell was named a Supreme Court judge by Richard Nixon, a position he held until 1987.

The novelty of this Memorandum is that Powell's fury wasn't directed so much at extremists, as moderates:

> We are not dealing with sporadic or isolated attacks from a relatively few extremists or even from the minority socialist cadre [. . .] The most disquieting voices joining the chorus of criticism come from perfectly respectable elements of society: from the college campus, the pulpit, the media, the intellectual and literary journals, the arts and sciences, and from politicians. [. . .] Although New Leftist spokesmen are succeeding in radicalizing thousands of the young, the greater cause for concern is the hostility of respectable liberals and social reformers. It is the sum total of their views and influence which could indeed fatally weaken or destroy the system.

(He continues, 'a chilling description of what is being taught on many of our campuses'.)

As happens to all those who prevaricate, from the Italian *Lega* who feel victimized by immigrants, to Israelis who feel victimized by the Palestinians, Powell also felt that American businessmen were victims, circled and in danger of extinction: 'One does not exaggerate to say that, in terms of political influence with respect to the course of legislation and government action, the American business executive is truly the "forgotten man".'

The businessmen must, therefore, equip themselves for something to which they are not accustomed: '[They] are not trained or equipped to conduct guerrilla warfare with those who propagandize against the system, seeking insidiously and constantly to sabotage it.' As such, 'it is essential that spokesmen for the enterprise system – at all levels and at every opportunity – be far more aggressive than in the past'. And the main battlegrounds would be universities and the ideas that they produce because 'the campus is the single most dynamic source', and because the ideas learnt at university by 'these bright young men' will then be used 'to change a system which they have been taught to distrust', 'they seek employment in the centers of the real power and influence in our country, namely: (i) with the news media, especially television; (ii) in government, as "staffers" and consultants at various levels; (iii) in elective politics; (iv) as lecturers and writers, and (v) on the faculties at various levels of education'. And 'In many instances, these "intellectuals" end up in regulatory agencies or governmental departments with large authority over the business system they do not believe in.'

For this 'guerrilla warfare', William E. Simon (1927–2000), who was Secretary of the Treasury under Richard Nixon before becoming president of the Olin Foundation, coined the term *counterintelligentsia* (taken from the military notion of counterinsurgency) because 'Ideas are weapons – indeed, the only weapons with which other ideas can be fought.'[4]

Powell states that to fight this guerrilla war, 'business must learn the lesson, long ago learned by labor [. . .] This is the lesson that political power is necessary; that such power must be assiduously cultivated; and that when necessary, it must be used aggressively and with determination – without embarrassment and without reluctance [. . .]'. Once it has been established that 'strength lies in organization, in careful long-range planning and implementation, in consistency of action

---

[4] John J. Miller, *A Gift of Freedom: How the John Olin Foundation Changed America*. New York: W.W. Norton & Co., 2009, p. 56.

over an indefinite period of years, in the scale of financing available only through joint effort, and in the political power available only through united action and national organizations', Powell went on to articulate the objective of how to 'restor[e] the balance' in universities through the financing of courses, departments, professorial roles, textbooks, essays and magazines. He then broadened the remit to include secondary education, the media, television, advertising and politics, making justice for businessmen more palatable across the board. In short, he outlined 'total warfare', a von Clausewitz strategy for the reconquest of ideological hegemony.

## The Midwest Enters the Fray

Powell's appeal resonated.[5] Not in exactly the way he had proposed – a centralized, national coordination of counterintelligentsia by the US Chamber of Commerce, a sort of Leninist party of the businessmen – as that would have been a slavish (not to mention outdated) imitation of the early twentieth-century Bolshevik structures. It was instead taken up by a handful of billionaires from middle America.

We must be clear that we are not talking here of a plot; there are no hidden motives or conspiracy theories. Everything happened in broad daylight; the movement of funds are available to everyone, detailed official budgets that can be downloaded online. The objectives met and the methods with which to meet them – strategies and victories – are praised in numerous self-congratulatory articles by institutions that are the protagonists of this counterintelligentsia.

---

[5] The attack of the ruling classes on left-wing ideas certainly began before 1971. You just need to look at nineteenth-century newspapers to see that 'the war between capital and work', as they call it in the US, was already an age-old conflict. This 'narrative' from 1971 is actually like an autobiography of the reactionary right.

Of those financing the conservative revolution, we have already met John Olin who moved between Illinois and Missouri. The other five families who exerted the most influence on the reactionary counter-offensive were the Mellon Scaifes (Pittsburgh, Pennsylvania), the Bradleys (Wisconsin), the Coors (Colorado), the Smith Richardsons (North Carolina) and the Kochs (Kansas).

These are only the most aggressive and ostentatious of the 'assault foundations'. However, we could also include the foundations of the Earharts (Michigan) and McKennas (Pennsylvania), as well as the JM Foundation (Virginia). Soon to join the conservative front were the Waltons (Arkansas), the DeVoses (Michigan) and a myriad of other magnates.

Among these five families, the most considerable wealth is held in Pittsburgh by the four foundations of the Mellon Scaife family, which in 2017 were worth $1,764 million dollars (respectively: the Scaife Family Foundation: $79 million (data from 2012); Sarah Scaife Foundation: $746 million[6]; Colcom Foundation: $509 million[7]; and the Allegheny Foundation: $430 million).[8] The Mellons are bankers, oil tycoons (they own Gulf), majority stakeholders in Alcoa (aluminium) and big players in uranium. The foundation made its aggressive swing to the right when Richard Mellon Scaife was in charge of the family fortune, a man who, according to an article in the *Wall Street Journal*, was nothing less than the 'financial archangel of the intellectual conservative movement'. Over the years, Richard Scaife financed figures such as Barry Goldwater, Richard Nixon and Newt Gingrich (who in the 1990s led the Republican swerve to the right). Gingrich himself defined Scaife as one of the people 'who had truly created modern conservatism'. It might be useful to remember that already in the 1960s, Richard Scaife

[6]  https://www.documentcloud.org/documents/4490939-Sarah-Scaife-Foundation-Annual-Report-2016.html.

[7]  http://colcomfdn.org/files/2018/04/Financial-Statements-2017.pdf.

[8]  http://www.scaife.com/Alleg_2016.pdf.

and his conservative friends thought it inadequate to compare the decline of the United States to the fall of Rome, finding much more fitting its comparison to the fall of Carthage, which collapsed when its affluent elites refused to adequately support Hannibal who had reached the gates of Rome. As such, Scaife and his men founded a League to Save Carthage, which in 1964 became the Carthage Foundation and merged in 2014 with the Sarah Scaife Foundation.

After those belonging to the Mellon Scaifes, the wealthiest of the foundations is the Lynde and Harry Bradley Foundation, which, in 2017, had $893 million at its disposal.[9] The Bradley brothers founded the company of the same name dealing with industrial electric components, with its headquarters in Wisconsin. Their foundation was created in 1943, but it only became relevant in 1985 when the Bradleys deposited a large part of the profits from the sale of their family business to Rockwell. In 1958, Harry Bradley was one of the founders of the John Birch Society, an extreme right association that believed the United Nations was 'an instrument of global Communist conquest', the movement for civil rights an attempt to create an 'independent Negro-Soviet republic' and the Republican president (and commander-in-chief during the Second World War) Dwight Eisenhower 'a zealous and knowing agent of the Communist plot'. Other communist agents who had infiltrated the US state were, according to the John Birch Society, Secretary of State John Foster Dulles and the director of the CIA, Allen Dulles.[10]

Continuing in order of wealth, next we have the foundation of the Smith Richardson family of Vicks VapoRub fame, which

9  cdn2.hubspot.net/hubfs/4152914/Annual%20Report/2017%20Annual%20Re port.pdf.
10  John Savage, 'The John Birch Society is Back', *Politico*, 16 July 2017, https:// www.politico.com/magazine/story/2017/07/16/the-john-birch-society-is -alive-and-well-in-the-lone-star-state-215377.

was worth $707 million in 2016.[11] The foundation was created in 1935 but only decisively veered right and increased its activism in 1973, when Randolph Richardson became president.

Since 1873, the Coors family in Colorado have been producing what Paul Newman called 'the best American beer' (I beg to differ) but also running from its coffers is a river of money that has been watering the extreme right for 50 years. The Adolph Coors Foundation, with assets of $177 million in 2014,[12] was created in 1975 by Joe Coors (who had also previously supported the John Birch Society) and who, between 1993 and 2011, created his own sub-foundation, Castle Rock. This was how Joe Coors' obituary read in 2003:

> Joe Coors, was definitely a man of the right. He was a free-market enthusiast [. . .] He was also an early supporter of Mr. Reagan [. . .] He went on to become a member of Mr. Reagan's trusted 'kitchen cabinet.' Yet his most important legacy (lies) in philanthropy: Coors spent millions of dollars making sure people would hear from the right. The conservative movement simply would not exist in the form it does today without the profound influence of Joe Coors.[13]

The Koch family, however, are in a league of their own, with a long tradition of supporting the most extremist of conservative causes. The patriarch Fred Koch (1900–1967) was (him too!) one of the founders of the John Birch Society, even if he had initially made his millions in the USSR in the 1930s, extracting oil for the Bolsheviks. But the influence of the Kansas oil tycoons has grown exponentially only in the first two decades

---

[11] Smith Richardson Foundation Annual Report 2016, https://www.srf.org/p-con tent/uploads/2017/12/Final-2016-SRF-Annual-Report.pdf.

[12] 2014 tax return, https://www.guidestar.org/inDocuments/2015/510/172/2015 -510172279-0c7adc36-F.pdf.

[13] 'Joe Coors, RIP. He fermented barley, hops and conservative ideas', *The Wall Street Journal*, 20 March 2003.

of the twenty-first century, when the family fortune was left in the hands of his two sons, Charles (1935–) and David Koch (1940–2019). It was at this time that the two brothers financed, shaped and essentially invented the Tea Party movement. Up until then, the Kochs were rarely discussed, to the point that the exhaustive book *Invisible Hands* (2009) by Kim Phillips-Fein on the genesis of the conservative movement from the New Deal to Reagan[14] referenced only the Koch brothers' father, Fred, even if, by the early twenty-first century, their presence had become so outsized that the term 'Kochtopus' was often used to describe them. Since David's death in 2019, Charles has become the sole heir to the family's fortune, valued at $128 billion[15] in 2022, making it the third largest on the planet, with the Walton family of Walmart distribution chain fame claiming first place with their $224 billion (this is shared among various relatives though the three brothers hold the lion's share with around $65 billion dollars each[16]). The Kochs' power lies in the fact that Koch Industries is private (it has no public shareholders) and therefore does not have to notify anyone as to its investments or political donations.

## The Three Stages of the Reconquest

The strategy adopted by foundations like those belonging to Bradley, Olin, Mellon Scaife, Richardson and Koch following

---

[14] Kim Phillips-Fein, *Invisible Hands: The Making of the Conservative Movement from the New Deal to Reagan.* New York: Norton, 2009.

[15] https://www.investopedia.com/articles/insights/052416/top-10-wealthiest-families-world.asp.

[16] The 2022 Forbes list of the 2,268 billionaires on the planet (https://www.forbes.com/billionaires). Interestingly, their collective wealth is worth $12.7 trillion (+39.6% on 2018). To give you an idea of just how much $12.7 trillion actually is, the combined annual GDPs of Germany, the United Kingdom, France and Italy is $12.4 trillion (https://data.worldbank.org/indicator/NY.GDP.MKTP.CD).

Powell's memorandum was explained in detail in 1976 by a then 25-year-old Richard Fink, who would later become the president and director of various Koch foundations.[17] Fink gave Charles Koch *The Structure of the Social Change*,[18] a concise directive to determine how 'investment in the structure of production of ideas can yield greater social and economic progress when the structure is well-developed and well-integrated'.

In this brief text, Fink adopts a 'managerial' perspective: he considers ideas products of investment in a commodity to

[17] Just to give an example of the accumulation of positions, titles and appointments in the life of these 'entrepreneurs of ideas', here is Mr. Fink's list: he was executive vice-president and board member for Koch Industries Inc.; president of the board and CEO of Koch Companies Public Sector LLC, which provides legal relations, government, philanthropy and community services for the Koch companies. He was also director of Georgia-Pacific and Flint Hills Resources LLC, a refining and petrochemicals company; president of the Charles G. Koch and Claude R. Lambe charitable foundations and administrator of the Fred C. and Mary R. Koch Foundation. Before working for Koch Industries, Fink was an executive vice-president and associate professor at George Mason University. In 1979, at George Mason, he and Charles Koch founded the Mercatus Center, a university research organization. He was a member of the Mercatus board, which he presided over until 1990. Fink sat on the board for George Mason University from 1997 to June 2005. In 1984, Fink co-founded the Citizens for a Sound Economy Foundation and its affiliate company, Citizens for a Sound Economy. In 2003, the foundation changed its name to Americans for Prosperity Foundation; Fink was a member of the board. Together with David Koch and Art Pope, he founded Americans for Prosperity. He sat on the oversight board for the International Foundation for Research and Experimental Economics and was a member of the board for the Institute for Humane Studies, the Jack Miller Center and the Laffer Center for Global Economic Growth. Previously he served on the boards of the American Prosecutors Research Institute, the Bill of Rights Institute, the George Mason University Foundation, the Public Choice Center and the Reason Foundation. He was also member of the Consumer Advisory Council of the Board for the Federal Reserve and President Reagan's Commission for Privatization.

[18] The text was later published in *Philanthropy*, vol. 10, no. 1, Winter 1996, under the title 'From Ideas to Action: The Role of Universities, Think Tanks and Activist Groups'. I downloaded it from https://kochdocs.org/2019/08/19/1996 -structure-of-social-change-by-koch-industries-executive-vp-richard-fink/.

impose on the market, to be first produced and then sold. Fink wanted to answer the question of how foundations can choose who to give their money to when

> Universities, think tanks, and citizen activist groups all present competing claims for being the best place to invest resources [...] The universities claim to be the real source of change. [...] The think tanks and policy development organizations argue that they are most worthy of support because they work on real-world policy issues, not abstract concepts. [...] Citizen activist or implementation groups claim to merit support because they are the most effective at really accomplishing things. They are fighting in the trenches, and this is where the war is either won or lost.

(Note again how the bellicose metaphor is wound into commercial, managerial jargon.)

Fink explicitly refers to the production model put forward by Austrian economist Friedrich August von Hayek and lays out a strategy in three stages:

> The higher stages represent investments and businesses involved in the enhanced production of some basic inputs we will call 'raw materials.' The middle stages of production are involved in converting these raw materials into various types of products that add more value than these raw materials have if sold directly to consumers [...] [t]he later stages of production are involved in the packaging, transformation, and distribution of the output of the middle stages to the ultimate consumers.

Applied to the production and sale of ideas, this model translates into an initial phase that sees investment in 'intellectual raw materials, that is, the exploration and production of abstract concepts and theories. In the public policy arena, these still come primarily (though not exclusively) from the research done by scholars at our universities'. However, these theories are incomprehensible to the public and so – bring on the second stage:

> to have consequences, ideas need to be transformed into a more practical or useable form. [. . .] This is the work of the think tanks and policy institutions. Without these organizations, theory or abstract thought would have less value and less impact on our society. But while the think tanks excel at developing new policy and articulating its benefits, they are less able to implement change. Citizen activist or implementation groups are needed in the final stage to take the policy ideas from the think tanks and translate them into proposals that citizens can understand and act upon.

As Charles Koch summed it up: 'To bring about social change requires a strategy that is vertically and horizontally integrated' that must span from 'idea creation to policy development to education to grassroots organizations to lobbying to political action'.[19]

## Assault Think Tanks

In reality, the three stages outlined by Fink were undertaken separately only in theory. In practice, the several families from the Midwest enacted them simultaneously, overlapping all three.

In 1973, thanks to financial support from Joe Coors, what would become one of the most authoritative conservative think tanks opened its doors: the Heritage Foundation.

---

[19] Cited by Jane Mayer, *Dark Money: The Hidden History of the Billionaires Behind the Rise of the Radical Right* (2016). New York: Penguin Random House, 2017, p. 173.

However, the majority of donations to this foundation came from the Mellon Scaife family, who were naturally joined by Bradley, Koch, Smith-Richardson and all the other magnates until, at the beginning of the 1980s, the ironclad divisions of US capitalism began to appear among the Heritage's leading corporate financiers: Amoco, Amway, Boeing, Chase Manhattan Bank, Chevron, Dow Chemical, Exxon, General Motors, Mesa Petroleum, Mobil Oil, Pfizer, Philip Morris, Procter & Gamble, R.J. Reynolds, Searle, Sears-Roebuck, SmithKline Beecham, Union Carbide and Union Pacific.[20] But by that point, Ronald Reagan was already in the White House.

It is interesting how many similarities there are between Reagan and Donald Trump's stories. Not only are they both outsiders – one a b-list Hollywood actor, the other a real estate mogul with varying fortunes (and several failures) who became famous as a television star thanks to a reality show – but both were held to be entirely ignorant and unsuited to the presidency, and both were destined to be impeached within a matter of months. Both candidates were also shunned by the extreme right because they were considered unreliable, but were assisted and piloted after being elected.

The similarity between the way in which conservative think tanks remote-controlled Trump and Reagan is staggering. The term 'remote-controlled' should be taken literally. For example, on 3 July 2020, this was the title of the first article on the Heritage Foundation's website: *The Nation Under Attack – What Must We Do To Stop the Socialist Programme of the Left*. The next day, in a rally held in front of Mount Rushmore in South Dakota, Donald Trump stated that 'the nation's history is under siege from "far-left fascism"'.[21] But it

---

[20] Ibid., p. 108.
[21] 'US under siege from "far-left fascism", says Trump in Mount Rushmore speech', *The Guardian*, 4 July 2020, https://www.theguardian.com/us-news/2020/jul/04/us-under-siege-from-far-left-fascism-says-trump-in-mount-rushmore-speech.

is in the government programme in particular that the influence of the Heritage Foundation can be felt: '208 Heritage policy recommendations adopted by the Trump administration', the Heritage Foundation proudly boasts in its Annual Report 2017, released in May 2018. A few pages later under the heading 'The Price of Success', Heritage added: '[We] bid farewell to some great people in 2017. The Trump administration snapped up more than 70 of our staff and alumni.'[22] The smugness was repeated the following year (2019) with the boast regarding the Foundation's *Mandate for Leadership* and: 'the Trump administration's embrace of 64% of Heritage policy prescriptions through its annual budget, regulatory guidance, or other actions'.[23]

This self-congratulatory tone suggests that, beyond a whimsical, humorous appearance and a possibly disastrous end, even if Donald Trump's victory in the 2016 presidential elections was a surprise to even the most dogged US conservatives, they were entirely prepared to seize the opportunity presented by this unexpected opening. And the successive political action – the fiscal, environmental and religious in particular – was anything but improvised, actually appearing increasingly shrewdly manoeuvred.

One example is enough to demonstrate this. Just two weeks after Trump's inauguration at the White House, on 4 February 2017 the *New York Times* published the document *A Roadmap to Repeal: Removing Regulatory Barriers to Opportunity*, released by Freedom Partners (a group financed by billionaire brothers Charles and David Koch) in which it

---

[22] The Heritage Foundation, 2017 Annual Report, which can be found at https://www.heritage.org/sites/default/files/2018-05/2017_AnnualReport_WEB.pdf. The hunt continues: In March 2019, Donald Trump appointed Stephen Moore, a fellow of the Heritage Foundation, to the board of the Federal Reserve (the US central bank) and in June 2019 the ex-chief of staff at the Heritage was interim minister for Defence.

[23] https://www.heritage.org/about-heritage/impact.

was suggested to Trump that he repeal regulations and issue presidential decrees on various issues (such as repealing the moratorium on new coal mines or withdrawing from the Paris Agreement on the limitation of greenhouse gas emissions). In the margin, the *New York Times* observed how 'Congress approved this repeal the past week' and 'President Trump issued a presidential order on this last Friday'.[24] No sooner said than done.

The point here is that history is repeating itself. Already in 1980, Heritage had given Congress and the White House *Mandate for Leadership*, a voluminous dossier containing 1,077 pages listing more than 2,000 political recommendations for the Reagan presidency, from tax cuts to cuts to programmes helping minorities, and a disproportionate increase in military spending in order to finally free themselves 'from the tyranny of the Left' and save them from the strains of 'Liberal-Fascism'. In 1984, before Reagan's re-election, The Heritage Foundation reappeared and published *Mandate for Leadership II*, which recommended (among other things) the privatization of Social Security and the abolition of special funds for supporting the disabled in education. In 1985, the Heritage boasted that 60–65% of its recommendations (curiously, the exact same percentage it boasts of with Trump) had been enacted by the Reagan administration, which over the course of two mandates counted 36 employees from the Heritage among its staff (55 also came from the Hoover Institution and 34 from the American Enterprise Institute, which we shall come to shortly).[25] It is alarming that Reagan is remembered today as a great statesman that even Barack Obama considered a vital 'reference point'.[26]

---

[24] https://www.nytimes.com/interactive/2017/02/04/us/doc-lobby.html.
[25] Richard Bonney, *False Prophets: The 'Clash of Civilization' and the War on Terror*. Oxford: Peter Lang, 2008, p. 36.
[26] Michael Duffy and Michael Scherer, 'The Role Model: What Obama Sees in Reagan', *Time*, 27 January 2011, http://content.time.com/time/magazine/artic le/0,9171,2044712,00.html.

(We are overlooking the highly documented and incredibly dense network of funding, suggestions and logistical support between these think tanks and US foreign policy, including various actions by the secret services, a discourse that falls outside our remit here.)

As we might expect, the Western nation that has produced the most politically efficient think tanks that most resemble their US counterparts has been the UK. The most noteworthy are the Bow Group, founded in 1951 to fight communism; the Institute of Economic Affairs (IEA), founded in 1955 by the businessman Anthony Fisher (1915–1988); the Centre for Policy Studies whose founders in 1984 included Margaret Thatcher; and finally, the Adam Smith Institute. The last three were decisive in shaping the politics of the Iron Lady. Furthermore, in 1981, Anthony Fisher founded the Atlas Economic Research Foundation (later called the Atlas Network) in the US, which produced another 150 conservative think tanks around the world and today connects more than 500 similar institutions throughout the five continents.

The think tank is a peculiar entity whose extensive use dates back to the aftermath of the Second World War. The *2020 Global Go To Think Tank Index Report* counts 11,175 institutes of this kind throughout the globe, of which 47% (2,932) can be found in Europe and North America. Of the 2,397 North American think tanks, 92% (2,203) are American. But rather more interesting is that 89.9% of think tanks were founded after 1950, that their number doubled in the US between 1980 and 2020, and that the golden decade for the creation of think tanks was the 1980s, when 20% of them were brought to life. Over the last decade, there has instead been a slowdown in their growth in the US and North America.[27]

---

[27] James G. McGann, *2020 Global Go To Think Tank Index Report*, Think Tanks and Civil Societies Program (TTCSP), University of Pennsylvania, 2020, pp. 20 and 10 (some historical data is taken from the previous edition), https://repository.upenn.edu/think_tanks/18/.

To use Louis Althusser's terminology, the think tank is a new kind of 'ideological apparatus' that sits upstream of the traditional ideological apparatuses (school, church, military indoctrination) and even the more recent ones (mass media, especially radio, TV and, today, social networks).[28] The aim of this particular institution is to supply, feed, provide theses and arguments to both traditional ideological apparatuses (schools) and modern ones (mass media and social networks).

Think tanks have existed for a long time – just think of the Brookings Institution (founded in 1916) or the Hudson Institute (1961). With regard to these august institutions, the novelty of the Heritage Foundation and the other think tanks that appeared on the scene in the 1970s and 1980s was their barely disguised factionalism, their openly taking sides and support for the most extreme causes in a full-on collision with the previous façade of bipartisan phariseeism (even if this did disguise a deep-rooted conservatism). These new 'combat' think tanks held, and continue to hold, a role of primary importance when it comes to providing an intellectual arsenal to the conservative revolution. It would be useless, and tedious, to list them all, but we must name at least four: the Manhattan Institute for Policy Research (MI), the Cato Institute, the Hoover Institution and the American Enterprise Institute (AEI).

The Manhattan Institute was launched in 1977 by Englishman Anthony Fisher, whom we have already met, and William Casey (1913–1987), who would go on to direct the CIA between 1981 and 1987. Its funders include the foundations of Bradley, Smith Richardson, Scaife, Koch, CastleRock, Olin,

---

[28] Demonstrating the abyss separating us from 50 years ago, Althusser's 1969 list of ideological apparatuses appears irrevocably outdated: religious (the various churches and religions); scholastic (public and private schools); family; legal; political (the various parties); trade unions; informative (printed press, TV, etc.); and cultural (literature, fine art, sport, etc.) in 'Ideology and Ideological State Apparatuses (Notes Towards an Investigation)', p. 83.

Earhart, Walton and Bill & Melinda Gates.[29] As we will see, its hand can be seen in all right-wing ideological campaigns of the last 40 years.

The Cato Institute was founded in 1977 by the Koch brothers. Its name recalled the libertarian ideal of the Roman Cato (first Carthage, now Cato – the problems of ancient empires was a real obsession!). Freedom from all legal binds and regulations, including those establishing a minimum wage, limiting overtime, banning child labour, obstructing monopolies, fighting pollution and governing the use of resources; it is against all such 'restraints' that the Cato Institute fights. They have made a utopia of minimal state supported at that time by Robert Nozick and his extreme interpretation of individual rights (Nozick believed that 'a free system will allow [the individual] to sell himself into slavery').[30] This meant that the Cato Institute campaigned against the welfare state, against the healthcare system, to limit the role of the state as much as possible, and therefore reduce taxation as much as possible (for Nozick, income tax was nothing but 'forced labour'),[31] for the privatization of Social Security, the federal electricity system, the entire scholastic apparatus, the postal service and NASA. The Cato Institute is also against US intervention in foreign affairs and is firmly against 'corporate welfare' (the taxpayer-funded subsidies given to large corporations).

The Hoover Institution is one of those cases in which the billionaires of the Midwest brought about a robust swerve to the right in a venerable institution. The Hoover Institution on War, Revolution and Peace was founded in 1919 by future president Herbert Hoover and since then, it had been a club for Republican lawmakers, its fellows including the former

---

[29] Source: www.sourcewatch.org.
[30] Robert Nozick, *Anarchy, State, and Utopia*. Oxford: Blackwell, 1974, p. 331.
[31] Ibid., p. 169.

secretaries of state Condoleezza Rice and George Shultz, former attorney general Edwin Meese and former secretary of defence James Mattis. Beginning in the 1970s, however, when regular funds began to arrive from reactionary foundations, the Hoover Institution became more markedly conservative. According to sourcewatch.org, between 1985 and 2012 the Hoover Institute received $11.7 million from Scaife; $5.8 million (up to 2005) from Olin; $5.2 million from Walton; $4.8 million from Bradley; $3.8 from Smith Richardson; $900,000 from Carthage and so on.

The case of the American Enterprise Institute is especially interesting on this score. Created in 1938 as the American Enterprise Association, it was renamed AEI in 1962. In 1964, the upper echelons of the AEI took a leave of absence to organize the presidential campaign for the ferociously anti-communist Arizona senator Barry Goldwater, against the 1964 Civil Rights Act, which would outlaw all discrimination based on race, skin colour, sex, religion or national origin. Goldwater was voted for by all the racists of the South (a somewhat ironic fate for the grandson of Polish Jew Michael Goldwasser who emigrated after having taken part in the revolutionary uprisings of 1848), but he was soundly defeated on a national scale by the democrat Lyndon Johnson (38% to 62%).

This defeat calmed the boiling fervour of the AEI until a turning point in the 1970s, when its finances were reinvigorated by conservative magnates, and again in the 1980s, when those same magnates complained that the AEI was too centrist. And just think that until 1982, the editorial director of the AEI magazine *Regulation, Journal on Government and Society* was Antonin Scalia, the extreme right-wing judge who would be appointed to the Supreme Court and go on to organize the constitutional coup against Al Gore in the presidential elections of 2000. After these complaints, AEI got back in line and the funds started flooding in once more. And it will not surprise you to hear that among the foundations that financed and/or finance the AEI, we find Bradley, Scaife, Smith Richardson, Olin and Koch.

P.S. In the last 20 years it has become more difficult to follow the money trail tying billionaire families to the think tanks, often because the donations no longer pass directly from the foundations to the think tanks, but transit through intermediaries who have a similar status to the foundations in terms of their fiscal regime, but have the advantage of guaranteeing anonymity to their contributors. For example, the US contributors to British foundations ultimately transited through the Donors Trust (founded in 1999), an entity affiliated with the Donors Capital Fund. You can get an idea of their most important donors from the fact that their president and CEO since 2015 has been Lawson Bader, who had previously been vice-president of the Mercatus Center founded by Charles Koch and Richard Fink.

Contributions to electoral campaigns have also become untraceable following the Supreme Court ruling in the case of *Citizens United v. Federal Election Commission* in 2010, which made unlimited anonymous donations legal. We will talk about this in more detail in chapter 7.

# 2

# Ideas Are Weapons

In 1974, the year after the founding of the Heritage Foundation, the Nobel prize for economics was awarded jointly to Swedish social-democrat Gunnar Myrdal (1898–1987) and Austrian conservative Friedrich August von Hayek (1899–1992). This double consecration marked the last moment of precarious equilibrium between the declining fortunes of Keynesianism and the ascent of the new monetary orthodoxy developed in particular by the University of Chicago, where von Hayek had taught for 12 years before being employed by the Hoover Institution at Stanford. Just two years later, in 1976, the Nobel was awarded solely to Milton Friedman, one of von Hayek's disciples. From this moment on, the so-called Chicago boys (including Gary Becker, Ronald Coase, Eugene Fama, Robert Fogel, Lars Peter Hansen, Robert Lucas, Theodore Schultz and George Stigler) were showered with Nobel prizes.

The wind had changed irrevocably, the Zeitgeist shifted from the Keynesian orthodoxy of the period immediately following the Second World War, to the point that in his first State of the Union address in 1977, Democratic President Jimmy Carter launched an attack on the welfare state using words von Hayek had written for him: 'Government cannot solve our problems [. . .] Government cannot eliminate poverty or provide a bountiful economy or reduce inflation or save our cities or cure illiteracy or provide energy [. . .]'.[1]

One of the factors that contributed to this change in direction was the very creation of the Nobel prize for economics, which is . . . not a Nobel prize. As we know, these prizes were the legacy of the inventor of dynamite, Alfred Nobel, who established in his will that, after his death (in 1896), his fortune should be used to assign five prizes (just five) a year for literature, chemistry, medicine, physics and peace. The prizes for chemistry and physics are assigned by the Royal Swedish Academy of Sciences, the prize for literature by the Swedish Academy, the price for medicine is decided by the Norwegian Karolinska Institutet, and the Norwegian Nobel Committee assigns the prize for peace.

Economics was not mentioned anywhere. It was not until 1968 that the prize was invented out of thin air by the Swedish Central Bank, as the 'Sveriges Riksbank Prize in Economic Sciences in Memory of Alfred Nobel', in order to commemorate the bank's 300th anniversary. Or rather, with hindsight, to delegitimize Swedish social-democratic politics and destabilize their governments, particular that of Olof Palme. As such, it is a prize that cloaks the economic policy pursued by a central bank in the prestige of a Nobel. The fact that over the following 30 years the overwhelming majority of prizes were awarded to the Chicago Boys and their acolytes is not due to the superior quality of the theories and studies of those economists, but the result of wilful political action. In a certain sense, this is yet another manifestation of the politics of the reactionary foundations, in this case embodied by a central bank. It is worth mentioning that Gunnar Myrdal himself, Sweden's leading

---

[1] Jibran Khan, 'Government Cannot Solve Our Problems', *National Review*, 10 May 2018, https://www.nationalreview.com/2018/05/jimmy-carter-more-conservative-administration-than-history-remembers/.

economist, a social democrat, recommended that the prize for economics be abolished.

The Nobel prize for economics was used, therefore, to legitimize extreme neoliberalism, not unlike that of the DOC labels used on wines or the UNESCO seal of 'World Heritage' given to sites, monuments and cities.

A second, less bombastic way of spreading the teachings of the Chicago School was the Chilean *coup d'état* of 11 September 1973 by the armed forces led by general Augusto Pinochet against the democratically elected government of President Salvador Allende, who died during the attack on the presidential palace (the bodies of 11 of his advisors and assistants were exhumed in 2010). This coup of unprecedented ferocity was the prototype and example for all successive coups and 'Condor plans' for annihilating the left in Latin America. Supporters of the opposition were corralled in sports stadiums, where at least 2,130 are reported to have died, 1,248 disappeared and 28,459 were tortured, including 3,621 women (3,400 raped by their incarcerators), 1,244 minors and 176 children under the age of 13 (these numbers are those given by the official commissions and do not take into account the murders witnessed but not recorded, including the other thousands of miners killed by the military).[2] It was in Chile that the technique of throwing opponents from aeroplanes was first used, a technique later employed in Argentina and Brazil. At least 150,000 dissidents were exiled.

As soon as it had taken power, the military acted with maximum urgency on the economic programme laid out in a report known as *El Ladrillo* (the Brick), of which a bard

---

[2] These are: (1) the *Comisión Nacional de Verdad y Reconciliación* (National Commission for Truth and Reconciliation, presided over by Raúl Rettig Guissen), 1990–1991; (2) the *Comisión Nacional sobre Prisión Política y Tortura* (National Commission into Political Imprisonment and Torture, Comisión Valech), 2003–2011. Both commissions held supplementary investigations. There were also other commissions.

of neoliberalism, Arnold Harberger, said 'I do not think it an exaggeration to say that the studies and debates leading up to El Ladrillo played for the subsequent revolution in Chilean economic policy a role not unlike that of the Federalist Papers in shaping the constitutional framework of the United States.'[3]

*El Ladrillo* was based on the work of a group of economists at the Pontificia Universidad Católica de Chile who had studied under professors from the University of Chicago and/or had studied in Chicago since the end of the 1950s as part of a scholarship system. It was these Chilean economists who were called the Chicago Boys, a name that was then extended to the entirety of the American neoliberal school. It was this 'handful of heroes', as Harberger refers to them, who were able to enact the economic reforms thanks to the actions of the military. As one of these 'heroes', Pablo Barahona, who was minster for the economy under Pinochet, said himself: 'I have no doubts that [. . .] in Chile an authoritarian government – absolutely authoritarian – that could implement reform despite interests of any group, no matter how important, was needed.'[4]

But while the genealogy of Chilean military neoliberalism leads us to Chicago, that of US–Chicago neoliberalism can be traced back to two (aristocratic) Austrian economists who emigrated to the US and deeply influenced conservative thought in the country: Ludwig von Mises (1881–1973) and, in particular, Friedrich von Hayek, whose book on the dangers of state intervention in the economy, *The Road to Serfdom* (1944), was popularized by the abridged and simplified version published in the *Reader's Digest* in 1945 with a circulation

---

[3] Arnold C. Harberger, 'Secrets of Success: A Handful of Heroes', *The American Economic Review*, vol. 83, no. 2, May 1993, pp. 343–50, p. 345.

[4] Genaro Arriagada Herrera and Carol Graham, 'Chile: Sustaining Adjustment during Democratic Transition', in Stephan Haggard and Steven B. Webb (eds.), *Voting for Reform: Democracy, Political Liberalization, and Economic Adjustment*. New York: Oxford University Press for the World Bank, 1994, pp. 242–89, p. 245.

of a million copies. Von Hayek's political position was made clear in his statement that 'social justice [is] entirely empty and meaningless',[5] a judgement that foreshadowed Margaret Thatcher's famously apodictic statement that 'There is no such thing as society.'[6] Even clearer was the justification given by von Hayek for his personal visit to see the Chilean dictator Augusto Pinochet in 1981: 'Personally, I prefer a liberal [meant here as "neoliberal"] dictator to a democratic government that is lacking in this regard' (interview with *El Mercurio*, 12 April 1981).

And yet von Hayek was considered too moderate by his supporters at DuPont de Nemours when he founded the Mont Pelerin Society in 1947 to promote the free market, so much so that for the society's second conference they forced him to involve the older Ludwig von Mises, who was considered more reliable when it came to neoliberalism.[7] Among the founders of Mont Pelerin were Walter Lippmann, the philosopher of science Karl Popper and two of the so-called Chicago Fathers, Milton Friedman and George Stigler. Schweizerische Kreditanstalt (today Crédit Suisse) paid 93% of the conference's total costs, some 18,062 Swiss francs).[8]

In the 1960s, Friedman (1912–2006) would be the only named economist to openly support Barry Goldwater's economic plan (in his *New York Times* article of 11 October 1964). After that, from 1968 onwards, his column in *Newsweek* would bring him

---

[5] Friedrich August von Hayek, *The Mirage of Social Justice: Law, Legislation and Liberty*, vol. 2. Chicago, IL: University of Chicago Press, 1976, pp. xi–xii.

[6] 'There is no such thing as society', interview in *Woman's Own*, 23 September 1987, https://www.margaretthatcher.org/document/106689.

[7] The society's name comes from the location of its first meeting, a castle on Mont Pelerin, close to Vevey in Switzerland. For more on the birth of the association, see Phillips-Fein, *Invisible Hands*, pp. 43–52. The managing director of DuPont de Nemours who found von Hayek too centrist was Jasper Crane.

[8] Dieter Plehwe, 'Introduction', in Philip Mirowski and Dieter Plehwe (eds.), *The Road from Mont Pelerin: The Making of the Neoliberal Thought Collective*. Cambridge, MA: Harvard University Press, 2009, p. 15.

to prominence among a much broader audience. It is worth highlighting that he was awarded the Nobel prize by the Bank of Sweden in 1976, after he voluntarily offered himself as an economic advisor to general Augusto Pinochet in 1975, whose politics were defined by Friedman as 'the Chilean miracle'.

As a result of the Nobel prize and his work with Pinochet, Friedman became the official guru of the American extreme right. When the president of the Olin Foundation, William Simon (the one who said 'ideas are weapons') published *A Time for Truth* in 1978, he asked Milton Friedman to write the preface and Friedrich von Hayek to provide the introduction. As payment, in 1980 the Scaife Foundation contributed $650,000 to produce the TV version of the book by Milton and Rose Friedman, *Free to Choose*, which had been financed by the Olin Foundation. Friedman was not only the most trusted economic advisor of Reaganism (and Thatcherism), but, as we will see, his ideas also inspired the conservative revolution in other fields.

In its two guises – German ordo-liberalism and US neoliberalism – neoliberalism has been the object of much criticism and little understanding. I will not delve into the differences between the two schools;[9] in the following pages (except for the odd reference) I will concentrate on US neoliberalism, which is generally considered to be simply an extreme version of classical liberalism, a total refusal of state interference, only more intransigent and sectarian than in the past; and a more systematic and radical form of hatred for the state, or 'state phobia'. In reality, neoliberalism is much more than this. It is a genuine epistemological revolution in the

---

[9] On the differences between the various neoliberal schools of thought, and between the German ordo-liberalists and US neoliberals, see Alessandro Roncaglia, 'Il mito della mano invisibile: i neoliberismi' [The myth of the invisible hand: the neoliberals], in *L'età della disgregazione. Storia del pensiero economico contemporaneo [The Age of Disgregation. History of Contemporary Economic Thought]*. Rome-Bari: Laterza, 2019, pp. 201–51.

paradigm of classical economics (that of the market, of supply and demand), and it has shaped a new ideology, a little like the US evangelical sects that are new religions in comparison to traditional Christianity (whether Catholic or Protestant).

Michel Foucault was the first to recognize this with extraordinary far-sightedness, as demonstrated by the course he offered at the Collège de France between January and April 1979,[10] when Europe seemed to be dealing with the aftershocks following 1968, yet before Reagan had come to power. Indeed, as Perry Anderson observed in 2000, hardly anybody recognized that 'the principal aspect of the past decade', meaning the 1990s would 'be defined as the virtually uncontested consolidation, and universal diffusion, of neoliberalism'. Although the years 1989–91 saw the destruction of Soviet-bloc Communism, it was not immediately obvious – even to its champions – that unfettered free-market capitalism would sweep the board in East or West'.[11] Even so, as Anderson himself held, the prevailing view among the Western left was that the neoliberal (abbreviated hereafter as 'neolib') revolution represented no more than an extreme form of classical liberalism, market fundamentalism, rather than a true rupture with respect to its tenets, practices and political implications.

The first rupture between liberalism and neoliberalism regards the political sphere. The policies put forward by American neoliberalism are entirely contrary to the spirit (if not the practice) of political liberalism, as we can clearly see

---

[10] Michel Foucault, *The Birth of Biopolitics: Lectures at the Collège de France, 1978–1979*. New York: Picador, 2010. Contrary to what the title might suggest, (1) these lectures only fleetingly refer to biopolitics, focusing on ordo-liberalism and US neoliberalism; and (2) the lectures were held in 1979 and not from 1978 to 1979. The expression used above – 'state phobia' – was coined by Foucault in these lectures.

[11] Perry Anderson, 'Renewals', *New Left Review*, no. 1, January–February 2000, pp. 5–24, https://newleftreview.org/issues/II1/articles/perry-anderson-rene wals.

by the enthusiasm shown by von Hayek and Friedman for a
dictator such as Pinochet.

The second rupture is philosophical, epistemological. The
key concept of classical economic theory was the market as
the location and mechanism of exchange, starting with the
famous myth of the origins of political economy, the 'certain propensity in human nature [. . .] to truck, barter and
exchange one thing for another', as Adam Smith says at
the beginning of *The Wealth of Nations*.[12] Adjacent to this
primacy of the market and exchange is the notion of the
equivalence, if not the equality of agents of the market. In
a perfect market, agents exchange money and goods in a
reciprocal manner that presupposes a condition of equality.
In neoliberalism, however, the central idea is competition,
not as a natural fact, a primordial condition of humanity (like
the mythical barter economy), but as an ideal to be achieved
that is precarious and difficult to maintain. Inequality not
equality is inherent in competition, as competition infers a
winner and a loser (otherwise what kind of competition would
it be?!). And competition is not only based on inequality, but
creates it.

The individual is therefore considered a market operator,
but only insofar as he or she is a competitor in the competition.
But who competes in capitalist competition? Enterprise. So,
the theory's foundation is no longer the market-system, but
single enterprises. There is a discontinuity between these two
concepts: the market is a self-regulating system; an enterprise
is not. As Ronald Coase states, the market is 'not an organization, but an organism', while an enterprise introduces an
element of planning and conscious direction that is foreign to
the logic of price adjustment through the mechanism of supply
and demand. According to a colourful metaphor from Dennis
H. Robertson, in enterprises we find 'islands of conscious

---

[12] Adam Smith, *The Wealth of Nations*, p. 9.

power in this ocean of unconscious co-operation like lumps of butter coagulating in a pail of buttermilk'.[13] As such, it is these 'lumps of butter' that are competing amongst themselves.

As a competitor, every individual is considered an entrepreneur, an enterprise even: their own manager. In neolib anthropology, the unit-individual is an enterprise-unit and the individual is their own proprietor. The idea of entering into a relationship with oneself based on ownership is certainly not one that occurs naturally to human beings. I personally have never seen myself as my own proprietor, I have never looked at myself in the mirror to evaluate my property or my own properties. Indeed, the term 'property' seems extraordinarily inappropriate when applied to the individual's relationship with themselves.

The first consequence of this definition is that we are all owners, from the Mexican labourer to the black South African miner to the Wall Street banker. But what exactly are we owners of when, for example, we possess no money or material objects? We are owners of ourselves, we constitute our own capital. Each of us is our own proprietor, of our own human capital, of our own enterprise, of ourselves as investors of our own capital – hence the notion of human capital: 'The distinctive mark of human capital is that it is a part of man, and it is capital because it is a source of future satisfactions, or of future earnings, or of both.'[14]

Human capital is to the economy what the soul is to religion; just as various faiths hold every person has a soul (you can't see it but it's there), each of us has 'capital', which however invisible and immaterial, is intrinsic to each one of us as entrepreneur of ourselves. We are, therefore, all capitalists, from the immigrant dish-washer to the Russian oligarch.

---

[13] Ronald H. Coase, 'The Nature of the Firm', *Economica*, vol. 4, no. 16, November 1937, pp. 386–405; the quote from Robertson is on p. 388.

[14] Theodore W. Schultz, *Investment in Human Capital: The Role of Education and of Research*. New York: Free Press, 1971, p. 48.

If the proletariat is also made up of capitalists (even if the former only has human capital), there is no longer then the capitalist on the one side who buys work as a commodity from the proletariat, and the proletariat, on the other, who sells their labour as a commodity to the capitalist. Rather there are simply two capitalists who each, in different ways, create an income from their capital, one from economic capital, the other from human capital. Workers aren't exploited by capitalists. They self-exploit insofar as they themselves are worker-capitalists. In that way, all of those traditional conceptual categories, such as exploitation and alienation, lose their meaning. And the loss of these categories, in turn, undermines the workers' movement. In the process, the parties and trade unions that provided the workers with political representation also disappear. In the notions of political economy that arise from this defeat, how to conceptualize excess profits or wage squeeze or income redistribution? In Spain, they used to say *todos caballeros*, now in the best of all possible markets we say *todos capitalistas*! In effect, class struggle ceases to exist because there are no longer different classes. There are only capitalists.

This concept of human capital, and therefore of work as capital income, has cascading consequences. If you see an African migrant in a boat off the Mediterranean coast or a Latin American desperately attempting to cross the US border through the tunnels dug by *coyotes*, don't be fooled: what you are actually seeing are investors treating migration as '*increasing the productivity of human resources*, [as] an investment which has costs and which also renders returns'.[15] Migration has costs because moving around has costs. True, while migrants are on the move, they are not earning and their insertion into a new environment carries a psychological cost.

---

[15] Larry A. Sjaastad, 'The Costs and Returns of Human Migration', in *Investment in Human Beings, Journal of Political Economy*, vol. 70, no. 5, part 2, 1962, pp. 80–93; citation from p. 83.

But all of these and other costs are accepted in view of making an improvement in one's status and income. These costs are thus an investment. In sum, the migrant is an entrepreneur, spending in order to obtain an improvement.

If you see a passer-by buying an ice cream, or a woman going into a dressmaker's, you are not looking at a buyer, at one of the two terms of exchange and the supply and demand ratio, but rather, before you is someone producing a non-economic income (in this case, a 'satisfaction') through economic commodities: 'In this framework, all market goods are inputs used in production processes of the nonmarket sector. The consumer's demand for these market goods is [. . .] analogous to the [. . .] demand by a firm for any factor of production.'[16]

Just as a building company buys cement to produce a building, the individual human consumer enterprise buys ice cream to produce satisfaction. From this perspective, Foucault notes,

> the classical analysis trotted out a hundred times of the person who is a consumer on the one hand, but who is also a producer, and who, because of this, is, as it were, divided in relation to himself, as well as all the sociological analyses [. . .] of mass consumption, of consumer society, and so forth, do not hold up and have no value in relation to an analysis of consumption in the neoliberal terms of the activity of production.[17]

Obviously the most immediate, most literally innate form of human capital is the genetic code, DNA:

> [. . .] given my own genetic make-up, if I wish to have a child whose genetic make-up will be at least as good as mine, or as

---

[16] Robert T. Michael and Gary S. Becker, 'On the New Theory of Consumer Behavior', *Swedish Journal of Economics*, vol. 75, no. 4, December 1973, pp. 378–96; citation from p. 381.

[17] Foucault, *The Birth of Biopolitics*, p. 226.

far as possible better than mine, then I will have to find someone who also has a good genetic make-up. The mechanism
of the production of individuals, the production of children,
can encounter all sorts of economic and social problems starting with the scarcity of good genetic traits. And if you want
a child whose human capital, understood simply in terms of
innate and hereditary elements, is high, you can see that you
will have to make an investment, that is to say, you will have
to have worked enough, to have sufficient income, and to have
a social status such that it will enable you to take for a spouse
or co-producer of this future human capital, someone who has
significant human capital themselves.[18]

Genetics is understood in terms of accumulation and improvement of human capital.

All aspects of human life, starting with the family, must be
read through the lens of human capital. From this perspective,
people only marry because marriage is 'a long-term contract, between spouses that enables them to avoid constantly
renegotiating at every moment the innumerable contracts
which would have to be made in order to function. "Pass me
the salt; I will give you the pepper"'. Foucault recalls how in the
1800s, Pierre Rivière, who had slit the throats of his mother,
sister and brother, described the relationship between his parents in the following way: 'I will work on your field, the man
says to the woman, but on condition that I can make love with
you. And the woman says: You will not make love with me so
long as you have not fed my chickens.'[19]

Divorce and family conflicts are attributed to 'imperfect
information': 'Participants in marriage markets hardly know
their own interests and capabilities, let alone the dependability,

---

[18] Ibid., p. 228.
[19] Ibid., p. 246. Michel Foucault edited the book *I, Pierre Rivière, having slit the throats of my mother, my sister and my brother: a Case of Parricide in the 19th Century*. Lincoln, NE: University of Nebraska Press, 1982.

sexual compatibility and other traits of potential spouses. Although they date and search in other ways to improve their information, they frequently marry with highly erroneous assessments, then revise these assessments as information improves after marriage.' It is necessary, therefore, to study both 'the various consequences of imperfect information and uncertainty' and 'the divorces that sometimes result when information becomes available after marriage. Information acquired during the first few years of marriage is frequently responsible for the quick termination of marriages'.[20]

The value of maternal love also changes:

> The mother–child relationship, concretely characterised by the time spent by the mother with the child, the quality of the care she gives, the affection she shows, the vigilance with which she follows its development, its education, and not only its scholastic but also its physical progress, the way in which she not only gives it food but also imparts a particular style to eating patterns, and the relationship she has with its eating, all constitute for the neoliberals an investment which can be measured in time [. . .] human capital, the child's human capital, which will produce an income. [. . .] It will be a psychical income. She will have the satisfaction a mother gets form giving the child care and attention in seeing that she has in fact been successful.[21]

There are many more examples. Medical treatments and all activities that involve people's health can be seen as tools with which to improve, use and conserve human capital for as long as possible.

---

[20] Gary Becker, *A Treatise on the Family* (1981). Cambridge, MA: Harvard University Press, 1991, pp. 324–5.
[21] Foucault, *The Birth of Biopolitics*, pp. 243–4.

Generalisation of the 'enterprise' form [. . .] involves extending
the economic model of supply and demand and of investment-
costs-profit so as to make it a model of social relations and
of existence itself, a form of relationship of the individual to
himself, time, those around him, the future, and the family.[22]

Starting a new cult is launching a 'start-up' in the religious
market. As such, the faithful are not (only) believers manifest-
ing their faith, but investors in a sector of the religious economy.
And the new believers really do invest a huge amount of time,
energy and money in their faith, sometimes even their own lives
(martyrs). But if 'religious behaviour [. . .] is generally based on
cost/benefit calculations', and if it 'is therefore rational behaviour in precisely the same sense as other human behaviour is
rational',[23] then the question that neoliberalism must ask itself
when applied to religion is: what is a believer earning from their
investment? The response given by Rodney Stark and other
scholars of this field is: 'They earn the investment itself'.

This answer seems tautological, and it is, just like the
consumption that produces a resource called 'satisfaction', or a mother who sacrifices herself because she earns
a 'psychological income' as a result. But we must be careful
not to underestimate tautologies, because this tautological
response – 'the income the believer makes from their religious
investment is the investment itself' – helps us to understand
why the most demanding faiths, those that demand more sacrifice, more time, more effort from their own believers, are
those that have the highest number of converts, while religions
that demand less from their members are in decline. And it is
with this decline in demands that Stark explains the dramatic
drop in Catholic vocations that accelerated after the Second
Vatican Council, when in the US, for example, the number of

---

[22] Ibid., p. 242.
[23] Rodney Stark and Roger Finke, *Acts of Faith: Explaining the Human Side of
Religion*. Berkeley, CA: University of California Press, 2000, p. 56.

nuns went from 181,421 in 1965 (the year the Council ended) to 153,645 in 1970 and 92,107 in 1995. And again, between 1965 and 1995, the number of monks went from 12,225 to 6,578, while seminarians dropped from 48,046 to 5,083.[24] According to Stark, the reason for this is that the Second Vatican Council opened the doors of heaven not just to Christians, the baptized, believers, but to 'all men of good will',[25] but in doing so, it had essentially made the real priesthood useless. If it was enough to simply be good in order to get to heaven, what need was there to convert and observe the teachings of the Church? And, more importantly, what need was there to become a priest, nun or missionary if conversion was no longer necessary for saving one's soul? Instead, the more the Pentecostals demand of their own affiliates, both in economic terms and in terms of personal involvement, the more proselytes convert and the more these churches expand, particularly in Latin America and Africa.

In short, nothing in human life escapes the economy, defined by the Chicago School as the discipline that studies all finalized behaviour implying a strategic choice of means, ways and tools: so, all rational behaviour. In a 1984 article published with the significant title 'Economics – The Imperial Science?', George Stigler writes that the reach of this theory has been compared 'to Copernicus' theory of the movements of the heavenly bodies. Heavenly bodies are better behaved than human bodies, but it is conceivable that his fantasy will

---

[24] Ibid., p. 169.

[25] *Gaudium et spes*, Pastoral Constitution promulgated by Pope Paul VI (Giovanni Battista Montini) on the penultimate day of the Council, 7 December 1965: 'The Christian [. . .] will hasten forward to resurrection in the strength which comes from hope. All this holds true not only for Christians, but for all men of good will in whose hearts grace works in an unseen way' (chap. I, paragraphs 30–31). The Council pushed itself to the point of stating that: 'Indeed, the Church admits that she has greatly profited and still profits from the antagonism of those who oppose or who persecute her' (Chapter IV, 23). Available for download from the Vatican website, https://www.vatican.va/arc hive/hist_councils/ii_vatican_council/documents/vat-ii_const_19651207_gau dium-et-spes_it.html.

be approached through the spread of the economists' theory of behaviour to the entire domain of the social sciences'.[26]

A more sardonic vision of this empire is provided by the American economist Deirdre McCloskey: 'Comparing non-economic with economic matters is another sort of novelty, apparent in the imperialism of the new economics of history, law, politics, crime, and the rest, and most apparent in the work of the Kipling of the economic empire, Gary Becker. Among the least bizarre of his many metaphors, for instance, is that children are durable goods, like refrigerators.'[27]

At the risk of freezing our children and falling madly in love with the refrigerator (it's always possible to get confused), the scope of the Chicago Boys' doctrine is incredibly serious and ambitious. It provides nothing short of a totalizing interpretation of society and human history in all of its aspects, including the cultural and the criminal. It could be defined as a real *ideology*, given that it shapes the individual's relationship 'to himself, time, those around him, the future'.[28]

## State phobia

We don't know if the bountiful billionaires of the Midwest were aware of the totalizing nature and the global world vision of the ideas they were supporting. Their objective was much more immediate: they wanted a free hand, meaning fewer state controls. On its website, the Heritage Foundation declares that its mission is to fight for free enterprise and 'limited government'.[29] The declared objective is to dismantle the state

[26] George J. Stigler, 'Economics – The Imperial Science?', *Scandinavian Journal of Economics*, vol. 86, no. 3, 1984, pp. 301–13, p. 313.

[27] Deirdre McCloskey, *The Rhetoric of Economics* (1985). Madison, WI: University of Wisconsin Press, 1998, p. 42.

[28] Foucault, *The Birth of Biopolitics*, p. 242.

[29] 'Heritage's mission is to formulate and promote public policies based on the principles of free enterprise, limited government, individual freedom,

('our movement must destroy the prevalent statist paradigm' as Charles Koch said in 1978)[30] until it reaches the 'minimal state' yearned for by Nozick, a state whose social role is limited to that of a 'night watchman' and that in economic matters does nothing more than regulate the flow of money. Naturally, the primary and most urgent interest of those magnates financing the conservative revolution was that of reducing taxes for themselves.

But with the reduction of taxes, the billionaire philanthropists did not just want to keep a little more money for themselves (though this never hurts). Theirs was also a political objective, one that Foucault ironically referred to as a 'frugal state'[31] and which US conservatives had renamed much more ferociously (though much more realistically) *starve the beast*: to cut taxes in a way that forces the state to reduce public services lest it end up getting into debt and being blackmailed by creditors. Alan Greenspan, president of the Federal Reserve from 1987 to 2006, explicitly supported this before the Senate Finance Committee in 1978: 'Let us remember that the basic purpose of any tax cut program in today's environment is to reduce the momentum of expenditure growth by restraining the amount of revenue available.'[32]

---

traditional American values, and a strong national defense.' Heritage Foundation Mission Statement, available at: https://www.heritage.org/about -heritage/mission.

[30] Mayer, *Dark Money*, p. 355.

[31] Foucault, *The Birth of Biopolitics*: 'we are entering what could be called the epoch of frugal government', p. 28. 'The question of the frugality of government is indeed the question of liberalism', p. 29. Forty years later, the adjective 'frugal' met with great success, to the extent that some countries of the European Union (Austria, Denmark, Netherlands, Sweden) paraded it like a title of merit and adopted it to define their own negotiations for the concession of loans to countries in difficulty.

[32] Bruce Bartlett, 'Tax Cuts and "Starving the Beast"', *Forbes*, 7 May 2010, https:// www.forbes.com/2010/05/06/tax-cuts-republicans-starve-the-beast-columni sts-bruce-bartlett.html.

It is thanks to the action of conservative think tanks that the idea of a 'frugal' state was sold so successfully to the American public and electorate. For example, it was the Smith Richardson Foundation that, at Irving Kristol's suggestion, financed the bestseller, *The Way the World Works* (1978) by Jude Wanniski, which popularized the expression 'supply-side economics' and put the phrase 'Laffer's curve' on everyone's lips, according to which fiscal revenue diminishes beyond a certain level of taxation.

The billionaires' dream of a world without taxes draws ever closer, thanks to successive cuts from the 1980s to date. In the US, the maximum marginal tax rate was 94% after the Second World War (one of the reasons so many 'charitable' foundations allowing for the deduction of donations were created). Between 1981 and 1986, under President Reagan, this dropped to 28%. But the tax cuts continued under Bush Jr. when a bipartisan vote led to taxes on dividends being cut from 39.6% to 15%, and those on capital gains from 20% to 15%, while the last cut made by Trump lowered corporate taxes from 35% to 21%, creating a hole in federal finances. The US public deficit for the 2019 fiscal year broke the trillion-dollar upper limit, and in 2022, it reached $1.38 trillion.

Clearly, this ever-more frugal state (this increasingly starved beast) progressively reduced the services it provided (as was the aim established by the neolibs). But in order to deprive citizens of the public services guaranteed by Roosevelt's New Deal and Lyndon Johnson's reforms, it was first necessary to create a consensus around these cuts. It was therefore necessary to feed what Foucault called 'state phobia'. Already in 1979, the French philosopher was able to state: 'All of those who share in the great state phobia should know that they are following the direction of the wind and that in fact, for years and years, an effective reduction of the state has been on the way, a reduction of both the growth of state control and of a "statified" and "statifying" (*étatisante et étatisée*) governmentality.'[33] Foucault had sensed the wind in April 1979, which, one month after he gave the last lesson in his course, had brought Margaret Thatcher to power in the United Kingdom and had, less than two years later, seen Ronald Reagan inaugurated as the President of the United States.

The traditional line of attack against the state, already practised against Roosevelt's New Deal, had been to denounce the inevitable decline into totalitarianism of all state intervention, with the idea that the state has an infinite power for expansion, a dynamic that, once unleashed, becomes unstoppable: 'For example, an analysis of social security and the administrative apparatus on which it rests ends up, via some slippages and thanks to some plays on words, referring to the analysis of concentration camps.'[34] This was essentially the nucleus of the argument used by von Hayek in his *Road to Serfdom*. It begins with welfare programmes against poverty and ends up with concentration camps and gulags.

But this strategy was no longer enough. It was now necessary to convince those using the services that the tax money given to the state was being badly managed, wasted, and that it would be better spent if managed by private entities (such as foundations). They had to therefore be convinced, according to Reagan, that 'Government is not the solution [. . .] it is the problem'. Hence, (1) the 360° attack on the welfare state; and (2) an unprecedented exaltation of the heroic virtues of all NGOs. A linguistic parenthesis is required here: in the US, government does not refer to 'governmental' but to 'federal state'. As such, the acronym NGO does not mean 'non-governmental' organization, so one that is independent of the changing majorities in government, but 'non state', meaning private.

---

[33] Foucault, *The Birth of Biopolitics*, pp. 191–2. The French text uses the word 'gouvernementalité'.

[34] Ibid., pp. 187–8.

The attack on the state unfolded through thousands of TV broadcasts, radio programmes, articles, all generously provided by the conservative foundations and encouraged by their think tanks, which specialized in the financing of books that sat halfway between academic treatises and ideological pamphlets. There was no text that influenced US political debate behind which we would not find the generous support of those foundations. The most symbolic publication is *Losing Ground: American Social Policy 1950–1980* (1984), written by Charles Murray when he was employed by the Manhattan Institute and receiving the support of the Olin, Bradley and Smith Richardson foundations. Its thesis is that all social programmes run by the US state had increased poverty rather than alleviating it, because they had created incentives for short-sighted behaviour that imprisons people in poverty in the long run. According to the apologetic John Miller, the book's power lay in its 'perfect' tone: 'rather than taking a perverse delight in the failure of government to relieve the suffering of the poor, it approached the subject with heartfelt regret and unyielding resolve'.[35]

*Losing Ground* set in motion the most powerful of the three rhetorical devices which the insufficiently appreciated political economist and philosopher, Albert Hirschman, identified as foundational to reactionary discourse. The first of these rhetorical *topoi* was perversity, the second, futility and, the third, jeopardy. Perversity suggests that any attempt to resolve a problem exacerbates it, any reform aimed at improvement is revealed to make things worse. Futility suggests that any reform only scratches the surface because the structure of domination remains unaltered, and therefore everything stays the same as before, while jeopardy indicates that the cost of

---

[35] John J. Miller, *Strategic Investment in Ideas: How Two Foundations Reshaped America*, Washington, DC: Philanthropy Roundtable (publishing house financed by these foundations), 2003. Available at: https://search.issuelab.org/resources/28631/28631.pdf.

the proposed reform is too high, because it jeopardizes some previous precious conquest.[36]

*Losing Ground* is the perfect example of a manual of perversity. As Murray writes: 'We tried to provide more for the poor and instead produced a greater number of people in poverty. We tried to remove the barriers to escape from poverty, and inadvertently built a trap.'[37] Ten years later, in 1994 alongside psychologist Richard Herrnstein, Murray published *The Bell Curve: Intelligence and Class Structure in American Life*, which correlated low IQ tests and race in order to maintain that black people would have less chance than white people of joining the 'cognitive elite'. The book met with such indignation that he was fired from the Manhattan Institute, but thanks to the Bradley Foundation, he was quickly re-employed by the American Enterprise Institute.

In one way or another, the device of perversity is used by all material churned out by the reactionary think tanks: public healthcare ends up shortening the average lifespan, public education makes the population more ignorant and so on. Linda Chavez was senior fellow of the Manhattan Institute when she published *Out of the Barrio: Toward a New Politics of Hispanic Assimilation* (1991), in which she charged public welfare with being responsible for the 31% male unemployment and 50% births out of wedlock in the Puerto Rican *barrio* of New York.

Perversity is also used in the most bizarre cases, as illustrated by the book *More Guns, Less Crime* (1998) by John Lott, who at the time was a researcher at the University of Chicago with a grant from the Olin Foundation. If more guns mean less crime, then, with a perverse effect, any limitation on guns

---

[36] Albert O. Hirschman, *The Rhetoric of Reaction: Perversity, Futility, Jeopardy*. Cambridge, MA: The Belknap Press of Harvard University, 1991.

[37] Charles Murray, *Losing Ground: American Social Policy 1950–1980*. New York: Basic Books, 1984, p. 9.

implies more crime. It is entirely coincidental that the Olin Corporation owns the Winchester gun factory.

Jeopardy is instead used by Marvin Olasky in *The Tragedy of American Compassion* (1994), published with the help of the Bradley Foundation and distributed by Newt Gingrich to all newly elected Republican members of Congress in 1995. Olasky maintains that philanthropy worked better when it was religious, family-owned and private, and that the welfare state jeopardizes true social, private and religious solidarity. It was Olasky who coined the phrase 'compassionate conservatism', which became George Bush Jr.'s electoral slogan in 2000. It should be noted that in Europe the thesis of perversion has never worked particularly well and has instead been heavily substituted by jeopardy, especially in the European Union and particularly in the wake of the 2008 crisis: excessive social spending jeopardizes the economy and risks destroying hard-won wellbeing.

## The Campus as a Battleground

But naturally, the decisive battlefield for the war on ideas was the university, the place where protests had exploded in the 1960s. This was not the first time the foundations had financed universities: in 1865, Cornell University (in the state of New York) was founded with the money of Ezra Cornell, telegraph industrialist and the founder of Western Union; in 1890 the University of Chicago was created with Rockefeller's dollars. Many medical schools were built with money from the foundations, and some foundations had already funded conservative spokespersons, with the salaries of both von Mises at New York University and von Hayek in Chicago paid by the Volcker Foundation. But in the 1970s, a new strategy was enacted, referred to by James Piereson, director of the Olin Foundation from 1985 to 2005, as the 'beachheads strategy'. 'Conservative beachheads' were established in the most influential universities in order to obtain maximum leverage: 'Establishing beachheads at the nation's elite colleges and universities was exponentially more valuable than backing lesser-known schools.'[38] But conservative intellectuals were to be supported in a way that would not 'raise questions about academic integrity'. Rather than dictate a faculty appointment, conservative donors were to support those like-minded faculty members whose influence could be expanded through outside funding, though it was 'essential for the integrity and reputation of the programs that they be defined not by ideological points of view'.[39]

This strategy was implemented with enormous success. I will give just two examples. At the University of Chicago, the Olin Foundation began to finance Allan Bloom (1930–92), who was known at the time as a scholar of Plato, Jonathan Swift and Jean-Jacques Rousseau. With Olin's support, Bloom published his article 'Our Listless Universities' in the *National Review* in 1982, which opens with the following words:

> I begin with my conclusion: students in our best universities do not believe in anything, and those universities are doing nothing about it, nor can they. An easy going American kind of nihilism has descended upon us, a nihilism without terror of the abyss, The great questions – God, freedom, and immortality, according to Kant – hardly touch the young. And the universities, which should encourage the quest for the clarification of such questions, are the very source of the doctrine which makes that quest appear futile.[40]

---

[38] Miller, *Strategic Investment in Ideas*, p. 17.

[39] James Piereson, 'Planting the Seeds of Liberty', *Philanthropy*, May–June 2005.

[40] Allan Bloom, 'Our Listless Universities', *The National Review*, 10 December 1982, https://www.nationalreview.com/2006/09/our-listless-universities-willi umrex/.

At that time, Michael Joyce was at the helm of the Olin
Foundation, making way in 1985 for Piereson and going on
to direct the Bradley Foundation (which had fully supported
Charles Murray of *Losing Ground* and *The Bell Curve*).
According to Forbes, Joyce 'was inspired by Antonio Gramsci.
He wanted to effect radical transformation'.[41]

After initially financing Bloom with $25,000 in 1981, the
following years Joyce and Piereson supported a donation of
$100,000, making Bloom Olin's first, fruitful 'beachhead'. In
1983, Olin signed a check for $1.1 million to create the Olin
Center for Inquiry into the Theory and Practice of Democracy,
co-directed by Bloom. The name given to the centre responded
perfectly to the demands for neutrality, not to appear partisan, as Piereson had wanted. In 1985, Olin donated another
$1.85 million, followed by $1.8 million in 1988 and so on. The
dollars continued to flow in even after Bloom's death in 1992:
$750,000 in 1994, $810,000 in 1996, $1.4 million in 1998. By
2001, the Olin Foundation had given the Centre more than
$9 million.[42]

So, let's think about this for a moment: 'rough and ready'
billionaires from the American Midwest, caustic soda and
Winchester rifle manufacturers, financing a university centre
to the tune of millions of dollars in which seminars on Rousseau
and *Gulliver's Travels* are given by a flamboyant classicist.
In effect, Bloom turned out to be a good investment. In 1987
his book, *The Closing of the American Mind: How Higher
Education Has Failed Democracy and Impoverished the Souls
of Today's Students* expanding on the thesis of his 1982 article,
was published and jumped to the top of bestseller lists. In the
US, it sold more than a million copies. If it didn't deal a mortal
blow to the progressive consensus on campus, it seriously
damaged its hegemony. Scarcely two years later, in February

---

[41] Mayer, *Dark Money*, p. 125.
[42] Miller, *A Gift of Freedom*, pp. 152, 156.

1989, Francis Fukuyama would give his famous lesson on the 'end of history' with the support of and in Bloom's Olin centre.[43] It would first appear in published form the following summer as an article in Irving Kristol's journal, *The National Interest*, as if an augury of the fall of the Berlin Wall eight months later.

On the same issue of universities, in 1991 Dinesh D'Souza published *Illiberal Education: The Politics of Race and Sex on Campus*, a text that applied the argument of perversity to affirmative action: all of the actions taken to improve the situation of minorities on campus ended up exacerbating them.

But probably the best academic 'beachhead' was found by the Olin Foundation: Samuel Huntington (1927–2008). Ex-*enfant prodige* of Harvard University, where he had started teaching at age 23 and where he stayed until he died, Huntington was first noticed by conservative (and military) circles in 1957 thanks to his book *The Soldier and the State: The Theory and Politics of Civil–Military Relations*, still studied in military academies, in which he held that the best way civilians can control the military is not to place limits on their autonomy but to professionalize them. The memory of 1951 was still fresh when, faced with the risk of a descent into Bonapartism, president Harry Truman had stood down Douglas MacArthur as commander in chief during the Korean war. In the elections of the following year, Truman was defeated by another general, Dwight Eisenhower.

However, Huntington achieved global notoriety in 1975 when (together with Michel Crozier and Joji Watanuki) he presented the report titled *The Crisis of Democracy: Report on the Governability of Democracies* to the tri-lateral Commission subsequently published by New York University Press.[44] This spoke to the ungovernability of Western nations,

---

[43] The conference transcripts are available online at https://apps.dtic.mil/dtic/tr /fulltext/u2/a228233.pdf.

[44] A discussion group founded in 1973 by the banker David Rockefeller, the Trilateral Commission was an alternative and globalist capitalist response to Lewis Powell's 'Manifesto' of 1971. Its first director was Zbigniew Brzezinski

attributing it to an 'excess of democracy', and underscoring the incompatibility between economic efficiency and social equality that would signal the logic of the victory of efficiently authoritarian governments that had as its underlying logic the vision of a Singapore as the utopia and final state of world history. In the Carter administration, Huntington was still on what we might call middle ground, serving on the White House Security Planning coordinator for the National Security Council. After Carter's resounding defeat however, at the beginning of the 1980s, he received his first contributions from the Smith Richardson and Bradley foundations to open what would become the Olin Institute for Strategic Studies at Harvard, to which Olin would donate $8.4 million over the years. 'The foundation kept track of those who passed through Huntington's Olin program, proudly noting that many went into public service and academia. Between 1990 and 2001, 56 of the 88 Olin fellows at the Harvard program continued on to teach at the University of Chicago, Cornell, Dartmouth, Georgetown, Harvard, MIT, Penn, and Yale. Many others became public figures in government, think tanks, and the media.'[45] The dissemination of reactionary ideas was guaranteed. In summer 1993, Huntington published 'Clash of Civilizations?' in *Foreign Affairs*, the essay that three years later would become a book by the same name but without the question mark, a title that seemed to be confirmed by the September 11, 2001 attacks on the Twin Towers in New York.

(1928–2017), future security advisor to Jimmy Carter. Other members of the Trilateral Commission were Paul Volcker and Alan Greenspan, future presidents of the Federal Reserve, and Jean-Claude Trichet, future president of the European Central Bank. The Trilateral has been the subject of various conspiracy theories, not least from Barry Goldwater and the John Birch Society, before being substituted in conspiracy mythology by the Bilderberg Group in the role of the hypothetical occult centre of world power.

[45] Jane Mayer, 'How Right-Wing Billionaires Infiltrated Higher Education', *The Chronicle Review*, 12 February 2016, https://www.chronicle.com/article/how-right-wing-billionaires-infiltrated-higher-education/.

Allan Bloom and Samuel Huntington are just two of the most famous 'beachheads' established by Olin. Also at Harvard, the Olin Foundation contributed \$3.3 million to the Mansfield Program on Constitutional Government created by Harvey Mansfield, another imitator of Leo Strauss (1899–1973), the German philosopher and *maître à penser* of all US neo-conservatives, the political equivalent of what Mises and von Hayek were to the economy.

It would be useless here to run through the hundreds of millions, if not billions donated by the foundations to various universities. Let me give just one example: George Mason University in Washington is for the most part financed by the Koch brothers, to the point where the law department has been re-dedicated to judge Antonin Scalia (see above). The George Mason University also hosts the Mercatus Center, another Koch think tank, defined 'the motor of deregulation' at Washington, whilst researchers and faculty at this university are among the strongest opponents of policies that would combat global warming.

But these are sectorial battles fought in defence of specific interests that are only the collateral products of the 'war of ideas'. It is, however, worth focusing on what is considered Piereson and the Olin Foundation's masterpiece: the redefinition of the concept of justice and their imposing of a new idea of law on the world.

# 3

# The Justice Market

In 5,000 years of history, no one had thought of it. Justice and law had been discussed at length, by asking is justice the defence of the weak against the strong? Or is it the weapon of the strongest against the weakest, as maintained in the fifth century by the sophist Thrasymachus?

> I say that justice is simply what is good for the stronger [. . .] Every ruling power makes laws for its own good. A democracy makes democratic laws, a tyranny tyrannical laws, and so on. In making these laws, they make it clear that what is good for them, the rulers, is what is just for their subjects. If anyone disobeys, they punish him from breaking the law and acting unjustly. That's what I mean [. . .] when I say that in all cities the same thing is just, namely what is good for the ruling authority. This is where the power lies, and the result is [. . .] that the same thing is just everywhere – what is good for the stronger.[1]

---

[1] Plato, *The Republic*, 338c–339a, Cambridge: Cambridge University Press, 2000, pp. 15–16. Available at: http://160592857366.free.fr/joe/ebooks/ShareData/The%20Republic%20by%20Plato.pdf.

But finally, at the end of the 1970s in Chicago, the age-old quandary was put to bed: *just is what makes the market happy*, the formula (in economic terms) closest to Thrasymachus' thesis. This is the central proposition of the doctrine known as 'Law and Economics'. According to philosophical dictionaries, this doctrine maintains that the law should be considered a tool that promotes economic efficiency, affirming that economic analysis and the ideal of efficiency can guide legal practice. Law and Economics studies how legislation can be used to improve market conditions. This means that it studies how the rationality of the market *must* shape the law and how the law *must* facilitate the market. Behind these definitions is an entire anthropology, a doctrine of humankind, of the individual-entrepreneur, that presupposes the assumption that human beings are 'rational maximizers' of their own individual satisfactions and, as such, respond to incentives. A 'rational maximizer' of personal satisfaction adjusts the means to the end in the most efficient way. We are not talking here of solely monetary matters; there are other kinds of satisfactions. Every potential satisfaction is implicated in the calculation of economic satisfactions and can therefore be investigated according to the rationality of the means with respect to the ends or of the balance between cost and benefit.

We have already seen that with this approach, economic calculation becomes the main tool, often (in the last instance) the only tool, with which to study, understand, *narrate* and judge all spheres of human action. It is therefore an ideology that, like all other ideologies, is presented as non-ideological, a-ideological, *scientific*, using equations and mathematical formulae.

As such, Law and Economics meets all of Piereson and the Olin Foundation's requirements when searching for a conceptual beachhead. As Piereson candidly states to the *New York Times*, 'I saw [Law and Economics] as a way into the law schools – I probably shouldn't confess that, [. . .]

Economic analysis tends to have conservatizing effects'.[2] In a later interview, Piereson clarifies: 'If you said to a dean that you wanted to fund conservative constitutional law, he would reject the idea out of hand. But if you said you wanted to support Law and Economics, he would be much more open to the idea', he confided. 'Law and Economics is neutral, but it has a philosophical thrust in the direction of free markets and limited government. That is, like many disciplines, it seems neutral, but it isn't in fact.'[3]

The school had started to take form at the University of Chicago in the 1950s, when von Hayek was teaching there. In this context, the phrase we have already quoted – 'social justice is meaningless' – was premonitory, with the emphasis now placed on the term 'justice' rather than the adjective 'social'. Those driving this new discipline were Aaron Director (who like von Hayek was also financed by the Volcker Foundation) and Ronald Coase, whom we have already encountered in our discussion of the relationship between enterprise and the market. In 1958, they founded and co-directed the *Journal of Law and Economics*, the school's official mouthpiece. The conservative Coase was in 'academic exile' from a post-war Britain hegemonized by Keynesian thought, and which under the Labour government led by Clement Attlee (1945–1951) had set in practice one of the most progressive social states in Europe, planned by William Beveridge. With a typically Anglo-Saxon sense of humour, Coase later recounted: 'When I came to the University of Chicago, I regarded my role as that of Saint Paul to Aaron Director's Christ. He got

[2] Jason Deparle, 'Goals Reached, Donor on Right Closes Up Shop', *The New York Times*, 29 May 2005, https://www.nytimes.com/2005/05/29/politics/goals-reached-donor-on-right-closes-up-shop.html.

[3] Mayer, *Dark Money*, p. 108. On Olin's financing of Law and Economics, as well as this text (pp. 130–4), see also Miller, *Strategic Investment in Ideas*, pp. 22–8. All subsequent information will be taken from these two sources unless otherwise specified.

the doctrine going, and what I had to do was bring it to the gentiles.'[4]

## Optimum Pollution

The 'Letter to the Gentiles' with which the apostle Ronald Coase brought the word of Law and Economics to the world was the 1960 article that would win him the Nobel and which would be decisive for the future of the discipline: 'The Problem of Social Cost'. Coase dealt in particular with the issue of environmental costs, for example 'contamination of a stream. If we assume that the harmful effect of the pollution is that it kills the fish, the question to be decided is, Is the value of the fish lost greater or less than the value of the product which the contamination of the stream makes possible?'. Coase therefore believed there to be an error in

> the suggestion that smoke-producing factories should, by means of zoning regulations, be removed from the districts in which the smoke causes harmful effects. When the change in the location of the factory results in a reduction in production, this obviously needs to be taken into account and weighed against the harm which would result from the factory remaining in that location. The aim of such regulations should not be to eliminate smoke pollution but rather to secure the *optimum amount of smoke pollution*, this being the amount which will maximize the value of production.[5]

---

[4] Speech given at a roundtable on 'Intellectual History of Law and Economics' held in Los Angeles on 21–23 March 1981, referred to by Edmund W. Kitch, 'The Fire of Truth: A Remembrance of Law and Economics at Chicago, 1932–1970', *Journal of Law and Economics*, vol. 26, April 1983, pp. 163–234, p. 192.

[5] Ronald H. Coase, 'The Problem of Social Cost', *Journal of Law and Economics*, vol. 3, October 1960, pp. 1–44. Reprinted in Ronald H. Coase, *The Firm, the Market and the Law*. Chicago, IL: University of Chicago Press, 1988, pp. 95–156. The citations are from pp. 96 and 153 of this book. My italics.

(And again: what is the optimum pollution if the smoke pouring from those chimneys causes lethal disease in children and genetic defects in future generations?)

As you might imagine, Coase's words are music to the ears of large, polluting companies that contribute generously to the billionaires' philanthropy.

In 1968, in an article whose title – 'Crime and Punishment' – was a self-deprecating quote from Fyodor Dostoevsky, Gary Becker extended the concept of Coase's 'optimum pollution' to the entire problem of law breaking. Becker saw himself as a kind of Aristotle for neoliberalism, as he applied his method to all social science fields (consumption, criminality, family life, etc.), a bit like how the Stagirite had taught metaphysics, zoology, logic and politics, though, as we have seen, Deirdre McCloskey instead defined him somewhat more mischievously as the 'Kipling' of the neolib epistemological empire (Kipling was consumed with the burden that the white man had to bear, the man to whom fell the thankless task of civilizing his ungrateful subjects).[6]

According to Becker, crime is any action that leads the individual to run the risk of being condemned to punishment: 'a person commits an offense if the expected utility to him exceeds the utility he could get by using his time and other resources at other activities. Some persons become "criminals," therefore, not because their basic motivation differs from that of other persons, but because their benefits and costs differ'.[7]

---

[6] 'The White Man's Burden' is the title and the refrain of a poem written by Rudyard Kipling in 1899, with the subtitle 'The United States and the Philippine Islands', when the Filipinos resisted US invasion with their tenacious guerrilla warfare. The poem can be found on many websites, here is a significant verse: 'Take up the White Man's burden / And reap his old reward: / The blame of those ye better, / The hate of those ye guard – / The cry of hosts ye humour / (Ah, slowly!) toward the light: – / "Why brought he us from bondage, / Our loved Egyptian night?"'.

[7] Gary Becker, 'Crime and Punishment: An Economic Approach', *Journal of Political Economy*, vol. 76, no. 2, March–April 1968, pp. 169–217, p. 176.

The criminal is also an investor who reasons in terms of costs and benefits, and who must evaluate what benefit they will gain from their crime based on the cost it implies, meaning the risk (the probability) of being punished. Justice's task is not to abstractly define what is lawful and what is not, but to issue laws that it is possible to enforce, and to then ensure they are respected with maximum cost to the criminal and, at the same time, minimal cost to the collective. Once again, the issue is one of min/max, of optimization, as the title of Stigler's article, 'The Optimum Enforcement of Laws', explicitly states: 'The goal of enforcement, let us assume, is to achieve that degree of compliance with the rule of prescribed (or proscribed) behavior that the society believes it can afford. There is one decisive reason why the society must forego "complete" enforcement of the rule: *enforcement is costly*.'[8] A classic example is that of department stores: halving thefts is easy with more CCTV, surveillance and improved magnetic markings on the merchandise. But reducing thefts by 90% is much more costly, while reducing thefts by 95% is almost prohibitive. At that point, the value of the stolen goods is less than the cost involved with stopping the theft in the first place. As such, it is worth accepting an 'optimal' percentage of thefts and incorporating the loss into the sales price.

The cost is a relevant problem because magistrates, police and prisons are all financed through taxation (and so we return to the crux of the problem). Expressed in even more vivid terms by Becker, the question is: 'How many resources and how much punishment should be used to enforce different kinds of legislation? Put equivalently, although more strangely, how many offenses should be permitted and how many offenders should go unpunished?'[9] So, from a penal perspective also,

---

[8] George J. Stigler, 'The Optimum Enforcement of Laws', *Journal of Political Economy*, vol. 78, no. 3, May–June 1970, pp. 526–36. Citation from pp. 526–7 (my italics).
[9] Becker, 'Crime and Punishment', p. 170.

Law and Economics is therefore the reduction of justice and its administration to a problem of minimums and maximums.

At the beginning of the 1970s when the Olin Foundation entered the scene, though still marginal in the academic field, Law and Economics had already churned out its own research corpus: in 1973 Richard Posner had systematized the subject matter in his treatise *Economic Analysis of Law* (Little Brown and Co.), and the following year, Becker and Landes edited the miscellaneous collection, *Essays in the Economics of Crime and Punishment* (Columbia University Press).

As well as financing the *Journal of Law and Economics*, Olin began to support Henry Manne, who in 1965 had published an article on corporate mergers in which, going against the grain, he denied that mergers were anticompetitive.[10] This 'pioneering' text was to Corporate Law what 'The Problem of Social Cost' had been to the subject of crime and punishment, laying the groundwork for what has been defined as a true 'revolution of corporate law': 'The term "revolution" is invoked all too often in popular culture, but [. . .] it is entirely apt in this case. The revolution in corporate law has been so thorough and profound that those working in the field today would have considerable difficulty recognizing what it was like twenty-five to thirty years ago.'[11] But Manne's real talent was for organization, to the point that it was to him that the term 'intellectual entrepreneur' was first applied. Thanks to Olin, in 1974 Manne founded the Law and Economics Centre (LEC) in Miami, which then moved to Emory University in Atlanta, Georgia, before settling at the Koch-financed George Mason University in Fairfax, Virginia, where Manne would later become Dean. But 'while the Olin programs represented a "Fabian" strategy of slowly burrowing into mainstream institutions,

[10] Henry Manne, 'Mergers and the Market for Corporate Control', *Journal of Political Economy*, vol. 73, no. 2, April 1965, pp. 110–20.

[11] Roberta Romano, 'After the Revolution in Corporate Law', *Journal of Legal Education*, vol. 55, no. 3, September 2005, pp. 342–59, p. 342.

GMUSL [George Mason University School of Law] follows a "Gramscian" approach of creating a parallel institution where more libertarian professors could hone their ideas without the compromises associated with elite institutions'[12]: yet another example of how the counterintelligentsia appropriates the categories of the workers' movement.

According to Manne, from a Law and Economics perspective, corporate law had an enormous academic market before it: 'Almost every corporation today has considerable in-house legal work; the general counsel has become an increasingly important figure [. . .]. Thus a law school especially designed to serve the needs with which these men are familiar could strike a sympathetic chord that many other law schools do not.'[13]

LEC would soon become a forge for conservative judges. From 1976, thanks to donations from 'philanthropists' (which, over the years, included not only Olin but also the Charles Koch Foundation, Shell, Exxon Mobil, the pharmaceutical giant Pfizer and insurance company State Farm), LEC organized summer schools on Law and Economics in which magistrates were put up for two weeks in luxury resorts such as the Ocean Reef Club in Key Largo, Florida. After a few hours of lectures, the judges could relax on the golf course, in the swimming pool and at the bar. In just a few years, 6,660 judges, including 40% of the federal judges and various Supreme Court judges, had taken part in these holidays. The fact that a phalanx of judges follows a particular interpretation of the law, and in a particular way of writing law, is pivotal in all places where Common law is in force (so in all Anglo-Saxon countries), where the legal system is based on precedent rather than codes, as happens in countries where Civil law is used. Every sentence creates law and the influence of a legal doctrine grows exponentially.

[12] Steven M. Teles, *The Rise of the Conservative Legal Movement*. Princeton, NJ: Princeton University Press, 2010, p. 207.
[13] Ibid., p. 103. The paragraphs discussing him are titled 'The Birth of an Intellectual Entrepreneur: Manne at Rochester'.

In the meantime, Olin was financing the most prestig-
ious universities to the tune of $68 million, with more than
$10 million going to Harvard, $7 million to Yale and Chicago,
and more than $2 million going to Columbia, Cornell and
Georgetown.

Between 1985 and 1989, Olin paid for 83% of all Law and
Economics programmes in US law schools. For Olin, however,
the real skeleton key that would open the door to all other campuses was the $18 million the foundation donated to Harvard
in 1985 to open the John M. Olin Center for Law, Economics
and Business at Harvard Law School. Not least because this
centre upturned the direction of Harvard's law school, which
had until then been predominantly liberal-progressive and
dominated by Critical Legal Studies (CLS), the most dynamic
current for leftist lawyers. With the Olin Centre, Harvard's law
school was placed in the hands of Law and Economics conservatives. At that point, other universities followed suit and,
by 1990, around 80 law schools offered Law and Economics as
part of their studies. The conservatives were able to celebrate:
'Law and Economics is the most successful intellectual movement in the law of the past thirty years, having rapidly moved
from insurgency to hegemony.'[14]

Olin continued to finance scholarships for law students spe-
cializing in this doctrine, in particular through the Federalist
Society, a conservative law students' association founded in
1982, with a donation of $5.5 million from Olin and equally
large gifts from foundations linked to the Kochs, the Scaife
Mellons and other usual suspects. Over time, the Federalist
Society became a powerful professional network of 65,000
right-wing lawyers with 150 chapters in campus universities
and 90 for practising lawyers. All current conservative judges
of the Supreme Court are members, as are ex-US Attorney
Generals Edwin Meese and John Ashcroft and former

---

[14] Ibid., p. 216.

vice-president Richard Cheney. Twenty-five out of the thirty
Court of Appeals judges nominated by Donald Trump in the
first two years of his mandate were members of the Federalist
Society. [15] During his presidency, Trump had nominated 174
district federal judges (out of a total 677) and fifty-four federal
appeal judges out of 177. [16]

But we would not be able to recognize just how crucial the
subject of justice is to neoliberals if we did not consider a
shrewd observation by Michel Foucault:

> For in fact there is a privileged connection between a society
> orientated towards the form of the enterprise and a society in
> which the most important public service is the judicial institu-
> tion. The more you multiply enterprises, the more you multiply
> the centers of formation of something like an enterprise, and
> the more you force governmental action to let these enterprises
> operate, then of course the more you multiply the surfaces
> of friction between each of these enterprises, the more you
> multiply opportunities for disputes, and the more you multiply
> the need for legal arbitration. An enterprise society and a judi-
> cial society, a society orientated towards the enterprise and a
> society framed by a multiplicity of judicial institutions, are two
> faces of a single phenomenon. [17]

Fewer civil servants, more legal staff (judges, lawyers, police,
etc.). Not only do we have a more judicial society, but a judiciary
that needs greater economic skills due to the 'boom in litigation,
economic deregulation, and mergers and acquisitions' (see

---

[15] Website of The Federalist Society, Lawyers Division, https://fedsoc.org/divi
sions/lawyers, and David Montgomery, 'Conquerors of the Courts: Forget
Trump's Supreme Court picks: The Federalist Society's impact on the law goes
much deeper', *The Washington Post Magazine*, 2 January 2019, https://www
.washington-post.com/news/magazine/wp/2019/01/02/feature/conquerors
-of-the-courts/.

[16] Figures updated on 20 June 2020, by Ballotpedia.org.

[17] Michel Foucault, *Birth of Biopolitics*, p. 155.

Manne) and 'the increase in complex financial agreements'[18]: on one hand, economic activity becomes increasingly subject to legal arbitration, while on the other, justice increasingly defers to financial expertise. It is no coincidence that, in 1977, Richard Posner was one of the founders of the economic consultancy firm Lexecon, which provided economic expertise and analysis on legal cases and normative issues. When it was acquired by Compass in 2008, Lexecon had more than 100 employees, offices in five cities and clients that included many of the US's major corporations. Today, Compass Lexecon has more than 750 employees over four continents and offices in twenty-one cities.

But the impact of Law and Economics on our world is even more cogent, because it becomes the legal doctrine of the empire dominating the world (Foucault entirely missed – or systematically avoided – the theme of empire in our time). And as the Ancient Romans were well aware, law is one of the lynchpins of empire, as it governs those who impose not only their justice, but the way in which they administer justice. What has happened since the Second World War is that US civil law has been imposed the world over and all trade deals are negotiated and signed only in exchange for the application of US law in case of disagreement. As a result of its proselytizing among US magistrates (particularly at a federal level) and lawyers, Law and Economics has shaped the very understanding and administration of justice throughout the world. It changes our law without us even realizing.

## Free Baby Market

It would be impossible to grasp all the implications – philosophical, political and social – of Law and Economics

---

[18] Teles, *The Rise of the Conservative Legal Movement*, p. 101.

if we did not cite the thesis that caused the most uproar, presented by Elisabeth Landes and Richard Posner in a 1978 article titled 'The Economics of the Baby Shortage', in which they candidly proposed the free commerce of children as the most efficient method of adoption.[19] And to think that, as he himself explains, Posner had been a liberal until at least 1968:

> People like George [Stigler] and Aaron [Director] and Milton [Friedman], Gary Becker, Harold Demsetz were extremely conservative [. . .] I'd been very liberal up until then, but I didn't like the student unrest of the late sixties and the general leftism . . . I didn't have any particular belief in the Vietnamese, all this left-wing stuff and riots and all that, so I was unsympathetic, but as late as '68 I did vote for Humphrey [the Democratic Party candidate]. I didn't vote for Nixon, but gradually I swung around [so that] in the seventies I was very conservative.[20]

Here we have another one for whom the student uprising was a real 'road to Damascus' moment. Just like what happened to the industrialist John Olin, who was scandalized by the sight of the armed black students at Cornell University, and as happened to a progressive German theologian by the name of Joseph Ratzinger who was converted to conservatism by the protests of his students at Tübingen University, before being made pope as Benedict XVI.

Landes and Posner's thesis was that the adoption system regulated in the US by state agencies created a lack of children to adopt, increased costs (particularly in terms of waiting lists, sometimes years-long) and generated a flourishing black

[19] Elisabeth M. Landes and Richard A. Posner, 'The Economics of the Baby Shortage', *Journal of Legal Studies*, vol. 7, no. 2, 1978, pp. 323–48.
[20] Interview with Steven M. Teles in *The Rise of the Conservative Legal Movement*, p. 98.

market. Furthermore, 40 years later and with hindsight, we see how there is already a market for surrogate human uteruses and sperm.

The Chicago Boys believed in the need to always underscore how deregulation is the most efficient system for allocating resources, even in the trade of newborns. As such, the most rational way of allocating available children would be the free baby market, the free buying and selling of infants (the authors point out that this would, of course, be in line with all limitations forbidding abuse against minors): 'In a legal and competitive baby market, price would be equated to the marginal costs of producing and selling for adoption babies of *a given quality*' (my italics).[21] It seems absurd, but when presented in the context of technical terminology, diagrams, curves, tables and equations, the expression takes on its own lab-like sterility.

Of course, Landes and Posner admit, 'were baby prices quoted as prices of soybean futures are quoted, a racial ranking of these prices would be evident, with white baby prices higher than nonwhite baby prices': 'prices for babies are racially stratified as a result of different supply and demand conditions in the different racial groups but perhaps bringing this fact out into the open would exacerbate racial tensions in our society'.[22]

The authors warn: 'Some people are also upset by the implications for the eugenic alteration of the human race that are presented by baby selling', 'for any market will generate incentives to improve the product as well as to optimize the price and quantity of the current quality level of the product'.[23] In reality, this eugenicist drift is already visible in the artificial insemination market, if it is true that 50% of all human sperm

---

[21] Landes and Posner, 'The Economics of the Baby Shortage', p. 339.
[22] Ibid., pp. 344–5.
[23] Ibid., p. 345.

imported into Great Britain comes from Denmark ('Viking sperm').[24] But Landes and Posner raise the issue of race, tacked on at the end of the article, criticizing public agencies for their 'exclusive control over the supply of both "first-quality" adoptive children and "second-quality" children residing in foster care'.[25]

The entirety of the political agenda underpinning the proposal of a free baby market becomes clear in a second article written by Posner nine years later as a response to the widespread criticism the authors were met with – theirs was compared to Jonathan Swift's *Modest Proposal* (1729) in which the author of *Gulliver's Travels* suggested, with great seriousness and compunction, that in order to solve their economic problems the Irish should sell and butcher the country's infants to bring great relief to public finances and healthy improvements in their diet. Given that 'for heuristic purposes (only!) it is useful to analogize the sale of babies to that of an ordinary good, such as an automobile or a television set',[26] Posner tries to clear the field and set some boundaries. He admits that, unlike a television, when it comes to newborn infants the defective product cannot be exchanged: a 'limitation on a baby market concerns remedies for breach of contract. In an ordinary market a buyer can both reject defective goods and, if the seller refuses to deliver and damages would be an inadequate remedy for the refusal, get specific performance of the contract'. 'For the same reason (the child's welfare) neither natural nor adopting parents should be allowed to sell their children after infancy, that is, after the child has established a bond with its parents.'[27]

---

[24] Stewart Lee, 'Denmark sows seeds of discontent over Brexit', *The Guardian*, 2 September 2018, https://www.theguardian.com/global/commentisfree/2018/sep/02/denmark-sows-seeds-of-discontent-over-brexit.

[25] Landes and Posner, 'The Economics of the Baby Shortage', p. 346.

[26] Richard A. Posner, 'The Regulation of the Market in Adoptions', *Boston University Law Review*, vol. 67, 1987, pp. 59–72, p. 64.

[27] Ibid., p. 67. In the previous article, Landes and Posner got away with the issue of age limits: 'We are speaking only of sales of newborn infants, and do not

But above all, the article reveals the political values inherent in the anxiety over the lack of children available for adoption: 'The supply of babies for adoption has been dramatically affected by the increase in abortions since the Supreme Court's decision in *Roe v. Wade.*' If the children were paid for, as abortion is nothing more than a woman's last option, 'for little more than the maintenance and medical expenses of pregnancy plus any lost earnings, and often for less, many women might be induced to forgo an abortion and give up the baby for adoption'.[28] Accordingly, the buying and selling of children turns out to be a way to reduce the number of abortions and therefore meet the requests of the US's Christian conservatives, who are fervently anti-abortion and for whom *Roe v. Wade* had been like a red rag to a bull for 39 years until it was overruled in June 2022 by the now majority conservative Supreme Court.

Finally, Posner clarifies the proposal's other political message: 'Thus far I have implicitly been speaking only of the market for healthy white infants. There is no shortage of non-white and of handicapped infants' (To be noted here is the implied equivalence between healthy and white, and handicapped and non-white, as if not being white were a physical handicap.) 'Such children are substitutes for healthy white infants, and the higher the price of the latter, the greater will be the demand for the former.' (For Posner it is unthinkable that a white couple would choose for themselves to adopt a non-white or handicapped child.)

The rules and regulations governing the adoption of healthy white children such, says Posner, that they

suggest that parents should have a right to sell older children. The creation of such a right would require identification of the point at which the child is sufficiently mature to be entitled to a voice in his placement. However, the question is largely academic given the lack of any significant market for adopting older children' (p. 344).

[28] Posner, *The Regulation of the Market in Adoptions*, p. 63.

have increased the willingness of childless couples to consider adopting a child of a type not in short supply [. . .] The present system is, in any event, a grossly inefficient, as well as covert, method of encouraging the adoption of the hard-to-place child. If society wants to subsidize these unfortunate children, the burden of the subsidies would be borne, if not by the natural parents of the children, then by the taxpaying population at large – rather than by just the nation's childless white couples, who under the present unsystematic system bear the lion's share of the burden by being denied the benefits of an efficient method of allocating healthy white infants for adoption in the hope that this will induce them to adopt non-white, handicapped, or older children.[29]

These non-white children are so annoying! Their existence really is a bother!

The racist sub-text to the proposal for a free baby market is revealed in all its shameless glory: we must not make white couples pay too much for wanting to adopt a white child! Indeed, the state, by levies on the tax-paying population, should pay out to support their endeavour.

[29] Ibid., p. 65.

# 4

# Trigger-Happy Parents

U p until now we have seen the attack on regulation of the economy, universities, justice and, most recently, even the adoption system. But what must be uprooted is the idea that we can expect anything positive from the collective, from what is shared, from the public, the state or the government. And it must be uprooted from childhood: any later is too late. Children must be raised on white bread and neoliberalism, which will be impossible if the school remains public, because the teachers, paid by public finances, will not be able to bite the hand that feeds them (or at least only a minority will do so). It is therefore essential that school is privatized from primary level onwards, from nursery even. But how was it possible, to use Milton Friedman's terminology, to dismantle the 'nationalization of the education industry'?

The solution is formalized by Friedman himself in 1955:

> Governments could require a minimum level of education which they could finance by giving parents vouchers redeemable for a specified maximum sum per child per year if spent on 'approved' educational services. Parents would then be free to spend this sum and any additional sum on purchasing

educational services from an 'approved' institution of their own choice. The educational services could be rendered by private enterprises operated for profit, or by non-profit institutions of various kinds. The role of the government would be limited to assuring that the schools met certain minimum standards such as the inclusion of a minimum common content in their programs, much as it now inspects restaurants to assure that they maintain minimum sanitary standards.[1]

The voucher strategy is part of the wider idea, also proposed by Friedman, of 'negative tax'. The idea is simple: just as incomes below a certain threshold are exempt from taxation, and taxes are paid as a percentage of any income received above that threshold ('positive tax'), so anyone below that threshold should receive a subsidy proportionate to the disparity between their income and that minimum threshold. As with the positive tax, the calculation for the negative tax also takes into consideration the size of the family and number of children.

It is clear that this threshold is the poverty threshold, and that negative tax is a poverty subsidy. Put like that, this doesn't seem that bad an idea. However, we must analyse its implications and repercussions. First, the state that limits itself to handing out negative tax to the least well-off has given up trying to deal with the causes of poverty, choosing only to alleviate its most macroscopic effects. As Lionel Stoléru, a French political economist under Giscard d'Estaing, said: 'Negative tax is [. . .] entirely incompatible with the social understanding that wants to know why there is poverty before running in to help. Accepting negative tax means therefore accepting a universalist understanding of poverty founded on the necessity

[1] Milton Friedman, 'The Role of Government in Education', in Robert A. Solo (ed.), *Economics and the Public Interest*. New Brunswick, NJ: Rutgers University Press, 1955, pp. 123–44, downloaded from https://la.utexas.edu /users/hcleaver/330T/350kPEEFriedmanRoleOfGovttable.pdf.

to help those who are poor *without trying to understand whose fault it is*, founded, that is, on the situation and not the origin.'²

This is an understanding of the welfare state that is entirely different from that which inspired the social democratic systems and the New Deal. Any idea of wealth redistribution is abandoned. As Friedman wrote in 1962, 'The advantages of this arrangement are clear. It is directed specifically at the problem of poverty. It gives help in the form most useful to the individual, namely, cash. It is general and could be substituted for the host of special measures now in effect. It makes explicit the cost borne by society. It operates outside the market.'³

With the notion of the 'poverty threshold', any idea of 'relative poverty' – the idea of a divide between rich and poor that should be, if not closed then at least, reduced – is abandoned, and the idea of 'absolute poverty' is adopted. As the ineffable Stoléru bluntly puts it: '*The frontier between absolute poverty and relative poverty is that between capitalism and socialism.*'⁴

A, by no means secondary, consequence of this imposition is that 'this reintroduces that category of the poor and of poverty that all social policies, [. . .] all the more or less socializing or socialized policies since the end of the nineteenth century, tried to get rid of'.⁵

Finally, this negative tax (the deduction of medical expenses from the tax return is one form; the other is the deduction of one's children's school expenses) substitutes the provision of

---

² Lionel Stoléru, *Vaincre la pauvreté dans les pays riches [Vanquishing Poverty in Rich Countries]*. Paris: Flammarion, 1977, pp. 205–6 (my italics).
³ Milton Friedman, *Capitalism and Freedom* (1962), Chicago, IL: University of Chicago Press, 2002, pp. 191–2. Negative tax is explained on pp. 191–4 in a chapter with a significant title: 'Alleviation of Poverty'.
⁴ Stoléru, *Vaincre la pauvreté dans les pays riches*, p. 295 (my italics).
⁵ Foucault, *Birth of Biopolitics*, p. 211.

services by the state (public school, public healthcare, with publicly paid teachers, doctors and nurses), *public services for all citizens* therefore, with the emission of cheques the most-needy can use for similar services (albeit of obviously inferior quality). This means that education and health are no longer the rights of citizens but the goods these individual self-proprietors purchase, sometimes helped along by the collective when they really need it. Accordingly, the state, instead of providing services, would limit itself to financing private individuals (and only those in obvious need) so that they can purchase commercial services, such as paid-for education or healthcare, from private enterprises. No more national health service, but vouchers so that those most in need can obtain private treatment. The state no longer builds community housing but instead subsidizes those who need help with the rent market. And so on. These are called conditional cash transfers (CCTs) and they were what the Chicago Boys advised Pinochet to do in Chile.[6] That is not to say that when such initiatives were in fact adopted, for example by the avowed leftist, Inácio Lula da Silva, who when he was in his first term as president of Brazil, passed the *Bolsa Família*, there was not an outpouring of fury from the country's leading capitalists.

The question, then, is why did Brazilian capitalists so vehemently oppose a measure that was even used by the Chilean dictatorship? The explanation is provided by Milton Friedman himself in an article in 1967, in which having assured his critics on the right that 'my support of a negative income tax has been and remains entirely serious, neither tongue-in-cheek nor Machiavellian', he explains why he supports a negative tax: 'If we lived in a hypothetical world in which there were no governmental welfare programs at all and in which all assistance to the destitute was by private charity, the case for

---

[6] For a clear-headed analysis of the CCT, see Lena Lavinas, '21st Century Welfare', *New Left Review*, no. 84, November–December 2013, pp. 5–40.

introducing a negative income tax would be far weaker than the case for substituting it for present programs. For such a world, I might very well not favor it.'[7]

So, Milton Friedman supports the negative tax as a first step towards the total abolition of the welfare state and its substitution with private charity, while Lula considered the *Bolsa Família* the first step towards the construction of a welfare state (still largely non-existent in Brazil). That would explain why the Brazilian ruling classes were enraged by a measure initially conceived by the Chicago Boys!

But in less socially ferocious societies, it is not easy to convince citizens to do away with the notion of public services and resign themselves to being helped only through negative taxes. The transformation of universal public services into private loans only for those most in need must be gradual; it needs to be enacted gradually across the various sectors. And, from a certain point of view, the battle to privatize the school, to dismantle the 'nationalization of the education industry', is the 'mother of all battles'.

Since Jean-Jacques Rousseau, universal education has been at the heart of the notion of legitimate government; 'There can be no patriotism without liberty, no liberty without virtue, no virtue without citizens; create citizens, and you have everything you need; without them, you will have nothing but debased slaves, from the rulers of the State downwards. To form citizens is not the work of a day; and in order to have men it is necessary to educate them when they are children.'[8] This is why 'public education regulated by laws and directives prescribed by government, and overseen by magistrates established by the Sovereign, is one of the fundamental rules

---

[7] Milton Friedman, 'The Case for the Negative Income Tax', *National Review*, 7 March 1967, pp. 239–41.
[8] Jean-Jacques Rousseau, *Discourse on Political Economy*, available at: https://www.files.ethz.ch/isn/125495/5020_Rousseau_A_Discourse_on_Political_Economy.pdf, p. 11.

of popular or legitimate government'. According to Rousseau, public education is irreplaceable because we must not 'abandon to the intelligence and prejudices of fathers the education of their children'.[9]

Instead, the lock pick used to break open the institution of public school was *parental freedom* itself. Educational freedom: why should my daughter be forced to do homework for three hours a day when I would prefer she spent that time playing sport or painting? Why should my son have to go to a school where they will teach him that abolishing slavery is a good thing whilst I, like Nozick, believe that in a free society a free individual should be able to sell themselves as a slave? And finally, religious freedom (particularly in the United States): why should my daughter be indoctrinated in a secular school when my family want to instil in her a healthy devotion to the Christian, Muslim or Jewish faith? Would it not be better if the state provided me with vouchers so I can send my child to a Christian, Muslim or Jewish school depending on my choice? This last argument has the advantage of attracting infinite legions of religious fundamentalists of all stripes to the cause of vouchers.

All foundations have massively financed, and continue to finance, what is modestly known as 'education reform', a euphemistic way of describing its privatization. Here we see not only those foundations on the extreme right, which we have already encountered, but also those that are more discreetly (albeit doggedly) conservative, such as the richest foundation in the USA, that belonging to Bill and Melinda Gates, with assets worth $55.8 billion (as of year-end 2021), or another opulent foundation, that of the Walton family (the family behind Walmart), which in 2021 boasted a wealth of $4.9 billion[10] and that donated $665 million that year,

---

[9] Ibid., p. 12.
[10] 2021 Tax Return through form 990, (990-pf): https://8ce82b94a8c4fdc3ea6d -b1d233e3bc3cb10858bea65ff05e18f2.ssl.cf2.rackcdn.com/87/72/5f93d38048d3 acbabf7e05ded4aa/2021-wff-990-pf-final.pdf.

$235 million of which went to education. However, picking through the 201 pages of their tax return, we discover that $68 million of these $235 million went directly to charter schools (to whom the Foundation had already provided loans worth $134 million that same year), as well as the $30 million given to 'education reform' or educational 'choice', meaning $230 million were spent in just one year on the 'de-nationalization of the education industry'.

But there is no foundation owned by US billionaires that does not in some way finance the privatization of the school system. These foundations donate around one billion dollars a year to encourage education reform. Again, it is no coincidence that Donald Trump named Betsy DeVos (whose brother Erik Prince founded the mercenary company Blackwater) as Secretary for Education. The bigoted billionaire DeVos family are key players in the Koch brothers' political circle. What splendid irony: during the Trump administration, at the helm of public education was a billionaire who has always wanted to dismantle it.

But while vouchers are the tool of school privatization in the name of parent (or family) power, we discover that the most efficient intermediary objective isn't vouchers, but the affirmation of parent power. And so, over the last 20 years, these large foundations have financed grassroots movements pushing for the adoption of what are known as Parent Trigger laws in various states. This is how the US association for conservative legislators (ALEC) defined this kind of law: 'The Parent Trigger Act places democratic control into the hands of parents at school level. Parents can, with a simple majority, opt to usher in one of three choice-based options of reform: (1) transforming their school into a charter school, (2) supplying students from that school with a 75 percent per pupil cost voucher, or (3) closing the school.'[11]

---

[11]  https://www.alec.org/model-policy/parent-trigger-act/.

The 'Parent Power' campaign, too, reveals a racist sub-text, just like Posner's 'free baby market'. Having the freedom to choose the school or to privatize it implies being able to separate your white children from non-white pupils. There is always the idea that the schools attended by non-whites (or in Europe, by immigrants) is underachieving, incapable of increasing the human capital of one's own children and there-fore to be dismissed.

This idea of a devaluation of the market caused by 'racial depreciation' has ancient, but unexpected, roots. One of the most enlightened reforms of the New Deal was the creation, in 1934, of the Federal Housing Administration (FHA), which acted as a guarantor for the mortgages given to working-class buyers in order to make mortgage rates accessible without a need for onerous deposits, and so the terrible housing crisis caused by the Great Depression was resolved. But the FHA acted as an insurer that insured the houses at their *market value*. For this reason, the contracts included a covenant that forbade the new owners from selling their house to non-Caucasian buyers as the presence of 'inharmonious racial or nationality groups' would have reduced the desirability of the area and, as a result, the market value of the houses.[12] This clause was only declared unconstitutional in 1948, and it was only then that Jewish and Black people, Hispanics and Asians were allowed to buy houses in 'white' neighbourhoods.

It would be impossible to grasp the true dimension of US racism without considering its monetary component, that is, the translation of the racial factor into a market value, into money. The school reform plays on the same political terrain as all the other campaigns for deregulation and de-taxation, a terrain that is known in the US as the 'Southern Strategy': local fiscalism demands that taxes are spent where they are

---

[12] Kenneth T. Jackson, *Crabgrass Frontier: The Suburbanization of the United States*. New York: Oxford University Press, 1985, pp. 207–8.

collected, so that the contributions made by rich neighbour-hoods are not spent on subsidizing poor ones. Essentially, in the South of the US, this local fiscalism ensures that wealthy white people do not pay for black or Latino people, just like how, in Europe, fiscal federalism expresses nothing more than the refusal by prosperous regions to pay for those in difficulty, like how those in Italy's Veneto region do not want to subsidize those in the poorer South, and the Catalans do not want to pay for the Andalusians in Spain. So, power to the parents is not only a vehicle for the messages of conservative Christians, but also for those of white racists.

Parent Trigger Laws have already been approved in seven states: California, Connecticut, Indiana, Louisiana, Mississippi, Ohio and Texas. The approvals date back to 2010 and 2012. In reality, these laws allow the parents not only to close a school or sell it to private enterprise, but as long as there is a simple majority, they can also fire teachers and headteachers. And in fact, the campaign in favour of these laws is presented by the foundations as a campaign to improve the quality of teaching and the efficiency of the teachers.[13]

This strategy's success can be measured, not only in the US but also in European countries, by the increasingly widespread resistance, animosity and unrest among parents when it comes to teachers and 'protecting' their children. This ranges from the protests against too much homework to complaints about the lack of understanding, to the now regularly documented cases of physical attacks on teachers. The idea that parents are the most qualified to decide how their children should be taught has found new arguments and a new drive with distance learning, the 'teleschool' imposed by the Covid-19 epidemic which exponentially increased the pedagogical role of the

---

[13] On the role of Parent Trigger Laws, see Joanne Barkan, 'Plutocrats at Work: How Big Philanthropy Undermines Democracy', *Dissent*, Autumn 2013, https://www.dissentmagazine.org/article/plutocrats-at-work-how-big-philant hropy-undermines-democracy.

family, introducing the idea of vouchers into the European public debate. But the reassertion of the primacy of the family extends well beyond education, and can be found, for example, in the No Vax campaign against compulsory vaccinations. Again, underlying this is a reassertion of one's own individual autonomy and an implicit revolt against everything that is public, including its authority.

# 5

# The Tyranny of Benevolence

The beauty and elegance of this offensive against the public sphere is that the campaign for dismantling the state is waged with government money. In fact, almost 40% (39.6% to be precise) of the foundations' assets 'is diverted every year from the public treasury where voters would have determined its use'.[1] For example, in 2011, total donations by US foundations came to $49 billion,[2] but that same year, the tax subsidies for charitable works cost the US treasury some $53.7 billion,[3] meaning that US charitable donations gave $4.7 billion less than what they cost the US treasury, so technically they had used none of their own money but that belonging to others, to the taxpayers. It truly is an act of genius to use the state's own money in order to demolish it.

---

[1] Joanne Barkan, 'Wealthy philanthropists shouldn't impose their idea of common good on us', *The Guardian*, 3 December 2015, https://www.thegu ardian.com/commentisfree/2015/dec/03/mark-zuckerberg-priscilla-chan-init iative-billionaire-philanthropy.

[2] Foundation Center, data for 2011, data.foundationcenter.org.

[3] Rob Reich, 'Philanthropic institutions are plutocratic by nature. Can they be justified in a democracy?', opening speech of the forum, 'What Are Foundations For?', *Boston Review*, 1 March 2013, http://bostonreview.net/fo rum/foundations-philanthropy-democracy.

Not only are the donations on which the foundations feed tax-exempt, but so is the handsome income produced by their assets. And as this income is net, it accumulates rapidly with the result that the financing for non-profit organizations comes much less from donations and much more from the income created by the sale of goods and services and from state contracts (on which no taxes to that same state are paid). By now, almost 90% of the income from US charitable organizations comes from earnings and little less than 10% from donations. It is increasingly difficult to distinguish between normal for-profit enterprises and foundations, except for the fact that the latter are tax-exempt. [4] On the other hand, as we have seen over the course of this book so far, the one thing we cannot say is that the activities of the various foundations (Scaife, Koch, Bradley, etc.) are destined to 'promote wellbeing and advance civilization [. . .] to prevent and assuage suffering; and to promote every and all elements of human progress', as the official aims of the Rockefeller Foundation suggested in 1913.

But these now perverse destinations of the money distributed by foundations (such as, for example, the financing of a think tank that sponsors a book on the intellectual inferiority of black people (*The Bell Curve*)) are legitimate because the definition of what is 'charity' is expanded disproportionately until it covers almost everything. Up until the 1960s, in the US, tax-exempt status was limited to bodies involved in a well-defined field of charitable, educational and religious activities. But by the end of the last millennium, these well-defined aims had been replaced with much more general criteria: any organization carrying out non-illegal activities (including financial) could be exempt from taxes as long as they do not distribute dividends or profits to their shareholders

---

[4] Peter Dobkin Hall, 'Philanthropy, the Nonprofit Sector & the Democratic Dilemma', *Daedalus*, vol. 142, no. 2, Spring 2013, pp. 139–58, p. 152.

or managers. In practice, any organization can request to be exempt.

This perverse use of charitable foundations does make you reflect on their nature, their history, it makes you wonder why, after just a century, these kinds of institutions, initially controversial and even vilified, have become such a powerful player in our economic life and social organization.

Effectively, when at the beginning of the twentieth century the robber barons aimed to redirect most of their assets into foundations (the Carnegie Foundation was created in 1905, the Russell Sage in 1907, the Rockefeller in 1913), they met with violent criticism from all sides of the political divide. When an iron and railway magnate like Carnegie announced he wanted to create a foundation, everyone knew what was behind it.

In 1889, Andrew Carnegie had published a pamphlet that would come to be known as *The Gospel of Wealth*. The pamphlet began by applauding the beneficial virtues of inequality:

> The contrast between the palace of the millionaire and the cottage of the laborer with us today measures the change which has come with civilization. This change, however, is not to be deplored, but welcomed as highly beneficial. It is well, nay, essential for the progress of the race, that the houses of some should be homes for all that is highest and best in literature and the arts, and for all the refinements of civilization, rather than that none should be so. Much better this great irregularity than universal squalor. Without wealth there can be no Maecenas.[5]

Andrew Carnegie agrees with Jean-Jacques Rousseau: civilization is at the basis of all inequality, though he believes this to be a virtue of civilization.

---

[5] Andrew Carnegie, *The Gospel of Wealth*, 1889, p. 1. The text can be found here: https://www.carnegie.org/publications/the-gospel-of-wealth/.

But then, the next question he asks is: 'What is the proper mode of administering wealth after the laws upon which civilization is founded have thrown it into the hands of the few? And it is of this great question that I believe I offer the true solution. It will be understood that *fortunes* are here spoken of, not moderate sums saved by many years of effort.' Passing it on to one's descendants 'is the most injudicious' because inheritance often 'work[s] more for the injury than for the good of the recipients'.[6] Distributing it to the poor is equally unwise as 'neither the individual nor the race is improved by almsgiving'.[7] The best way to dispose of one's fortune is to finance organizations that help 'those who desire [. . .] to rise': universities, public libraries (Carnegie financed more than 3,000), ballrooms, concert halls, swimming pools. A man of wealth must become 'the mere agent and trustee for his poorer brethren, bringing to their service his superior wisdom, experience, and *ability to administer, doing for them better than they would or could do for themselves'.[8]

One example of how 'these mere trustees' behaved towards their 'poorer brothers' was given by an elite country club in Pennsylvania, the South Fork Fishing and Hunting Club, to which some sixty magnates belonged including Andrew Carnegie and the Andrew Mellon whose descendants would go on to create the Mellon Scaife foundations. The club, replete with its own cabins, was set around an artificial lake created from a dam upstream of a place called Johnstown. In 1889, the same year that the *Gospel* was written, exceptionally heavy rainfall caused the dam to burst. The dam had not been properly maintained, the members had instead simply patched it up, selling for profit its iron drainage tubes, which they had never replaced. The ensuing flood killed 2,209 'poorer brothers'

---

[6] Ibid., p. 6.
[7] Ibid., p. 13.
[8] Ibid., p. 12 (my italics).

that lived in Johnstown. But as they had rushed to organize the rescue, the honourable fishers and hunters managed to avoid paying any damages.

And again. Three years after the publication of his *Gospel*, Carnegie decided to get rid of the Amalgamated Association of Iron and Steel Workers from one of his most important ironworks in Homestead, near Pittsburgh, and forced a new contract stipulating a 35% pay cut on the workers. When the workers refused, he proceeded with a lockout and called on the Pinkertons (vigilantes from the Pinkerton company who acted as thugs for the robber barons). Sixteen workers were killed and the union was defeated.

The *Saturday Globe*, a weekly newspaper in Utica (New York State), published a cartoon that showed two Siamese Carnegies. One, smiling, was offering a library and a cheque, the other held a notice of salary cuts for his workers. The caption read: 'As the tight-fisted employer he reduces wages that he may play philanthropist.'[9]

You can understand then why Theodor Roosevelt declared himself against the new institute when he said: 'No amount of charity in spending such fortunes can compensate in any way for the misconduct in acquiring them.'

And Roosevelt is not an isolated case. President Taft knew what he was doing when he asked Congress to oppose the creation of foundations, describing this attempt as a 'bill to incorporate Mr. Rockefeller'.

John Rockefeller had always been ferociously opposed to the unionization of his own workers, and had demonstrated this in the Spring of 1914 at a mine he owned in Ludlow, Colorado. Eleven thousand miners that had been on strike since the previous September had been evicted from their

---

[9] Cited by Elizabeth Kolbert, 'Gospels of Giving for the New Gilded Age', *The New Yorker*, 28 August 2018, https://www.newyorker.com/magazine/2018/08/27/gospels-of-giving-for-the-new-gilded-age.

lodgings, but had resisted and survived the harsh winter in tents in the mountains until the Colorado national guard and their machine guns were called upon. Not only were 13 miners mown down, but the next day, the bullet-riddled bodies of 11 children and two women were found in a tent. At the end of the repression, there were 66 casualties among the strikers and their families.[10]

This is why when faced with the proposal of creating a philanthropic foundation, the president of the American Federation of Labour (AFL), Samuel Gompers, snarled: 'the one thing that the world would gratefully accept from Mr. Rockefeller now would be the establishment of a great endowment of research and education to help other people see in time how they can keep from being like him'. President of the American Civil Liberties Union, Rev. John Haynes Holmes said that 'this foundation, the very character, must be repugnant to the whole idea of a democratic society'.

The opposition to the very idea of the foundation was also shared at the highest levels. In 1915, the president of the US Industrial Relations Commission, Frank Walsh, said that 'the huge philanthropic trusts, known as foundations, appear to be a menace to the welfare of society'.[11]

Foundations and their magnates have come a long way in a century. For decades, the benefactor Olin was the hardened poisoner of entire swathes of the United States. Not only did he produce (in buildings rented from the US military, no less) 20% of all the DDT made in the US in Alabama (DDT was banned in 1970), but his factories poured more than

---

[10] One description of the Ludlow Massacre can be found in Howard Zinn, *A People's History of the United States: 1492–Present* (1980). New York: HarperCollins, 1999, pp. 354–6.

[11] Cited by Rob Reich in 'Repugnant to the Very Idea of Democracy? On the Role of Foundations', in *Democracies*, 2016, https://www.law.berkeley.edu/wp-con tent/uploads/2016/01/Repugnant-to-the-Whole-Idea-of-Democracy_On-the -Role-of-Foundations-in-Democratic-Societies..pdf, p. 4.

4 tonnes of mercury a year into the Niagara Falls, while in Saltville (Virginia), a township in Appalachia where he produced chlorine and caustic soda, his factories poured 280 kilos of mercury a year into the rivers for 20 years. Inspectors also found a swamp containing 50,000 litres of toxic waste. Who could possibly imagine why John Olin had generously financed research fighting environmental protections and legal disciplines that attempted to pinpoint the 'optimum level of pollution' (Coase)? No campaign against this slick charity has ever managed to succeed or gain any leverage with the wider public.

The same discourse could be used for the massive financing of research that denies or diminishes global warming by the Koch brothers, whose coal and oil industry has been described by Greenpeace as one of the world's 'major polluters'.[12] Everyone knows but there is no uproar, no real opposition. In fact, with the Trump administration they hit the jackpot and imposed their carboniferous vision on the world.

And there's worse. The Sackler family was, until 2017, the nineteenth richest family in the US, with a net wealth of $13 billion (according to Forbes) and were famous for their philanthropy. They have donated to the Smithsonian, the Tate Gallery, the Metropolitan Museum of Art, the Royal College of Art, the Louvre, the Berlin Jewish Museum, the Royal Opera House, as well as many research centres in various universities (MIT, Columbia, Cornell, Stanford, Oxford, Tel Aviv University, and so on). But the money for these generous donations comes from legal drug-trafficking. The Sackler family's fortune comes entirely from their pharmaceutical company, Purdue Pharma, which in turn thrived thanks to a drug, OxyContin, launched in 1995; since then, this drug

---

[12] Koch Industries Pollution, https://www.greenpeace.org/usa/fighting-climate -chaos/climate-deniers/koch-industries/koch-industries-pollution/.

alone has generated a turnover for the company of $35 billion.[13] OxyContin has a single active ingredient, oxycodone, which is a chemical cousin of heroin and twice as powerful as morphine. For years, before being defeated in court and forced into bankruptcy in 2019, Purdue promoted OxyContin with family doctors, not as a last resort for those terminally ill with cancer (as it had been previously prescribed), but as a catch-all medicine for any pain, big or small. The result: millions of drug addicts and, in 2017, according to the Centres for Disease Control and Prevention, 47,600 deaths caused by OxyContin and other opioids (68% of all US deaths by overdose). Between 1999 and 2018, 150,000 deaths[14] were caused by opiates from the oxycodone family, the active ingredient in OxyContin, before Purdue decided to remove it from sale to be prescribed by doctors.

It took more than 15 years of outcry and campaigning for some (not all) of the temples of culture, the so-called sacred places of art, the treasure chests and forges of human knowledge, to show any compunction about being financed by the drugs trade, regardless of how legal it may or may not have been.[15] It was only in 2022 that the Sacklers agreed to pay $6 billion in damages and give up ownership of Purdue. In doing so, that poor family saw their fortune reduced to just $5 billion. Nevertheless, despite the scandal, the trials and the guilty verdicts, even in 2021 and 2022 Oxford University still

[13] All the news on the Sackler family and the opioid crisis is from Patrick Radden Keefe, 'The Family That Built an Empire of Pain', *The New Yorker*, 30 October 2017, https://www.newyorker.com/magazine/2017/10/30/the-family-that-built-an-empire-of-pain, and 'Meet the Sacklers: The family feuding over blame for the opioid crisis', *The Guardian*, 13 February 2018, https://www.theguardian.com/us-news/2018/feb/13/meet-the-sacklers-the-family-feuding-over-blame-for-the-opioid-crisis.

[14] https://www.kff.org/other/state-indicator/opioid-overdose-deaths-by-type-of-opioid.

[15] *Financial Times*, 24 February 2023: https://www.ft.com/content/6a42e764-46a1-4bdf-a76e-d548d78db8fc.

continued to extend 'exclusive invitations to Sackler family members and accepted funds from a Sackler family charity, as it maintained the Sacklers' naming rights on university buildings and fellowships'. Twenty-six deaths in Colorado caused outrage in 1914, hundreds of thousands of overdoses struggle to make an impact in 2022.

The fact is that in 1913 a federal income tax was created (at the time, a flat tax of 3%). Naturally, the attitude of Congress and the Senate changed and in 1917, donors were guaranteed unlimited philanthropic deductions. Since then, the number of foundations multiplied in the US. In 1930 there were around 200 and they held an aggregate fortune of less than a billion dollars. In 1959, there were more than 2,000; in 1985, there were just under 30,000. In 2004, their number swelled to 76,000.[16] In 2015, the foundations numbered 86,203 with their combined wealth totalling $890 billion, their annual outgoing donations totalling $62.7 billion, and they received donations of $53.1 billion.[17]

These huge amounts of money can change the course of history if channelled in the right directions. It's enough to think of how private foundations that unleashed, directed and won the reactionary revolution at the time had just a few hundred million dollars each, not tens of billions, and yet their impact was decisive because those (relatively) limited resources were aimed at specific targets. To use the military metaphor so beloved of those 'philanthropists', a concentrated attack at a single point can break any line of defence. Imagine the effect of financial investments hundreds of times bigger!

And yet no-one, or only a few rare faultfinders, ask themselves about the patently anti-democratic nature of private foundations:

---

[16] Reich, 'Repugnant to the Very Idea of Democracy?', p. 8.
[17] Foundation Center, data for 2015, data.foundationcenter.org.

Foundations appear at odds with democracy, for they repre-
sent, by definition and by law, the expression of plutocratic
voices directed toward the public good. But why, in a democracy, should the size of one's wallet give one a greater say in
the public good and public policy? Why should this plutocratic
voice be subsidized by the public? And why should democracy
allow this voice to extend across generations in the form of
tax-produced assets? It would seem that foundations are a
misplaced plutocratic, and powerful, element in a democratic
society.[18]

What is disturbing about these benefactors is that they
reserve for themselves the right to define what is good. Because
they are, as Carnegie said, absolutely certain of '*doing for them
better than they would or could do for themselves*'.[19] And
the condition of these 'benefactors' is that they are beyond
reproach, subject to no verification. Especially not that at the
polls. It is no coincidence, given the pervasive action of his
foundation in the field of education, that Bill Gates has been
called the 'real secretary for education in the United States'.
Nor do foundations have to answer to anyone, unless their
actions can be legally pursued. 'When a foundation project
fails [. . .] the subjects of the experiment suffer, as does the
general public. Yet the do-gooders can simply move on to their
next project.'[20]

But what makes the foundations a real conceptual
'monstrosity' is that they appeal to a privatist conception of the
common good. They are founded on the neoliberal belief in the
private efficiency of the market as a place of competition, but,
in reality, they are not subject to any competition rules what-
soever, as noted by the Richard Posner we already encountered

---

[18] Rob Reich, *Just Giving: Why Philanthropy Is Failing Democracy and How It
Can Do Better*. Princeton, NJ: Princeton University Press, 2018, p. 151.
[19] Carnegie, *The Gospel of Wealth*, p. 12.
[20] Barkan, 'Plutocrats at Work'.

as the standard bearer for Law and Economics and advocate for the free buying and selling of children. Despite being a market fundamentalist and a paladin of rational expectation theory, he too is scandalized: 'A perpetual charitable foundation, however, is a completely irresponsible institution, answerable to nobody. It competes neither in capital markets nor in product markets [. . .] and, unlike a hereditary monarch whom such a foundation otherwise resembles, it is subject to no political controls either. [. . .] The puzzle for economics is why these foundations are not total scandals.'[21]

Even the economic fundamentalists of the Chicago School believe foundations to be an absurdity, a 'total scandal'! These private entities are effectively created, generated, maintained and provided for by the very government they abhor. In our relationship with these institutions, we are neither citizens, nor voters, nor clients, but mere supplicating beggars and grateful beneficiaries. These wealthy philanthropists never hear any criticism about the way they operate because they are surrounded only by courtiers and acolytes, *cronies*. They would make Adam Smith turn in his grave, given that when we address foundations, trusts with billions in capital, we are appealing to their *benevolence*. And it is they who call themselves the heirs of Smith that envision a world in which – to quote the father of neoliberalism – makes beggars of us all. No one seems to remember that the very famous quote about the butcher, the brewer and the baker ends with this ferocious statement: 'Nobody but a beggar chooses to depend chiefly upon the benevolence of his fellows-citizen.'[22]

---

[21] Charitable Foundations – Posner's Comment, in The Becker-Posner Blog, 3 December 2006, https://www.becker-posner-blog.com/2006/12/charitable-foundations--posners-comment.html.

[22] 'It is not from the benevolence of the butcher, the brewer, or the baker, that we expect our dinner, but from their regard to their own interest. We address ourselves, not to their humanity but to their self-love, and never talk to them of our own necessities but of their advantages. Nobody but a beggar chooses to depend chiefly upon the benevolence of his fellows-citizen.' Adam Smith,

Everyone lines up – artists, authors, conservatives, deans, ministers, the religious – to beg for a handout from poisoners, polluters and legal narco-traffickers.

And where the munificence of criminals is not being sought, the praises are being sung of the 'normal' billionaire: today, Bill Gates and Warren Buffett are the object not only of admiration, but also of civic, docile gratitude. Foundations have become a familiar part of our landscape; they are no longer a 'scandal' and we are no longer shocked that these 'charitable' institutions have for-profit activities for which they are tax-exempt. It is considered normal that they accumulate ever-expanding fortunes that are always tax-exempt, potentially for all future generations. This was perhaps less like science fiction than what Isaac Asimov was thinking in 1951 when he published his *Foundations* series, in which a 'foundation' would be able to halt the decline of the galactic empire and eventually govern solar systems, nebulae and the entire known universe.

*An Inquiry into the Nature and Causes of the Wealth of Nations* (1776), book i, cap. 2 (my italics). This can be found at http://geolib.com/smith.adam/won1 -02.html.

# 6

# *Capitale sive Natura*

But to endure without complaint, or rather with muted gratitude, the overwhelming power wielded by foundations is only a marginal corollary to the victory that the ideological counterintelligence of the Midwestern tycoons has achieved.

Much more devastating has been the effect on our culture, our expectations, our human relationships and those with society and even ourselves. Foucault, whom we have already referenced, had understood it all 40 years ago: 'This generalization of the "enterprise" form [. . .] involves extending the economic model of supply and demand and of investment-costs-profit so as to make it a *model of social relations and of existence itself, a form of relationship of the individual to himself, time, those around him, the group, and the family.*'[1]

It was not a sudden capsizing. It began with the hollowing out of the very idea of 'social justice'. We have taken von Hayek's statement describing social justice as empty and meaningless as a judgement, when in reality it is an exhortation,

---

[1] Foucault, *The Birth of Biopolitics*, p. 242 (my italics).

a performative act: social justice *becomes* an empty sentence as an effect of political action by those who follow the lead of von Hayek and his ilk: all action by the various Friedmans, Stiglers, Beckers and Posners was aimed at emptying 'social justice' of any content. When their anthropology confines us to the role of 'proprietor of our own person or capacities, owing nothing to society for them', society is automatically reduced to 'relations of exchange between proprietors'.[2]

With a retroactive mechanism, even the advocates of this crusade against 'society' became increasingly extremist over the years, much like the effects of their actions. Thirty years later, von Hayek himself would no longer endorse what he had written in 1944:

> But there are two kinds of security: the certainty of a given minimum of sustenance for all and the security of a given standard of life, of the relative position which one person or group enjoys compared with others. There is no reason why, in a society which has reached the general level of wealth ours has, the first kind of security should not be guaranteed to all without endangering general freedom; that is: some minimum of food, shelter and clothing, sufficient to preserve health. Nor is there any reason why the state should not help to organize a comprehensive system of social insurance in providing for those common hazards of life against which few can make adequate provision.[3]

---

[2] C.B. Macpherson, *The Political Theory of Possessive Individualism: Hobbes to Locke*. Oxford: Oxford University Press, 1962, p. 3.

[3] Friedrich von Hayek, *The Road to Serfdom* (1944) (The Reader's Digest condensed version as it appeared in April 1945). London: Institute of Economic Affairs, 2001, pp. 58–9, can be found at https://iea.org.uk/wp-con tent/uploads/2016/07/upldbook351pdf.pdf. Perhaps this cautious opening to the social state was the reason why, in 1947, the sponsors of the Mont Pelerin Society believed von Hayek to be too moderate and so wanted him flanked by von Mises in the second meeting (see above, p. 27).

When he visited Pinochet in 1981, von Hayek would no longer accept that the state should provide a universal health care system.

The first step taken to convince us that social justice is empty and meaningless was to undermine the very concept of justice. Already, Law and Economics had decided that what is just or unjust is relative, dependent on how much it costs to punish the wrongdoer ('how many offenses should be permitted and how many offenders should go unpunished' is, as we have seen, a central question for Becker). But there is more: given that competition produces inequality, as competition always has a winner and a loser, if free competition is humanity's most efficient way of organizing itself socially, that is, if the most efficient social asset is intrinsically iniquitous, then equality is incompatible with efficiency. And, therefore, iniquity is increasingly considered to be a 'price of progress', to then become – with a semantic slip from 'equality = inefficiency' to 'equality = obstacle to efficiency' to 'iniquity = necessary condition for efficiency' – the condition *sine qua non* for the wealth of nations, recalling Marx's extraordinary phrase in which 'the sycophant of capital, the political economist', 'in the interest of the so-called *wealth of the nation*, he seeks for artificial means to ensure the *poverty of the people*'.[4] Jean-Jacques Rousseau and Andrew Carnegie agree that the origin of inequality lies in the process of civilization, but while Rousseau believed this fact undermined the very legitimacy of the concept of civilization, for Carnegie and his followers, inequality is the principal benefit brought by civilization.

We have seen that even Jimmy Carter placed no faith in the state's ability to resolve the most pressing social problems

---

[4] Karl Marx, *Capital. A Critique of Political Economy. Volume 1*. London: Penguin Classics, 1976, Chapter 33: 'The Modern Theory of Colonisation', p. 932 (my italics).

(therefore, implicitly demanding that private entities attempt to do so). At the beginning of the 1990s, this rejection of the social state became 'common sense' even among the so-called liberals, and the thesis of the 'perversity' of welfare as put forward in *Losing Ground* was shared by Bill Clinton's New Democrats. In 1993 Clinton said of Murray: 'He did the country a great service. [. . .] I think his analysis is essentially right'⁵ (and the reform of the social state approved by Clinton made a significant step towards its demolition). This idea was embraced by those importing Clintonism into Europe, namely Tony Blair's New Labour and the epigones of the Italian Communist Party, until in 2012, the president of the European Central Bank, Mario Draghi (later hailed in Italy as the country's saviour) said in an interview with the *Wall Street Journal*: 'this could be the beginning of a new world for Greece [. . .] *the European social model has already gone'.*⁶

When spoken by the highest gatekeeper of monetary policies in the world's second largest economic bloc, this statement sounds not like an observation, but like a verdict, a sentence, a death sentence to be precise. In reality, the social state is already dead in the consciousness of those who should benefit from it but who instead allow themselves to be convinced that if a state becomes indebted, or fails, it is due to pensions that are 'too generous' and 'paid too early', paid holidays, maternity leave, free healthcare and 'excessive' education spending. Today, it is commonly held that anyone with a permanent contract with 'social benefits' attached is considered to be privileged, or rather, a bloodsucker exploiting the work of the 'real' workers.

---

⁵ Interview with NBC News on 3 December 1993, https://contemporarythinkers. org/charles-murray/commentary/talking-points-response-to-charles-mur ray/.

⁶ https://www.ecb.europa.eu/press/key/date/2012/html/sp120224.en.html, February 2012 (my italics).

As US philosopher Wendy Brown states:

> when everything is capital, labor disappears as a category, as does its collective form, class, taking with it the analytic basis for alienation, exploitation, and association among laborers. Dismantled at the same time is the very rationale for unions, consumer groups, and other forms of economic solidarity apart from cartels among capitals. This paves the way for challenging several centuries of labor law and other protections and benefits in the Euro-Atlantic world and, perhaps as important, makes illegible the foundations of such protections and benefits. One instance of this illegibility is the growing popular opposition to pensions, security of employment, paid holidays, and other hard-won achievements by public-sector workers in the United States. Another measure of it is the absent sympathy for the effects of life-threatening austerity measures imposed on Southern Europeans amid the 2011–2012 European Union crises. German Chancellor Merkel's infamous 'lazy Greeks' speech [in May 2011] during this crisis was important [. . .] for delivering as common sense the charge that Spanish, Portuguese, and Greek workers should not enjoy comfortable lives or retirements.[7]

Furthermore, it is evident that, if work is no longer the (only) thing the worker can sell to the capitalist, but rather the income they gain from the investment of their human capital, then the worker is no longer an employee but a freelancer providing a service, so the apprentice or dishwasher receives a fee just like the lawyer and the doctor. It is out of the question that the apprentice or dishwasher will receive healthcare, pension contributions, paid holidays, maternity or parental leave. After all, we don't pay for our lawyer's holidays, pension or

---

[7] Wendy Brown, *Undoing the Demos: Neoliberalism's Stealth Revolution*. New York: Zone Books, 2015, pp. 38–9.

healthcare. Instead, all of us capitalists *in pectore* feel antipathy and impatience towards those 'employees with a permanent contract' who enjoy social safety nets, because in our eyes they are capitalists who benefit from 'unnecessary' public subsidies. This conviction is both an expression and an effect of the symbolic violence exerted over us, and which, like all symbolic violence, ensures that the dominated internalize the very values that subjugate them (naturally, symbolic violence has effects that are not symbolic at all but are actually highly tangible and often lethal). As Pierre Bourdieu said: 'Symbolic violence is violence wielded with tacit complicity between its victims and its agents, insofar as both remain unconscious of submitting to or wielding it.'[8] As such, 'the dominated apply categories constructed from the point of view of the dominant to the relations of domination, *making them appear as natural*'.[9] Like how the woman subjected to patriarchal violence torments herself because she doesn't feel 'feminine' enough (that is, she does not correspond enough to the role the patriarchy has assigned her and to which it has confined her), or the soldier who is ashamed because he is not courageous enough to face the enemy (meaning he is not ready enough to die or make that sacrifice imposed on him as a moral duty), or how the fired worker justifies the actions of the boss who fired him because he has internalized the 'need to cut costs', and that is because he thinks of himself as a 'business cost': the small bankrupt capitalist understands the logic of the bankruptcy procedure.

One of the most symptomatic ways in which we can see this internalization of the capitalist dominion is in the words disappearing from the language. I don't even mention the term 'master', which has become a dirty word to be avoided in public. But even the more neutral words 'capitalism' and

---

[8] Pierre Bourdieu, *On Television*. New York: The New Press, 1999, p. 17.
[9] Pierre Bourdieu, *Masculine Domination*. Stanford, CA: Stanford University Press, 2001, p. 35 (my italics).

'capitalist' tend to vanish. No one has noticed, but these two words are not only no longer used but, when they have to be, it is done with a certain discomfort. The only polite way to use this term is to add an adjective to it: human capital, social capital, cultural capital, symbolic capital. Sweetened by an adjective, the term becomes acceptable, but when it is used alone, stripped of any predicate, it is just too crude. The moment in which it is drummed into us that we are all capitalists, all owners of our own human capital, in that same moment we no longer talk about capital in the strictly economic sense, and capital-as-money becomes unspeakable.

This phenomenon had already been noted by Roland Barthes in reference to the bourgeoisie: ours – he wrote – is a bourgeois society by 'its profound status – a certain regime of ownership, a certain order, a certain ideology'; and yet the bourgeoisie 'makes its status undergo a real ex-nominating operation: the bourgeoisie is defined as the social class which does not want to be named'.[10]

What Barthes wrote about the bourgeoisie in 1957 is even more true today for the capitalists. The ex-nomination of capital is even more shocking and thunderous the more capital the capitalists possess. We have already seen that the 2,668 billionaires on the planet possess more than $12,000 billion. A more precise measure of the 'capitalist' class is provided by Deloitte in its 2017 report on the global art market,[11] in which it defines those with an investable capital (excluding their home and all consumables) of more than $30 million as 'Ultra-High Net Worth Individuals (UHNWI)'. We are talking here about capital in its true sense, as investable money. The most current statistics on this category (from the beginning

[10]  Roland Barthes, *Mythologies*. London: Vintage Books, 2000, pp. 137–8.

[11]  Deloitte ArtTactic, Art & Finance Report 2017, https://www2.deloitte.com /content/dam/Deloitte/at/Documents/finance/art-and-finance-report-2017. pdf.

of 2022)[12] estimate the total number of UHNWI on the planet to be 392,410 with a collective fortune of $41,800 billion (averaging out at $106 million of investible wealth pro capita). Finally, we know exactly how many masters of the world there are: 392,410 (one for every 20,053 humans living on Earth, if anyone were interested).

But it is not polite to call them capitalists, we must refer to them using a convoluted acronym – UHNWI. Capital is unspeakable, much better that we paraphrase it using the plural: 'the markets', 'the decision of the markets', 'the sentence of the markets'.[13] Indeed, anyone who accidentally says the words 'capitalist', 'capitalism' or 'capital' is met with embarrassed disapproval, as if they had broken a tacit rule of linguistic behaviour, and is immediately consigned to the zoological species of dinosaurs, still linked to the categories of the past.

The reason for capital's unspeakable nature is the same Barthes uses to explain the ex-nomination of the bourgeoisie: our media, our films, our conversations (and chats), 'our remarks about the weather, a murder trial, a touching wedding, the cooking we dream of, the garments we wear, everything, in everyday life, is dependent on the representation which [capital] *has and makes us have* of the relationships between man and the world'.[14] Capital invades, saturates and influences all of our social relationships, to the point of becoming invisible: not *Deus sive Natura*, as Spinoza's motto would have it, but *Capitale sive Natura*, in the double sense that capital both

---

[12] https://www.barrons.com/articles/global-ultra-high-net-worth-population-has-fallen-by-6-in-2022-01667949736.

[13] It is telling that the only country in which the word 'capital' is used outside its specific technical meaning ('increase in capital', 'initial capital') is the United States, whose press gives to the term 'capital' a right to citizenship, but only within a single phrase: 'war (battle, conflict) between capital and labour'.

[14] Barthes, *Mythologies*, p. 140: I substituted the word 'bourgeoisie' with the word 'capital'.

permeates our entire social universe and manages to access a certain divine quality.

Capital effectively acquires the attributes of a divinity: omnipresence, omnipotence, ineffability. And severity: capital is as jealous and vengeful as Yahweh, and any lack of respect for its will unleashes its fury, with exemplary and merciless punishments, as countries who fall behind on their debt payments know far too well:

> both persons and states are expected to comport themselves in ways that maximize their capital value in the present and enhance their future value, and both persons and states do so through practices of entrepreneurialism, self-investment, and/or attracting investors. Any regime pursuing another course faces fiscal crises, downgraded credit, currency or bond ratings, and lost legitimacy at the least, bankruptcy and dissolution at the extreme. Likewise, any individual who veers into other pursuits risks impoverishment and a loss of esteem and creditworthiness at the least, survival at the extreme.[15]

In reality, this new, severe monetary pantheism lacks the sharp clarity and stringent logic of Spinoza. Because in this religion (albeit one formalized by equations), there is an animist element: we have already noted (with a straight face) that 'human capital' is the behaviouralist and economistic equivalent of what the Ancients called 'soul'. But here we play on the ambivalence of the term 'capital': on the one hand, when we talk about human capital, about capital-as-soul, everything is capital. Singing in tune is 'capital', as is having a hand for drawing, a prodigious memory or a capacity for observation (in a Pascalian sense, Cleopatra's capital was her nose), while on the other hand, when we talk about capital-as-money, capital-as-Yahweh, the vengeful god who punishes sinners (debtors,

---

15 Brown, *Undoing the Demos*, p. 22.

as the Germans would say), then we enter the reign of the ineffable and the unspeakable. As we know, in German, the word 'debt' is *Schuld*, which literally means 'guilt'.

The laws of capitalism are likened to the divine laws, but in the form these take in modern times, that of natural laws. We are no longer talking about a rather recent economic regime (a few hundreds of years), but about a paradigm that might forever regulate (in the past and the future) the behaviour of humans, just as Maxwell's equations regulate the propagation of light and Newton's laws the forces of gravity. Just as the most primitive superstitions have been filtered from human consciousness over the course of tens of thousands of years, arriving at the discoveries of modern science, so the human being has roamed the darkness of primitive exchanges and mythical 'bartering', before discovering the crystalline clarity of the capitalist economy, the law of supply and demand, the criteria of marginal utility and the ecstasy of perfect competition.

And here it becomes clear why I have introduced Roland Barthes to the argument, because the function of myth is to transform a precise and transitory historical situation into an unchanging and perennial state of nature, making 'contingency appear eternal'.[16] White Europeans dominated (and enslaved) black Africans for three centuries? Then the myth transforms this temporary domination into eternal and intrinsic superiority, by which black people have always been and always will be inferior to whites. The myth is not concerned with the fact so many whites are much more stupid and less creative than so many black people. Were some Jews pushed into the role of moneylenders by historical circumstances? The myth transforms this experience into an immutable Jewish vocation for usury of which Shylock becomes a timeless example.

---

[16] Barthes, *Mythologies*, p. 142.

**Table 1.** Healthcare spending per capita in dollars and in % of GDP (2020)

| Countries | Total Healthcare Expenditure | | Government Healthcare Expenditure |
|---|---|---|---|
| | In $US per capita | In % of GDP | In $US per capita and as % of the total expenditure |
| United States | 11,702 | 18.82 | 6,643 (56.7%) |
| Germany | 5,930 | 12.82 | 4,652 (78.4%) |
| Sweden | 6,028 | 11.38 | 5,179 (85.9%) |
| Iceland | 5,637 | 9.56 | 4,956 (87.9%) |
| United Kingdom | 4,926 | 11.98 | 4,123 (83.7%) |
| France | 4,768 | 12.81 | 3,659 (76.7%) |
| Italy | 3,057 | 9.63 | 2,326 (76.1%) |
| Brazil | 1,031 | 10.31 | 313 (44.7%) |

Likewise, the myth of the efficiency and rationality of the market couldn't give a damn about any proof to the contrary. The US private healthcare system costs double per person than the European public healthcare systems (see Table 1), with a shorter life expectancy and worse health on average for its citizens? Who cares! The beauty of the myth is that any evidence to the contrary is entirely immaterial.[17]

---

[17] Indeed, as we can see from Table 1, the government's share of the US healthcare system absorbs just 57% of the total, yet it is equal to more than the per capita healthcare expenditure of all European countries, countries in which, however, this constitutes more than three-quarters of the total, reaching four-fifths in Iceland, Sweden and the United Kingdom. For the year considered here, 2020 (the most recent available), the data should, however, be considered with caution as they are biased by it being the first year of the Covid-19 pandemic. This data is from the World Health Organization (WHO) https://www.who.int/data/gho/data/indicators/indicator-details/GHO/domestic-general-government-health-expenditure-(gghe-d)-per-capita-in-us; https://apps.who.int/gho/data/view.main.GHEDCHEpcUSSHA2011v?lang=en; https://www.who.int/data/gho/data/indicators/indicator-details/GHO/current-health-expenditure-(che)-as-percentage-of-gross-domestic-product-(gdp)-(-).

The myth of the beneficial effects of reducing taxes clashes with the undeniable observation that the countries with the lowest taxation are the damned of the Earth. For example, in Pakistan, only 0.57% of the population pay income tax, and Pakistanis are certainly not better off than the Swedes. Similarly, in the Democratic Republic of Congo tax revenue corresponds to just 7.6% of GDP as opposed to 34.3% in OECD countries, and again, life in Congo is not better than in Austria or Portugal.[18] What does it matter? The myth insisting that the private ownership of firearms reduces the number of homicides is contradicted by all statistics, which show a murder rate that is five times higher in the US than in Western European countries (5 victims per 100,000 inhabitants in the US vs. 1.2 in France and the UK, 0.9 in Germany, 0.6 in Italy and Spain),[19] but what does that matter? The myth only partially reflects historical reality, which loses any relevance when this contingent experience is given back to us as an immutable essence, as a fact of nature.

This is why 'any number of radical theorists from Brecht through to Foucault and Badiou have maintained, emancipatory politics must always destroy the appearance of a "natural order", must reveal what is presented as necessary and inevitable to be a mere contingency, just as it must make what was previously deemed to be impossible seem attainable'.[20] *So, trying to change the world is not futile.*

At this point, the *topos* of *futility* connects unexpectedly with the reactionary rhetoric defined by Hirschman and the concept of myth in Roland Barthes: if the superiority of white people over black people (or men over women) is an

---

[18] On the Democratic Republic of the Congo: https://www.oecd.org/tax/tax-po licy/revenue-statistics-africa-congo-dem-rep.pdf.

[19] Data for 2018 from the United Nations Office on Drugs and Crime, https://da taunodc.un.org/content/data/homicide/homicide-rate.

[20] Mark Fisher, *Capitalist Realism: Is There No Alternative?* Winchester: Zero Books, 2009, p. 17.

immutable natural law, then any attempt to change the power relations between blacks and whites, women and men, is useless and *futile*. The mythification of a situation, let's say a social relationship, reveals itself as the indispensable condition for triggering the argument of futility. Any action to change the world (the society) proves *futile* if the world is at it is not by historical contingency, but by the natural law: if the actual situation is translated into myth, if, for example, the colonial domination of Africa by white Europeans is replaced by the myth of 'natural' white supremacy. It is by the same token that women 'must know their place' and 'people shouldn't meddle with things they don't understand'.

## Business Ontology

The idea that capital '*has and makes us have* of the relationships between man and the world' (Barthes) is therefore viewed with the same inexorability as the laws of nature (the Texans say of themselves that they are so individualist that they don't even obey the laws of gravity). Margaret Thatcher's statement – 'there is no alternative' – has the same value (that of a prophecy making itself true) as von Hayek's decree that social justice is an empty phrase: everything has been put in place so that the only future that can be conceived is a capitalist one.

Mark Fisher calls this widespread conviction that there is no alternative, 'capitalist realism': 'Over the past thirty years, capitalist realism has successfully installed a "business ontology" in which it is simply obvious that everything in society, including healthcare and education, should be run as a business.'[21]

This observation by Fisher touches a nerve that escapes the superficial critics of the neoliberal counter-revolution.

---

[21] Ibid., p. 17.

They confuse the 'statephobia' discussed by Foucault with the apparently anarchic utopia invoked by Nozick. Certainly, for purely propagandistic aims, neolibs brandish the famous introduction by Thomas Paine to his book *Common Sense; Addressed to the Inhabitants of America* (1776):

> Some writers have so confounded Society with government, as to leave little or no distinction between them; whereas, they are not only different, but have different origins. Society is produced by our wants, and government by our wickedness; the former promotes our happiness positively by uniting our affections, the latter negatively by restraining our vices. The one encourages intercourse, the other creates distinctions. The first is a patron, the last a punisher. Society in every state is a blessing, but Government even in its best state is but a necessary evil; in its worst state an intolerable one [. . .]. Government like dress is the badge of lost innocence; the palaces of kings are built on the ruins of the bowers of paradise.[22]

But in reality, no follower of the Chicago Boys has ever considered destroying the state (not for nothing did they admire Pinochet). Their palaces may well be built on the ruins of the shacks of paradise, but neither Thomas Paine nor today's neoliberals would wander around naked simply because clothes are the mark of lost innocence. For however much Charles Koch insisted he wanted to 'roll back the state', the real goal of the neoliberal counter-revolution is not to abolish the government (the Koch brothers were not the new Bakunin)

---

[22] The full title is: *Common Sense; Addressed to the Inhabitants of America, on the following interesting Subjects. i. Of the Origin and Design of Government in general, with concise Remarks on the English Constitution. ii. Of Monarchy and Hereditary Succession. iii: Thoughts on the present State of American Affairs. iv. Of the present Ability of America, with some miscellaneous Reflections. Written by an Englishman* (Printed, and Sold, by R. Bell, in Third-Street, Philadelphia, 1776), downloadable from Library of Congress, loc.gov/item/2006681076.

but to remodel it, remould the state in order to ensure it works for the system of free enterprise. As Antonin Scalia said at the inaugural meeting of the Federalist Society in 1982: 'I urge you, then [. . .] to keep in mind that the federal government is not bad but good. *The trick is to use it wisely.*'[23]

The wise use of the Federal government proved to be fully functional to the neolib project during the very crises that should have threatened it: both the financial crisis of 2008 and the Covid-19 pandemic of 2020 were dealt with by governments and not by the markets. Indeed, during these emergencies, the markets became extraordinarily discreet, retreating behind the scenes and leaving centre stage to the governments before reappearing at the helm, stronger than ever, once the crises had passed.

This 'wise' use of the state explains the apparent incongruity of the globalization process that, while it unifies the economy, exacerbates the separation between states. As Matteo Vegetti writes,

> the planetary adoption of the State form does not in any way contradict the interests of the globalized economy, but instead represents for the latter the opportunity to place national pro-ductive and fiscal systems, credit and local development models in competition with one another. No matter how obvious it might seem, the strategies of delocalization and re-localization of the transnational companies that shape contemporary economic geography would make no sense in places where political diversity and social inequalities were cancelled out on a global scale.[24]

---

[23] Antonin Scalia, 'The Two Faces of Federalism', *Harvard Journal of Law and Public Policy*, vol. 6, no. 1, 1982, pp. 19–22 (my italics).
[24] Matteo Vegetti, *L'invenzione del globo. Spazio, potere, comunicazione nell'epoca dell'aria [The Invention of the Globe. Space, Power, Communication in the Age of Air]*. Turin: Einaudi, 2017, pp. 137–8.

In other words, multinational companies have a vested interest in the existence of a multiplicity of states in order to play them against one another (at whose taxes are lower, who offers more incentives for localization, etc.). As such, neoliberalism not only demands one state that serves it but needs many states that compete to do so.

If states were not competing to ingratiate themselves to corporations, tax havens would not exist. It is interesting that this rhetorical device evoking safety is used to describe an anomaly, an exception, when tax havens are instead a cog, small yet indispensable, that allows the entire neolib global economic system to function smoothly: without tax havens, it would be much more difficult to 'starve the beasts'.

In archaic terms, it is not the merchants who trade to serve the emperor, but the various emperors who fight amongst themselves to govern at the merchants' service. While for the classical liberals of the nineteenth century the state governed *because* of the market, now neoliberals believe the state governs *for* the market. As Wendy Brown states: 'Neoliberal states thus depart from liberal ones as they become radically economic in a triple sense: The state secures, advances, and props the economy; the state's purpose is to facilitate the economy, and the state's legitimacy is linked to the growth of the economy [. . .] State action, state purpose, and state legitimacy: each is economized by neoliberalism.'[25] This means the state is judged by its success in favouring the market economy. Therefore, 'a State under the surveillance of the market, rather than a market under the surveillance of the state',[26] in which the market becomes the judge and jury for the state, deciding whether it is to be absolved or punished. This is an idea formulated with cold violence by the ex-governor of the German Central Bank,

[25] Brown, *Undoing the Demos*, p. 64.
[26] This phrase does not appear in the English translation, but can be found in the French original: Michel Foucault, *Naissance de la biopolitique. Cours au Collège de France, 1978–1979*, Paris: Gallimard-Seuil, 2004, p. 120.

the *Bundesbank*, Hans Tietmeyer, when in 1998 he praised national governments that privileged 'the permanent plebiscite of global markets' to the 'plebiscite of the ballot box'.[27]

The new orthodoxy does not, therefore, ask for *less* state; it may even create *more* state, only with radically different objectives and a revolutionized structure. In a triple sense:

(1) The objective of the state is to favour the market (while the aim of the merchants was once to expand and strengthen the empire). The state's performance is measured by the mark that it (like a fearful schoolboy) receives from the ratings agencies (the new strict teachers). Its success is sanctioned by the triple AAA it achieves, and therefore by the credit it will enjoy, whilst its failure is made official through its 'downgrading'.

(2) The function of the state is to extend the business and accountancy model to all sectors of society, education, healthcare and scientific research. The credit system in universities is a striking example. Universities become 'credit institutions': students have an academic 'bank account' that is credited with the credits they get, with 60 available per year in the European system (ETCS) and 30 in the US. Each credit corresponds to 50–60 hours in the US system and 25–30 in the ETCS, hours that make up the student workload and spent attending lectures, seminars, tutorials, practicals, completing homework, coursework projects, examinations, and so forth. In both systems this totals between 1,500 and 1,800 study hours a year, which ensure that by the end at least 180 credits are deposited into the student's 'account' that can be exchanged for a degree, and up to 3,000 credits for postgraduate qualifications.

Here, the key event is the introduction of a financial concept, 'credit', into the university lexicon. And in fact, in order to obtain university 'credits', millions of US students

---

[27] Taken from Luciano Canfora, *Critica della retorica democratica [Critique of Democratic Rhetoric]*, Rome-Bari: Laterza, 2011, p. 33.

must indebt themselves and take out bank loans, so each credit corresponds to a debt. The total student loans debt in the US amounts to $1,757 billion (more than the GDPs of Canada, Russia or Australia), with more than 44 million students burdened with debt. The average debt is $39,950 dollars and 3.5 million Americans still have student debt after the age of 62 (data from 2022).[28]

The language used is never irrelevant: it is through language that narratives are imposed, and behind these, ideologies, as the manual for US marines teaches us. In Italy, the territorial headquarters for the national healthcare service were once called local healthcare units (Usl, *Unità sanitarie locali*). Then, a decree changed their name to local healthcare firms (Asl, *Aziende sanitarie locali*). At first glance, the change from a U to an A might seem irrelevant, but in reality, behind it all there was an ideological conversion. Once upon a time in Italy, anyone taking a train was called a 'traveller', those taken into hospital were known as 'patients'. Now, whether on a train or in hospital, we are all 'customers'. Even in school we are no longer students but customers, and as we all know, 'the customer is always right' and their happiness should always be ensured. But this has nothing to do with the quality of the education given or the skills the students leave the school with. A school can satisfy its 'customers' but teach very little to its 'students'.

(3) The third and decisive overturning of the idea of the state is that now the public entity *par excellence* must function like a private company: the state (just like every individual who is their own proprietor) must behave like a business, maximizing their own current value and increasing that to come, attracting investors and guaranteeing conditions that produce credit. Once again, this capsizing is revealed by words. Wendy Brown examines three of these: governance, benchmarking and best

[28] https://educationdata.org/student-loan-debt-statistics.

practices. We must note how these three English terms have entered the bureaucratic language of other European languages, such as Spanish, French, German and Italian.

Governance is originally a business term (corporate governance) and defines the management of the enterprise. As the OECD tells us:

> The purpose of corporate governance is to help build an environment of trust, transparency and accountability necessary for fostering long-term investment, financial stability and business integrity, thereby supporting stronger growth and more inclusive societies. [...] Corporate governance involves a set of relationships between a company's management, its board, its shareholders and other stakeholders. Corporate governance also provides the structure through which the objectives of the company are set, and the means of attaining those objectives and monitoring performance are determined.[29]

The point is that now governance is applied to the entire state apparatus, to healthcare, education, justice (curiously it is only the armed forces that escape, at least in part, the tyranny of governance). Governance substitutes *government*. With this simple linguistic substitution, the entire universe of private business is transferred wholesale to public administration, but in so doing it transfers the emphasis from the choice of objectives for public action to the choice of the cheapest and most efficient tools for meeting unspecified objectives, which are usually assimilated to market objectives: 'When governance becomes a substitution for government, it carries with it a very specific model of public life and politics [...] public life is reduced to problem solving and program implementation,

---

[29] *G20/OECD Principles of Corporate Governance.* Paris: OECD Publishing, 2015, pp. 7, 9, http://dx.doi.org/10.1787/9789264236882-en.

a casting that brackets or eliminates politics, conflict, and deliberation about common values or ends.'[30]

Governance introduces a business management model independent of the objectives of the institutions to which it is applied. Here, the concepts of benchmarking and best practice come into play. Benchmarking was presented in the 1970s as a method for improving the techniques and means of production within a company by comparing it to other companies achieving better results, and 'entailing some sort of comparison of performance based on agreed indicators. Typically, this leads to some form of ranking or scoreboards. Such benchmarking can be used to assess the performance of governments (national, regional, local, agencies or government services), within industry to compare the performance of different business divisions or between companies and installations'.[31]

Benchmarking creates classifications and points systems, then searches for management techniques and those for work organization structures that improve the firm's classification and points, and these techniques are now universally known as *best practices*.

> A key premise of benchmarking is that best practices can be exported from one industry or sector to another and that some of the most valuable reforms will happen by creatively adapting practices in one field to another. [. . .] The presumed interchangeability of processes and practices across industries and sectors and the consolidation of best practices out of many different sources have several important implications [. . .].

---

[30] Brown, *Undoing the Demos*, p. 127.

[31] CEPS (Centre for European Political Studies) Task Force Report, *Benchmarking in the EU: Lessons from the EU Emissions Trading System for the Global Climate Change Agenda*. Brussels, 2010, p. 5, https://www.ceps.eu/ceps-pub lications/benchmarking-eu-lessons-eu-emissions-trading-system-global-cl imate-change-agenda/.

First, in benchmarking, practices are separated from products. Productivity, cost effectiveness, or consumer satisfaction are understood to inhere in practices with little respect to what is being produced, generated, or delivered. This permits private-sector practices to move readily into the public sector; it allows, for example, educational or health care institutions to be transformed by practices developed in the airline or computer industries. Second, the reason practices are separable from products and are transferable is that the ultimate end of every organization is presumed to be the same: competitive advantage in a marketplace.[32]

The most interesting aspect (to which we will return) is that an expert in the field cited by Brown, Robert Camp, explicitly invokes war-like images to explain that 'solving ordinary business problems, conducting management battles and surviving in the market place are all forms of war, fought by the same rules [know your enemy and know yourself]'.[33]

As such, there is no dismantling of the state by capitalism (much less, that extinction of the state Marx hoped for). Instead, there is a reconfiguration of the state.

Proof that neolibs need more state, in spite of their pretentious proclamations to the contrary, can be found during times of crisis, such as (if we just consider recent events) the great financial recession of 2008 or the 2020 pandemic. In these difficult moments, when the entire market system seems set to rupture and the entire global economy appears on the brink of collapse, suddenly, out of the blue, 'the markets' fell incredibly quiet, almost inert and passive. This is what happened in 2008 with the quantitative easing manoeuvres utilized by all major central banks. Quantitative easing is the immaterial, financial equivalent of printing money in the past, though without any

---

[32] Brown, *Undoing the Demos*, p. 137.
[33] Ibid.

tangible compensation. Thousands of billions of dollars, euro, yen and yuan flooded the markets, like pamphlets thrown from an airplane. This is the famous metaphor of the money thrown out of the helicopter, also coined by Milton Friedman in 1969.[34] The Federal Reserve enacted this solution several times over in such a radical way that its president, Ben Bernanke, had already been nicknamed 'Helicopter Ben' in a previous crisis, that of 2001–2 following the attacks on the Twin Towers in New York on September 11, 2001 (proving how certain crises *se suivent mais ne se ressemblent pas*, they repeat but do not look the same, though the responses given are always the same).

The same happened with the 2020 pandemic, when the markets retired to the balcony to watch the states rushing to avoid social crises and getting up to their eyeballs in debt in order to 'get the markets going again'. In this case also, tens of thousands of billions were poured into global economies to stop it all from coming crashing down around us. The elegance of the helicopter system lies in the fact that, in order to come to the aid of private business, the financial system, private banks and insurance companies, states are not only burdened with debts they must then service, but they take away all their possible resources with which to honour them by cutting taxes for the wealthiest. And here we see the entirely modern novelty in an age-old story. Even in feudal times, when an emergency required it or the kingdom had to go to war, the sovereign created a special tax for the barons (it was in order to limit these compulsory tax burdens that the English barons forced John Lackland to sign the Magna Carta in 1215). However, no one has ever asked today's barons to pay a special contribution

---

[34] 'Let us suppose now that one day a helicopter flies over this community and drops an additional $1,000 in bills from the sky, which is, of course, hastily collected by members of the community': Milton Friedman, *The Optimum Quantity of Money, and Other Essays*. London: Macmillan, 1969, pp. 4–5. Available at: http://abdet.com.br/site/wp-content/uploads/2014/12/Optimum -Quantity-of-Money.pdf.

(the marquis of Boeing, the archduke of Facebook, the prince of Google, the landgrave of Amazon). On the contrary, their already incredibly modest fiscal burden has been lightened even further.

This is how the precept of Rahm Emanuel is put into practice, and 'no crisis is wasted', because every crisis is used to make the state even more 'frugal', to 'starve the beast', forcing it to take on tasks and functions for disasters for which it is not responsible.

We can see here how superficial the idea is that a growth in the power of corporations and multinationals would necessarily bring a reduction in the power of states. Contrary to this common misconception, says Saskia Sassen, the power play made on individuals is not a zero-sum game between the power of a national state and that of multinational corporations, it is not true that 'the global and the national [are] mutually exclusive'.[35] It is not true that the more power wielded over each of us by multinationals, the less power is wielded by the state, as if everything that is won by one were lost by the others, and vice versa. In reality, according to Sassen, the state 'reconfigures itself' in order to be functional for corporations. In order to better adhere to them, it loses some functions but acquires others, it specializes in certain tasks but the total power exercised by the state over us grows, like that of global corporations. Or as Gilles Deleuze and Félix Guattari had already observed almost 50 years ago: 'Never before has a State lost so much of its power in order to enter with so much force into the service of the signs of economic power.'[36]

Foucault had already noted that an ecosystem of free enterprise exponentially increases the judicial role of arbitration: fewer civil servants, yes, but many more judges.

[35] Saskia Sassen, *Territory, Authority, Rights: From Medieval to Global Assemblages* (2006). Princeton, NJ: Princeton University Press, 2008, p. 21.
[36] Gilles Deleuze and Félix Guattari, *Anti-Oedipus. Capitalism and Schizophrenia*. Minneapolis, MN: University of Minnesota Press, 2000, p. 252.

The end result is that, against all common assumptions, free enterprise needs *more* state, a state with even more eyes, one that is more punitive but that has different goals: a 'private' government.

# 7

# The Politics Pricelist

The control of this now 'private' state is entrusted to that bizarre activity called 'politics'. The aim of politics is to assume corporate control of the state, conceived as the main service enterprise. As such, not only is politics a market, but there is also a market of politics, in the sense that the candidates must be bought (by the interests they want to espouse) and sold (to the electorate that they must convince to vote for them). These dynamics cause the costs of representation to rise. In 1976, the average cost of winning a seat in the US Senate was $609,000, whilst in 2016 it was $19.4 million. 'Political spending in the 2020 election totalled $14.4 billion, more than doubling the total cost of the record-breaking 2016 presidential election cycle. While the presidential election drew a record $5.7 billion, congressional races saw a stunning $8.7 billion in total spending.'[1] These figures are only for federal elections and do not include those at state, county or city level. And added to the money spent during the electoral campaigns is the expenditure on

---

[1] https://www.opensecrets.org/news/2021/02/2020-cycle-cost-14p4-billion-do ubling-16/.

lobbying. Although lobbies have a long and illustrious history – their defenders appeal to the spirit of James Madison – the boom comes in the same years as the neolib revolution – no coincidence there. While in 1975, spending on lobbyists in Washington did not exceed $100 million, in 2022 it was $4.09 billion. And while there were only a few registered lobbyists in the 1970s, by 2022 there were 12,644.[2] Of these, 466 are ex-representatives or senators recycled from the other side of the revolving door.[3] According to the former Secretary of Labor under Clinton, Robert Reich, more than half ex-senators and 42% of ex-representatives become lobbyists.[4]

It is not clear then whether the neolib interpretation of politics was confirmation of what was happening in the United States or whether their vision, based on rational choice theory, contributed to American politics taking this particular path, as it imposed that specific, sectorial view that lobbyists have of politicians and politics as a universal paradigm. According to rational choice theory, 'politically rational man is the man who would rather win than lose, regardless of the particular stakes'.[5] Therefore, 'rational candidates' will choose 'their electoral strategy and subsequent legislative behavior conditional on electoral success'.[6] 'The hard-line rational choice theorists assume that voters and politicians are utility maximizers in a very narrow sense and, directly or indirectly, imply that this assumption is descriptively accurate and even normatively

[2] For the 1970s, see the already cited series by Robert Kaiser; for current data on lobbyists, see Lobbying Data Summary, https://www.opensecrets.org/federal-lobbying/.
[3] https://www.opensecrets.org/revolving/top.php?display=Z.
[4] Robert Reich, 'Lobbyists are snuffing our democracy, one legal bribe at a time', Salon, 9 June 2015, https://www.salon.com/2015/06/09/robert_reich_lobbyists_are_snuffing_our_democracy_one_legal_bribe_at_a_time_partner/.
[5] William H. Riker, The Theory of Political Coalitions. New Haven, CT: Yale University Press, 1962, p. 22.
[6] David Austen-Smith and Jeffrey Banks, 'Elections, Coalitions, and Legislative Outcomes', American Political Science Review, vol. 82, no. 2, 1988, pp. 405–22, p. 405.

appropriate. Voters, in choosing among candidates, look in an egotistical way for their material self-interest. Politicians, equally selfishly, are motivated to be elected and reelected.'[7]

This description reduces politics to a zero-sum game (the post one person wins is lost by another) that is entirely independent of its political content. As such, the strategies adopted by a fascist, a communist or a liberal-capitalist will all be the same, or at least inspired by the same principles. The key phrase here is 'regardless of the particular stakes': with breath-taking mental acrobatics, politics is also revealed to be subject to the interchangeability of best practices and the electoral result is nothing more than the umpteenth form of benchmarking, independently of the product that has been 'voted' for, whether right, left or centre.

As Riker writes, 'the theorist can neither believe what actors say are their goals nor trust his or her own attributions of them. Many people hide aggrandizement under the cloak of self-proclaimed altruism. The theorist may be gullible or cynical or both. Furthermore, utopian goals are necessarily modified in real interaction, so that action itself affects the form and order of goals.'[8]

Obviously, just as Gary Becker believed, so too did Riker – altruism does not exist, as the altruist always expects something in return for their sacrifice:

> It is, for example, misleading to describe any particular action as entirely altruistic. To do so covers up some relevant self-regarding motives. The loving mother endangering her own life for the sake of the child is nevertheless the carrier of genes that presumably direct such action for the survival of the

[7] Jürg Steiner, 'Rational Choice Theories and Politics: A Research Agenda and a Moral Question', *PS: Political Science & Politics*, vol. 23, no. 1, March 1990, pp. 46–50, p. 47.

[8] William H. Riker, 'The Political Psychology of Rational Choice Theory', *Political Psychology*, vol. 16, no. 1, 1995, pp. 23–44, pp. 25–6

genetic strain. The revolutionary at the barricades sacrificing himself or herself for social ideals is nevertheless also expecting to benefit in terms of office and honor when the revolution succeeds. Consequently, adequate description of behavior depends on disentangling such goals, determining how each one contributes to the outcome and so on.[9]

We will return to the circularity of this reasoning: if everything is done for individual profit and if an action produces no apparent profit (such as, for example, making a sacrifice), then *there must be* a hidden profit of some other kind that balances the books. It is clear that *ex post*, once the sacrifice has been carried out, a 'dark profit' can always be found (just as cosmologists hypothesize about 'dark matter' in order to account for things that would otherwise not make sense). This configuration makes explicit recourse to the sociobiology of Edward Osborne Wilson, which stated that no human, nor any animal species, is entirely altruistic, as:

> many species have a genetically determined propensity to extreme altruism (such as sacrifice of the actor's own life). But this altruism is only displayed in genetically advantageous ways. Thus, honeybees defend the hive with suicidal stings, birds lead predators away from nests, mammals defend offspring (even siblings) to the death, and chimpanzee warfare probably counts as defense of the extended family. But none of these creatures nurture a weakened or aged adult, apparently because there seems no genetic advantage in doing so.[10]

This reasoning ignores the fact that not all animals are 'political animals', particularly not birds of prey, and therefore this theory, though it may provide us with useful explanations

---

[9] Riker, 'The Political Psychology of Rational Choice Theory', p. 39.
[10] Riker, 'The Political Psychology of Rational Choice Theory', p. 37.

for certain aspects of politics, does not account for its specifics. And most importantly, it is entirely defenceless in the face of great social change.

As always in neoliberal thought, once the laws of economics have been applied and extended to all human decisions (even those that are seemingly non-rational), then all of these choices become economic choices, market choices in a strict sense, with 'accountable' profits and losses. And so, politics is a market, a specific one, but nevertheless a market that obeys market logic, just as the art market is different from that for raw materials, but they are still two markets. By this understanding, parties are 'political enterprises' and 'from the perspective of party *entrepreneurs*, votes were *resources* for gaining control of government offices'.[11] And our hotly contested politics can be defined as a political or electoral marketplace.

'Marketplace' is in fact a term used nine times by the US Supreme Court in the majority ruling that accompanied their historic sentence in January 2010 in the case of *Citizens United vs. Federal Election Commission*.[12] 'The Supreme Court ruled against government bans on corporate contributions to super PACS, political action committees formed to support a candidate outside the auspices of her or his campaign. Calling such bans an abridgement of free speech and giving corporations the standing of persons with an unqualified right to political speech, the ruling permits corporate money to overwhelm the election process.'[13]

First and foremost, it is worth noting that of the five judges that underwrote the sentence as a majority, four (the president

---

[11] Frances Fox Piven and Richard A. Cloward, *Why Americans Still Don't Vote: And Why Politicians Want It That Way*. New York: Pantheon Books, 1988, p. 52 (my italics).

[12] The opinion of the court was given by judge Anthony Kennedy and can be read here: https://supreme.justia.com/cases/federal/us/558/310/#tab-opinion-1963051.

[13] Brown, *Undoing the Demos*, p. 152.

of the Court John Roberts, Samuel Alito, Antonin Scalia and Clarence Thomas) were members of the Federalist Society, the one financed by the foundations (Olin, Bradley, Koch, etc.) to promote Law and Economics. The investment in justice paid off better than anyone could have imagined.

Secondly, as we have already seen in the Powell Memorandum of 1971, the powerful present themselves as victims and, indeed, in the opinion given by Justice Kennedy, corporations are portrayed as being targeted and victimized, their freedom of speech threatened: what must be ensured is that 'certain disfavored associations of citizens – those that have taken on the corporate form – are penalized' and prevented 'from presenting both facts and opinions to the public, [. . .] which is deprived of knowledge and opinion vital to its function'.[14] As Wendy Brown observes,

> Whether the speaker is a homeless woman or Exxon, speech is speech, just as capital is capital. This disavowal of stratification and power differentials in the field of analysis and action is a crucial feature of neoliberal rationality, precisely the feature that discursively erases distinctions between capital and labor, owners and producers, landlord and tenant, rich and poor. There is only capital, and whether it is human, corporate, financial, or derivative, whether it is tiny or giant, is irrelevant to both its normative conduct and its right to be free of interference.[15]

But the most shocking effect of this approach is that it suddenly makes the problem of corruption simply disappear from politics. Not small-scale corruption, the politician taking a holiday or buying a house with a banker's money, but large-scale corruption, that in which a mega-billionaire creates an entire party out of nowhere and literally 'owns a candidate'.

---

[14]  Ibid., p. 161.
[15]  Ibid.

It is no coincidence that Robert Reich refers to lobbying as 'legal racketeering'. Here we can see another circularity, that by which Becker's definition of crime can be perfectly applied to US non-corruption: we recall that Becker believes crime to be any action that causes an individual to run the risk of being sentenced to punishment. The moment lobbying becomes an activity regulated by laws and lobbyists are legally registered, the moment the bribe becomes legal, corruption is no longer a crime and it disappears from the penal code.

Moreover, if politics is a market in which 'votes' constitute resources, there is nothing unusual about someone wishing to further their own interests by buying the company (the enterprise-party) that supplies these resources. This is why in Brazil it was possible to send a politician like Lula da Silva to prison for supposedly having bought a small, out-of-town apartment, but entirely legitimate to elect a presidential candidate (Jair Bolsonaro) who was literally owned by the agri-food complex.

On the other hand, how can we talk of corruption – the buying and selling of candidates, nominations and posts – if politics itself is a market? It is worth revisiting an article written in *Vanity Fair* in 1930 by Walter Lippmann. He was the intellectual to whom the 1938 Paris meeting was dedicated, a meeting that was retrospectively named the precursor to the Mont Pelerin Society.[16] It was at this meeting that Alexander Rüstow coined the term 'neoliberalism'. The meeting was called 'Colloque Walter Lippmann' as it was held to discuss the book written by Lippmann, *An Inquiry into the Principles of the Good Society* (among his other lexical innovations, Lippmann coined the term 'stereotype' and later popularized the expression 'Cold War'). This is just one example of how

---

[16] The meeting organized by philosopher Louis Rougier was attended by, among others, the Frenchmen Raymond Aron and Jacques Rueff, Friedrich von Hayek, Ludwig von Mises, Wilhelm Röpke, Michael Polanyi (older brother of Karl Polanyi) and, of course, Walter Lippmann.

connections intertwine underground and resurface over time as tangled roots.

In his *Vanity Fair* article, Lippmann talks about Tammany Hall, the New York Democrat-affiliated political organization that by the end of the nineteenth century had become synonymous in the US with corruption: 'I think that Tammany, for example, is a kind of disease which has affected the body politic. There it is, to be sure; it has been there a long time, and the counterpart of it is to be found in virtually every American community. Nevertheless, we feel that it is not supposed to be there, and that if only we had a little more courage or sense or something we could cut away the diseased tissue and live happily ever after.' Once again today this is the sentiment shared by public opinion in all corners of the Earth. But, according to Lippmann, this public opinion is wrong: 'The implications of this notion seem to me to be false, and I believe that our political thinking would be immensely more effective if we adopted an entirely opposite theory.' 'As a matter of historical fact [. . .] corruption in the form of jobbery represents a decisive step upward in political life. I think it could be shown from the history of the Mother of Parliaments itself [England] [. . .] that corruption is the practical substitute for factional wars. [. . .] There are places in the world today where corruption is progress.'[17]

Already in 1930 Lippmann could see (albeit vaguely) that corruption was nothing more than a kind of 'political marketplace'. But the interesting thing is that, in an umpteenth application of the theory of double truths (there is one truth for the plebs and another for the 'wise', the 'philosophers', the 'best', the 'aristocrats', the 'masters', however you wish to put it), while the US Constitutional Court, in the name of Law and Economics, absolves mega-corruption, corruption as a

---

[17] Walter Lippmann, 'A Theory about Corruption', *Vanity Fair*, November 1930, pp. 61, 90.

political market system, at the same time corruption is used as a tool for putting politics in its place. However much the slogan 'down with corruption!' might stir our sympathies, it is necessary to state that any hunt for the corrupt, any 'clean hands' campaign always leads to the right. Just think: we have never seen an anti-corruption campaign end in a progressive solution or one that is 'on the left'. This is for the simple reason that the premise of every anti-corruption campaign is that politicians are corrupt and therefore we cannot allow them to manage the economy, meaning the economy must return to the hands of those who have the right to run it: the capitalists.

If politics is a market, there is only one licit form of corruption, and it is that waged by the capitalist over the entire system. At that point, however, it is no longer corruption but merely a legitimate acquisition of political firms (i.e., the parties) by financial and industrial companies.

## The Privatization of the Brain

If, however, there is one thing that those operating the market cannot do, it is change the market and its rules. In the neoliberal understanding of politics there is no place for transformations; the idea of being able to 'change the world' is entirely alien. This is the 'capitalist realism' that provokes (and is caused by) a reflexive impotence: not apathy, not cynicism, but rather the knowledge that 'They know things are bad, but more than that, they know they can't do anything about it. But that "knowledge", that reflexivity, is not a passive observation of an already existing state of affairs. It is a self-fulfilling prophecy.'[18]

If there is indeed something that constantly gnaws away at us, especially since the 2008 crisis, it is that we are seeing no

[18] Fisher, *Capitalist Realism*, pp. 17, 21.

signs of revolt. The question is: why the hell aren't we rebelling? Why aren't young people exploding with rage?

Yes, timid, feeble movements pop up here and there (and immediately retreat), but they are nothing but defenceless bellyaching against the blows the dominant rain down upon the dominated, against the beatings the masters of the world mete out to the plebs. Discomfort is returning; it brings to mind the astonishment that shook David Hume and Étienne de La Boétie when they were faced with the human vocation for subordination, acquiescence, subjecting themselves to the dominion of others.

The Scottish philosopher of the Enlightenment was dumbfounded:

> Nothing appears more surprising to those who consider human affairs with a philosophical eye than the easiness with which the many are governed by the few and the implicit submission with which men resign their own sentiments and passions to those of their rulers. When we inquire by what means this wonder is effected, we shall find that, as force is always on the side of the governed, the governors have nothing to support them but opinion. It is, therefore, on opinion only that government is founded, and this maxim extends to the most despotic and most military governments as well as to the most free and most popular.[19]

Looking around, we might have something to say about the idea that 'force is always on the side of the governed'. On the other hand, the object of the text you are reading is precisely how they are shaping our 'opinion'.

Two centuries earlier, Étienne de La Boétie, the humanist friend of Michel de Montaigne, had already registered his

---

[19] David Hume, 'On the First Principles of Government', *Essays and Treatises on Several Subjects*, 1758 edition', in *Political Essays*. Cambridge: Cambridge University Press, 1994, p. 16.

astonishment at the 'voluntary servitude' by which human beings submit themselves to tyranny: 'Surely a striking situation! Yet it is so common that one must grieve the more and wonder the less at the spectacle of a million men serving in wretchedness, their necks under the yoke, not constrained by a greater multitude than they, but simply, it would seem, delighted and charmed by the name of one man alone whose power they need not fear, for he is evidently the one person whose qualities they cannot admire because of his inhumanity and brutality toward them.' 'What vice is it, or, rather, what degradation?' the young La Boétie asked himself (he was twenty-four when he wrote these words), 'to see an endless multitude of people not merely obeying, but driven to servility? Not ruled, but tyrannized over?' His conclusion was desolate: 'It is therefore the inhabitants themselves who permit, or, rather, bring about, their own subjection, since by ceasing to submit they would put an end to their servitude. A people enslaves itself, cuts its own throat, when, having a choice between being vassals and being free men, it deserts its liberties and takes on the yoke, gives consent to its own misery, or, rather, apparently welcomes it.'[20]

However, both La Boétie and Hume were writing before the 'age of revolution' began. Just a few decades after Hume's words, people would repeatedly demonstrate, with a rapid succession of revolutions, that the many would not let themselves be so easily governed by the few and that they did not always 'enslave themselves and cut their own throats': France 1789, 1830, 1870; Haiti 1791; the whole of Europe 1848; Russia 1905, 1917; Germany 1919, 1989; China 1948; Cuba 1959 (I have not included the 'American Revolution' of 1765–83 because, strictly speaking, it was a war of colonial independence, not a revolution). Never, in the previous 5,000 years had human

[20] Étienne de La Boétie, *The Politics of Obedience: The Discourse of Voluntary Servitude* (1554), http://www.public-library.uk/ebooks/16/4.pdf, pp. 1–3.

history witnessed such a high number and frequency of revolutions.

On the other hand, it was only recently that the very term 'revolution' had stopped meaning the full rotation of a planet around the Sun and started to indicate a sudden and total regime change (such as the 'Glorious Revolution' in England of 1688). The uprisings that had naturally punctuated history had been described in other terms: disorder, tumult, revolt, upheaval, (the Ciompi in Florence, Cola di Rienzo in Rome, the Carnival in Romans in Delphine, Thomas Müntzer in Germany, Masaniello in Naples). Most importantly, never had so many revolutions been victorious. Of the only lasting (albeit partial) successes of the dominated, one dates back more than 2,000 years to the secession of the Roman people (*secessio plebis*) in 493 BCE, which achieved the creation of the 'plebeian tribunes', and the other to almost four centuries ago when the English became the first people in history to cut off their own king's head.

So, one hypothesis would be that the 'age of revolution' was very short, lasting a few centuries before coming to an end. But even if this were the case, we need to understand how and why it ended, what made it end, given that for two centuries human beings had hated 'voluntary servitude'. So how is it that after two centuries of people believing that the world could be changed did the *reflexive impotence* discussed by Fisher became so widespread?

One explanation is provided by Wendy Brown. Put plainly, the victory of the ideological counter-offensive of the last half century, of counterintelligentsia, has not privatized only railways, schools, healthcare, armies, police, motorways, but it has *privatized our brains*.

As neoliberalism converts every political or social problem into market terms, it converts them to individual problems with market solutions. Examples in the United States are legion:

bottled water as a response to contamination of the water table; private schools, charter schools, and voucher systems as a response to the collapse of quality public education; anti-theft devices, private security guards, and gated communities (and nations) as a response to the production of a throwaway class and intensifying economic inequality; [. . .] and, of course, finely differentiated and titrated pharmaceutical antidepressants as a response to lives of meaninglessness or despair amidst wealth and freedom. This conversion of socially, economically, and politically produced problems into consumer items depoliticizes what has been historically produced, and it especially depoliticizes capitalism itself. [. . .] Thus, the much-discussed commitment of neoliberalism to 'privatization' has ramifications that exceed the outsourcing of police forces, prisons, welfare, militaries, and schools on one side, and the corporate buyout of public endeavors and institutions on the other. Privatization as a value and practice penetrates deep into the culture and the citizen-subject. If we have a problem, we look to a product to solve it; indeed, a good deal of our lives is devoted to researching, sharing, procuring, and upgrading these solutions.[21]

The privatization of our heads goes beyond the picture painted by Wendy Brown. Not only does it transform the social solutions to problems into commodities, but the privatization of our brains has convinced all of us that collective action does not make any sense, that it produces nothing. It tells us the only salvation from our existential and social problems is individual, personal, that the only way of improving our lives is not to cooperate and act together but to elbow each other out of the way, push through, and that the only relationship

[21] Wendy Brown, 'American Nightmare: Neoliberalism, Neoconservatism, and De-Democratization', *Political Theory*, vol. 34, no. 6, December 2006, pp. 690–714, p. 703.

between human beings is that of the market with client and supplier on one side and competition on the other, forcing us to view our fellow human beings solely through these prisms. It is at this point, then, that 'there is no such thing as society' and that it no longer makes sense to talk of social justice. So, what should it be? Justice between clients, maybe? Between suppliers? Justice between competitors?

Once more we come back to *futility*, collective *political* action is 'futile' because what counts is individual economic action.

# 8

# Arsenic and Witchcraft I:
# The Remote-Control Society

It might be said that in attributing such a significant role to Midwestern magnates and the counterintelligentsia of reactionary think tanks, I am making the same mistake as Voltaire's hero who boasted that a well-advised mixture of prayers, spells and arsenic was a sure-fire way of annihilating his enemies, with the ideological struggle playing the role of the spells and the colossal power of global and globalized capital as the arsenic. It is true that in imposing the 'There is no Alternative' ideology on the entire planet Earth (and even the orbital space around it), capital has wielded an unprecedented, overwhelming power. As the prematurely departed David Graeber wrote over ten years ago in 2011,

> In fact, it could well be said that the last thirty years have seen the construction of a vast bureaucratic apparatus for the creation and maintenance of hopelessness, a giant machine designed, first and foremost, to destroy any sense of possible alternative futures [. . .] To do so requires creating a vast apparatus of armies, prisons, police, various forms of private security firms and police and military intelligence apparatus, and propaganda engines of every conceivable variety, most of which do not

attack alternatives directly so much as create a pervasive climate of fear, jingoistic conformity, and simple despair that renders any thought of changing the world seem an idle fantasy. [. . .] Economic freedom, for most of us, was reduced to the right to buy a small piece of one's own permanent subordination [. . .] we were left in the strange situation of not being able to even imagine any other way that things might be arranged. About the only thing we can imagine is catastrophe.[1]

It would be bizarre in this time of tumultuous technological progress, if the only sector that remained static were the technology of power. This has also taken giant leaps: the power exercised over each of us is infinitely greater, more pervasive, more constant, perhaps less crudely brutal but more implacable than that imposed even just a few decades ago, let alone a few centuries. But it is not only the quantity of power that has grown exponentially, it is also the quality of this power. The paradigm of power has changed, with a mutation similar to that separating neoliberalism from classical liberalism.

To use Foucault's taxonomy, the passage from feudalism to industrial capitalism corresponded to a transformation of power from sovereign power to disciplinary power. Royal power identified the sovereign ('the body of the king') and rendered the subject anonymous, and was a power that could be exercised at one and the same time, alongside other sovereign powers. The sovereign power of the *pater familias* (the name of the father) coexisted with that of the king and the pope. On the contrary, disciplinary power is a power that makes the disciplinarian anonymous but identifies the subject (through their work card, school reports, legal records, medical records). It is a total power in the sense that it overwhelms the person upon whom it is exercised to the exclusion of all other

---

[1] David Graeber, *Debt: The First 5,000 Years* (2011). London: Melvin House, 2014, pp. 382–3.

disciplinary powers: when you are at school, you are not at the factory; when you are in the mental hospital, you are not in the army. But it is a power limited to a place (the school, the barracks, the prison, the factory, the hospital) and a time (the duration of the detention, work hours, the length of the shift, etc.), as is the control it exerts. The Panopticon imagined by Jeremy Bentham in 1791 only ever watches over those being disciplined, as its original title explained: *Panopticon: or, the Inspection-House. Containing the Idea of a New Principle of Construction applicable to any Sort of Establishment, in which Persons of any Description are to be kept under inspection. And in particular to penitentiary-houses, prisons, houses of industry, work-houses, poor-houses, manufactories, mad-houses, hospitals, and schools. With a plan adapted to the principle.*

But these disciplinary powers are isolated from one another, the poor house from the prison, the hospital from the factory. This intersection of the various disciplinary powers passes through the sovereign power of the family. We leave the family to go to school, return to the family before joining up and go back to the family before leaving to go to work.

The same technological innovations of free time connected to disciplinary power tended to close the individual off, render them 'static' (as it were). The individual left where they were subjected to disciplinary power (the office, factory, school) and shut themselves back in their homes. And only when they were within its walls were they able to access the world first through the radio, landline telephones and record players, and later through televisions and cassette players. Suburban civilization was the apotheosis of this 'staticization' of humans.

Instead, today we are subjected to a power that is different from the disciplinary one, a ubiquitous 'remote-controlling' power. Firstly, because we are always trackable, always signed in, always intercepted. We do not realize the level of surveillance, of control over our lives. Just 40 years ago, a rebel could 'go underground', disappear, become anonymous and resurface elsewhere. Today, not only would this be impossible, it would be unthinkable: surveillance CCTV, the systematic intercepting of email, chats, SMS and telephone calls, documents requiring retinal and iris scans, the traceability of expenditure through credit and debit cards – you can forget Bentham's Panopticon! This demonstrates how the technologies of power are not mutually exclusive, and how remotely controlling power can enormously reinforce disciplinary power. Think of facial recognition software, only one of many technologies of control. It is already used in Georgia to gain access to the subway (instead of a season ticket), and in China in hotel receptions, hospital emergency rooms, airplane and train check-in, the entrances to banks and for maintaining discipline at school.[2] And, naturally, it allows for the identification (and therefore, the repression) of anyone and everyone taking part in a protest, even when there are hundreds of thousands of people present.

Any occasion is a good one. Obeying Rahm Emanuel's injunction, no crisis must be wasted when it comes to exercising control. Just think of how the acceptance of individual tracking devices, used by governments to monitor individuals, was promoted as an example of civic spirit, a manifestation of social virtue during the pandemic in 2020. Previously, they had been used discreetly, as a collateral product of our telematic society. But the Covid-19 virus promoted the voluntary acceptance of digital tracking as a laudable civic duty, and its refusal into an act of civil desertion. That same epidemic also gave a strong push for the extinction of cash, physical money, in favour of electronic money in the form of credit and debit cards, online transfers that allow for the infinitely more detailed control avoided by the crumpled and anonymous banknote.

---

[2] Yuan Yang and Madhumita Murgia, 'Facial recognition: how China cornered the surveillance market', *Financial Times*, 6 December 2019, https://www.ft.com/content/6f1a8f48-1813-11ea-9ee4-11f260415385.

The control is capillary, continuous and ubiquitous. And it is exerted in a synergic way by the large technology oligopolies and governments (as revealed to us by Edward Snowden), whereby we do not know whether it's the governments spying for oligopolies or oligopolies intercepting for governments, in which each of the two sides uses the other, just as Antonin Scalia advised, when referring to federal government: 'the trick is to use it *wisely*'.

It cannot be stressed enough just how much the new technological panorama is defined by neolib ideology, to the point that no relevant political force even thought about opening a public debate on whether (let alone proposing) the internet should be public. There has been so much talk of the 'information highway' but roads are public, no one wants to go back to tollbooths and taxes at every crossroads. And yet it is taken for granted that the enormous servers, providers, operators, motors and connectors are all in private hands, constituting gigantic oligopolies and even feudal structures; the archduke of Facebook, the prince of Google, the marquis of Alibaba, the count of Oracle, and so on.

But there is a second way – more subtle, sarcastic even – in which the large network operators have reinterpreted the concept of 'human capital'. In this new variety of capitalism, which Shoshana Zuboff calls 'surveillance capitalism', all of our public and private life, all of our experiences, communications, images, conversations, notes and searches become primary material that is used to predict our behaviour. And it is these predictions that surveillance capitalists sell to the market in a B-to-B (business-to-business) transaction where the users are the raw materials being extracted, and the commodity is the user: 'Once we searched Google, but now Google searches us. Once we thought of digital services as free, but now surveillance capitalists think of us as free.' The fact is that the big network operators have literally appropriated our data without asking anyone's permission. When Google decided to digitalize all the books printed to date without concerning itself with copyright, or when it photographed every street and house on the planet without asking anyone for permission, it acted just like 'Columbus' who 'simply declared the islands as the territory of the Spanish monarchy and the pope'.[3]

> Surveillance capitalism unilaterally claims human experience as free raw material for translation into behavioral data. Although some of these data are applied to product or service improvement, the rest are declared as a proprietary behavioral surplus, fed into advanced manufacturing processes known as 'machine intelligence,' and fabricated into prediction products that anticipate what you will do now, soon, and later. Finally, these prediction products are traded in a new kind of marketplace for behavioral predictions that I call behavioral futures markets.[4]

In this sense, our entire life has become original capital, 'human capital' in a literal sense, from which network operators profit. This new capitalism exploits and uses for profit all digital traces we leave behind – whether voluntarily or involuntarily – just like car engines leave trails of exhaust fumes. The process of creating these predictions begins with the harvesting of our 'data exhaust', the data generated by the users themselves, 'from the haphazard ephemera of everyday life, especially the tiniest details of our online engagements – captured, datafied (translated into machine-readable code), abstracted, aggregated, packaged, sold, and analyzed. This includes everything from Facebook likes and Google searches

---

[3] John Naughton, '"The goal is to automate us": welcome to the age of surveillance capitalism', *The Guardian*, 20 January 2019, https://www.theguardian .com/technology/2019/jan/20/shoshana-zuboff-age-of-surveillance-capitalism -google-facebook.

[4] Shoshana Zuboff, *The Age of Surveillance Capitalism: The Fight for a Human Future at the New Frontier of Power*. London: Profile Books, 2019, p. 8.

to tweets, emails, texts, photos, songs, and videos, location and movement, purchases, every click, misspelled word, every page view, and more'.[5]

> It has spread across a wide range of products, services, and economic sectors, including insurance, retail, healthcare, finance, entertainment, education, transportation, and more, birthing whole new ecosystems of suppliers, producers, customers, market-makers, and market players. Nearly every product or service that begins with the word 'smart' or 'personalized', every internet-enabled device, every 'digital assistant', is simply a supply-chain interface for the unobstructed flow of behavioural data.[6]

In this way, there is a ridiculous asymmetry between Google (or Facebook, or Twitter), who know everything about us, and ourselves, who are completely ignorant of having given away for free the knowledge of our entire lives. It is an asymmetry that Zuboff calls a 'coup from above'[7]: another form of the victorious revolt of the powerful against their subjects, as considered by Aristotle, has come to pass and we are experiencing it directly.

Furthermore, the technology of *coup d'état* has been refined, anaesthetized. In 1997, in order to overthrow the civilian government (for the fifth time since 1945), the Turkish army carried out the first 'postmodern coup' in history. Postmodern in that a simple announcement on television was sufficient to carry it out, without placing so much as one tank on the street. In recent years, judicial coups have multiplied, those in which the army or the elite use the judiciary to remove unpopular governments (oh, Thrasymachus, you again!). This

---

[5] Shoshana Zuboff, 'A Digital Declaration', *Die Frankfurter Allgemeine Zeitung Feuilleton*, 15 September 2014, available at: https://opencuny.org/pnmarchive /files/2019/01/Zuboff-Digital-Declaration.pdf.

[6] Shoshana Zuboff in an interview with John Naughton, cited above.

[7] Zuboff, *The Age of Surveillance Capitalism*, pp. 513–16.

has happened several times in Latin America, in 2016–19 in Brazil with the demolition of the Working Party (*Partido dos Trabalhadores*) government led by Lula, thanks to accusations of corruption that culminated in the return of military power under an electoral guise (one of the first acts by president Jair Bolsonaro, ex-paratrooper, was to celebrate the 55th anniversary of the 1964 military coup).

But there is another, deeper connection between the new technological panorama and the neolib counter-revolution, and it concerns our relationship with time, work and with the others. It is linked to the nomadic nature of new technologies which essentially do nothing more than bring with us, almost as an extension of our bodies, those technologies that had once been static, relegated to the domestic space or the office. The smartphone, iPod, tablet and laptop allow us to carry the tv, record player, radio, videogames and (no longer fixed) telephone with us. And everything that previously had been available in a well-defined space (house, office, cinema) becomes perpetually accessible anywhere. But the other side of the coin is that you can be reached anywhere. And this fact alone irreversibly alters your relationship with space, time and work. You are on an island in the Aegean, but you are also in your office (where they are calling you from). You are in a work meeting, but you are also next to the cot holding your child, who cries if you stop talking to them. You have emigrated to a distant land, yet you are still close to your loved ones with whom you dine through Skype or WhatsApp.

But this perpetual reachability changes your relationship with work. Firstly, the control exerted over you no longer has temporal or spatial limits, as delivery drivers and riders know only too well. These new slaves who bring us our pizza or Amazon packages are punished if their GPS show they are not keeping up with the timetable imposed on them and checked by satellite. Secondly, because free time is never totally free, just like how spatially you are never entirely in one place. When that phone rings, your work penetrates your free time, leisure time, the intimacy of your toilet. I remember when we would go on holiday and would call home once or twice a month when we found a payphone and coins to use in it. And, naturally, no one called you from your place of work. Not now. You work 24/7, or must at least be available to do so. In this light, we can better understand those enthusiastically singing the praises of remote working, known also as 'smart working' for a reason (let's not forget the implications Zuboff attributes to the adjective 'smart'). In this field also, the response to the 2020 epidemic enabled a colossal social engineering experiment, allowing us to experiment with 'remote working', 24/7 remote-control availability and reachability, anticipating a system of sanctions for those who cannot be reached, or punishment for 'desertion', for 'abandoning one's post'. This is a further demonstration of how new technologies exalt the need for the total 'flexibility' neolib capital requires of its subjects.

Finally, obviously, if you are not entirely in one place or entirely in one time, then neither are you totally together with someone. Even if you have them next to you, you are, in that moment, on your own; you are far away, with others, fully realizing what Guy Debord said was the ultimate aim of modern city planning: that 'the system requires that isolated individuals be recaptured and *isolated together*'.[8] Nothing better visually expresses this concept of 'isolated together' than a subway carriage in which everyone, absolutely everyone, is sitting next to one another, each staring at their own mobile phone: solitude, together. There is something almost sardonic about the expression 'social network'. Furthermore, these technological instruments are all devices aimed at exempting you from contacting others, from asking for help, from interacting. Even two decades ago, if you travelled to a foreign

---

[8] Guy Debord, *The Society of the Spectacle*, Critical Editions, 2021, para. 172, p. 93 (my italics).

country and wanted to ask for some information, you had to learn a few words in the language and then make contact with someone from the place and ask them for the knowledge you required, while also trying to understand the response. In short, you had to interact, no matter how primitively. Now, all you need are the indications provided by Google Maps and all human interaction can be avoided. That reduction of the social human into the isolated individual who is the cornerstone of neolib anthropology is fully realized ('there is no such thing as society').

P.S. Naturally, we are in no way suggesting here that it was neolib ideology that produced these new technologies, but among the varied and diverse directions that technological developments can take, in the end the road taken is the one best suited to the economic interests and ideologies of the society in which these technologies end up operating. It is very well known that the ancient Greeks built toys powered by steam, but it never occurred to them to power a mill or a galley that way, just as the Chinese did invent gunpowder but never created anything that could be called artillery. This was simply because these uses correspond neither to the economic structure of those societies, nor to the *forma mentis* that governed it. Closer to home, technology can either save work and be capital-intensive, or save capital and be labour-intensive. But the West has only developed the first type of technology, the one which saves work and is based on a broad availability of capital while, in order to develop the economies that were once referred to as Third World, those technologies that save capital and which are based on a wide availability of cheap labour would have been much more useful. But, funnily enough, the latter have never become widespread.

# 9

# Arsenic and Witchcraft II: Do Not Forgive Us Our Debts as We Do Not Forgive Those Indebted To Us

While the digital revolution provides us with the technological tools for remote control, it is the technology of debt that secures its economic dimension.

No matter how strange it might appear, the systematic and codified use of debt – both of private individuals and states alike – is fairly recent. Debt has, of course, been at the basis of human society since prehistoric times: the gift economy is based on the idea that whoever receives that gift feels *indebted* and has a duty to reciprocate. And certainly, sovereigns often accrued debts, especially to finance their wars, as Florentine bankers Bardi and Peruzzi learnt to their own expense in 1343 when their banks catastrophically collapsed due to the insolvency of the King of England, Edward III, whose war, which would become the Hundred Year War with France, they had recklessly financed.

As with many other issues, it was Marx who first understood the role that public debt would play in modern capitalism:

> The national debt, i.e. the alienation of the state – whether that state is despotic, constitutional or republican – marked

the capitalist era with its stamp. The only part of the so-called national wealth that actually enters into the collective possession of a modern nation is – the national debt. [. . .] Public credit becomes the credo of capital. And with the rise of national debt-making [*Staatsverschuldung*], lack of faith in the national debt [*Staatsschuld*] takes the place of the sin against the Holy Ghost, for which there is no forgiveness. The public debt becomes one of the most powerful levers of primitive accumulation. As with the stroke of an enchanter's wand, it endows unproductive money with the power of creation and thus turns it into capital, without forcing it to expose itself to the troubles and risks inseparable from its employment in industry or even in usury. [. . .] the national debt has given rise to joint-stock companies, to dealings in negotiable effects of all kinds, and to speculation: in a word, it has given rise to stock-exchange gambling and the modem bankocracy.[1]

But until the end of the nineteenth century, public debt remained an issue of money and goods. As such, Marx himself writes about it on various occasions with words that are striking today due to their currentness:

the faction of the bourgeoisie that ruled and legislated through the Chambers had a direct interest in the indebtedness of the state. The state deficit was really the main object of its speculation and the chief source of its enrichment. At the end of each year a new deficit. After the lapse of four or five years a new loan. And every new loan offered new opportunities to the finance aristocracy for defrauding the state, which was kept artificially on the verge of bankruptcy – it had to negotiate with the bankers under the most unfavourable conditions.[2]

---

[1]  Marx, *Capital*, Ch. 31, 'The Genesis of the Industrial Capitalist', p. 919.
[2]  Karl Marx, 'Class Struggle in France: 1848–1850', in Karl Marx and Friedrich Engels, *Selected Works in Three Volumes. Vol. 1.* Moscow: Progress Publishers, 1973, p. 206.

Marx spoke about the French state at that time:

> What conditions the accrual of state property to high finance? The constantly growing indebtedness of the state. And the indebtedness of the state? The constant excess of its expenditure over its income, a disproportion which is simultaneously the cause and effect of the system of state loans. In order to escape from this indebtedness, the state must [. . .] restrict its expenditure, that is, simplify and curtail the government organism, govern as little as possible, employ as few personnel as possible.[3]

In 1850, Marx had already noted that public debt forces the state to be 'frugal'. But here we are still in the arena of a domestic class struggle, in which public debt is the tool with which financial capital picks its tax-paying and bond-buying citizens' pockets.

It was only in the twentieth century that debt came to be used as an actual tool for political control. It does so first and foremost as a control over individuals and their families through the creation of the mortgage. In the nineteenth century, the use of a mortgage for buying a house as a disciplining tool of entire populations was still unknown. Anyone taking on a 15- or 30-year mortgage is highly unlikely to revolt, for two reasons: (1) the mortgage makes them houseowners, and therefore causes them to internalize the ideology of ownership; and (2) in a certain sense, the mortgage makes them their own debtor, prisoner of their own (future) ownership for years and decades to come. The 30-year mortgage on houses guaranteed by the state was one of the principal innovations of Franklin Delano Roosevelt's New Deal; he exclaimed: 'a nation of home owners, of people who own a real share in their own land, is

---

[3] Ibid., ch. 3, p. 270.

unconquerable'.[4] Before Roosevelt, the mortgage in the modern sense did not exist. Only with that reform was the deposit for the acquisition of a house lowered to 10% of the total price, and only then was the length of the mortgage extended to up to 30 years, reducing the cost of monthly rates and allowing millions of working- and middle-class families to buy their own house (by the 1950s, more than six in ten US families were already the owners of their own home).[5]

Today in the US, 68% of the debt belonging to family units continues to be the mortgage. But it is since the Second World War that family debt exploded in the US and, later, throughout (most of) the world. It is no coincidence that while the *mortgage* was the most significant harbinger of consequences between the two world wars, in the decades immediately following 1945, the most relevant financial innovation was undoubtedly the *credit card*. The first general credit card (meaning it was valid in more than one particular chain of shops or services) was Diners Club, founded in 1950. American Express then appeared in 1958. That same year, Bank of America launched the Bankamericard (known in France in the 1960s as *Carte Bleue*), which was renamed Visa in 1976. In order to counter the monopoly of the Bank of America, in 1969 a group of banks founded Master Change: The Interbank Card, which became Mastercard in 1979. So, the credit card was also invented, popularized and imposed in and by the US.

Mortgage and credit cards offer at least a partial explanation for the incredible expansion in private loans after the Second World War. In 1950, household debt represented 23% of US gross domestic product; today it constitutes 75% (having reached 95% in 2008). And while in 1960, family debt was equal

---

[4] Marco d'Eramo, *Il maiale e il grattacielo. Chicago: una storia del nostro futuro* (1995). Milan: Feltrinelli, 2020. English edition: *The Pig and the Skyscraper. Chicago: A History of Our Future*. London: Verso, 2002, p. 127.

[5] PK, Historical Homeownership Rate in the United States, https://dqydj.com /historical-homeownership-rate-in-the-united-states-1890-present/.

to 60% of their annual income, in 1980 this rose to 75%, then 95% in 1995 and in 2021 it was 145%.[6]

Debt has become a given for almost all families in developed countries. We get into debt with our mortgages, to buy a car, to study at university, to go on holiday, to get dental work done. But the most illuminating case is undoubtedly that of student debt, agreed to in order to pay for university education in the US.

In the third trimester of 2019, this debt totalled $1,757 billion (more than Spain's GDP), with 44 million Americans burdened by student debt. For 'student' debtors, the rate of insolvency (caused by a payment delay of more than three months) is 7.2%.[7] It is useful to note that in the last ten years, the number of people aged sixty and over (so, more than 30 years after graduating from university) who still have student debt has quadrupled, going from 700,000 to 2.8 million people. The annual borrowing has gone from $7.6 billion (adjusted for inflation) in 1975–6, to $110.3 billion in 2012–13, with an increase of 1,472%.[8] Among the many causes for this, two are particularly relevant. The number of university students has more than doubled (+223%) and this rise is due to an increase in less-wealthy students, and therefore a higher number in

---

[6] The data for 1950 can be found at https://tradingeconomics.com/united-st ates/households-debt-to-gdp, which also provides international statistics, while the data for 1960, 1980 and 1995 are from Juliet B. Schor, *The Overspent American: Why We Want What We Don't Need.* New York: Harper, 1999, pp. 231–2. The numbers on current debt levels are provided by https:// www.firstrepublic.com/insights-education/average-american-debt. It is also worth noting that, according to the International Monetary Fund (IMF), in 2021 household debt to GDP was higher in some countries than in the US: in Canada it was 107.5% of GDP, in South Korea 105.7%, in the Netherland 101.5%, in the UK 86.1%, while in others it was far smaller: Japan 68.8%, France 66.6%, Spain 58.4%, Germany 56.7% and Italy 43.6%. https://www.imf.org/external/datamap per/HH_LS@GDD/CAN/GBR/USA/DEU/ITA/FRA/JPN/VNM.

[7] Data from https://educationdata.org/student-loan-debt-statistics.

[8] Sandy Baum, *The Evolution of Student Debt in the U.S.: An Overview,* The Urban Institute, George Washington University, October 2013, http://www.up john.org/stuloanconf/Baum.pdf.

need of a loan in order to study. But most significantly, tuition fees have tripled. For the 1975–6 academic year, annual tuition for four-year university courses (both private and public) cost on average $7,513 (in constant-dollars, 2016); this rose to $12,274 in 1985–6 and was $26,593 in 2016–17. In private universities average annual tuition cost $13,745 in 1975–6, rising to $20,578 in 1985–6 and was $54,501 for the 2020–1 academic year. And the times of crisis obviously have a dramatic effect on this debt: if students finished their studies in a period of crisis (2008–12) or after an epidemic (2020–2), they faced a work market in recession, drastically reducing the possibility of being hired, leading them towards insolvency, a kind of generational bankruptcy.

The philosopher who best understands the implications of this debt is Maurizio Lazzarato. He writes:

> Student indebtedness exemplifies neoliberalism's strategy since the 1970s: the substitution of social rights (the right to education, health care, retirement, etc.) for access to credit, in other words, for the right to contract debt. No more pooling of pensions, instead individual investment in pension funds; no pay raises, instead consumer credit; no universal insurance, individual insurance; no right to housing, home loans. [. . .] Education spending, left entirely to students, frees up resources which the state quickly transfers to corporations and the wealthiest households, notably through lower taxes. The true welfare recipients are no longer the poor, the unemployed, the sick, unmarried women, and so on, but corporations and the rich.[9]

Furthermore, 'Students contract their debts by their own volition; they then quite literally become accountable for their

[9] Maurizio Lazzarato, *Governing By Debt*. South Pasadena, CA: Semiotext(e), 2015, pp. 66–7.

lives and, to put it in terms of contemporary capitalism, they become their own managers'. As an act of disciplinary control,

> factory workers, like primary school students, are controlled within an enclosed space (the factory walls) for a limited time and by people and apparatuses, which remain exterior to them and are easily recognizable. To resist, they might rely on their own resources, on those of other workers, or on the solidarity between them. Control through debt, however, is exercised within an open space and an unlimited time, that is, the space and time of life itself. The period of repayment runs to twenty, sometimes thirty, years, during which the debtor is supposed to manage his life, freely and autonomously, in view of reimbursement. The question of time, of duration, is at the heart of debt. Not only labor time or 'life time', but also time as possibility, as future, it anticipates and pre-empts the future. Students' debt mortgages at once their behavior, wages, and future income. This is the paradigm of liberal freedom [. . .] Credit produces a specific form of subjectivation. Debtors are alone, individually responsible to the banking system; they can count on no solidarity except, on occasion, on that of their families, which in turn risk going into debt. Debtors interiorize power relations instead of externalizing and combatting them.[10]

As such,

> Debt is the technique most adequate to the production of neoliberalism's *homo economicus*. Students not only consider themselves human capital, which they must valorize through their own investments (the university loans they take out), but they also feel compelled to act, think, and behave as if they were individual businesses. Debt requires an apprenticeship in certain behaviour, accounting rules, and organizational

---

[10]  Ibid., pp. 69–70.

principles traditionally implemented within a corporation on people who have not yet gone on the job market.[11]

Here, the doctrine of human capital is taken to its most extreme and literal consequences, in the sense that the debt itself forces you to think of yourself in terms of capital, investment and depreciation. The power exerted on the individual is therefore ever more total and more economic, in the double sense of the word: it is increasingly based on the economy and is less expensive, requiring less effort to be exerted. The yoke is replaced with an 'automatic' leash (or rather, a sort of virtual electronic bracelet), the disciplinary control of the factory and the prison are replaced with the collar of defaulting debt: 'If the figure of discipline was the worker-prisoner, the figure of control is the debtor-addict.'[12] The debtors are forced to discipline themselves, becoming their own jailer, their own watcher, and are therefore placed in a punitive, suspicious relationship with themselves.

While Foucault had been far-sighted enough to understand the (counter)revolutionary nature of neoliberalism, Gilles Deleuze showed an equal foresightedness when in 1990 he identified debt as the new neolib power's main tool for dominion, no longer based on discipline but on control: 'Man is no longer man enclosed, but man in debt'. 'We no longer find ourselves dealing with the mass/individual pair. Individuals have become "dividuals," and masses, samples, data, markets or "banks".'[13]

But being dominated by debt is not only personal; it is also public, national. It was in the 1970s, in lockstep with the neolib counter-revolution, that debt became an essential tool

---

[11] Ibid., pp. 70–1.
[12] Fisher, *Capitalist Realism*, p. 25.
[13] Gilles Deleuze, *Postscript on the Societies of Control* (1990), available at: https://theanarchistlibrary.org/library/gilles-deleuze-postscript-on-the-societies-of -control.

of geopolitics. With hindsight, we could say that debt has been the most effective tool for imposing the neo-colonial order and sweeping away what it saw as a faddish fixation with real independence in former colonies turned formally independent in the 1960s (the so-called 'Third World'). It was then, in the name of the 'fight against poverty', that wealthy countries began to lend increasingly large amounts of money to the struggling economies of those countries euphemistically referred to as 'developing'. This new strategy was named after Robert McNamara (1916–2009) who, having overseen the entire first phase of the US escalation of the war in Vietnam (from January 1961 to November 1967) as defence secretary of the Kennedy and Johnson administrations, was the president of the World Bank from 1968 to 1981. Under McNamara's guidance, World Bank loans rose from $1 billion in 1968 to $13 billion in 1981. Many billions more were offered to potential debtors by the banks that found themselves with piles of petrodollars, which grew exponentially following the oil crisis in 1973.

The first debt crisis exploded in summer 1982 when that country, Mexico, that is 'too close to the United States and too far from God',[14] declared itself insolvent. The creditors, collectively known as the 'Paris Club',[15] came to the rescue with new loans that were, however, accompanied by drastic conditions euphemistically called 'structural reforms', meaning fiscal austerity, privatization of public companies, reduction of commercial protectionist barriers, deregulation of industrial legislation, and more favourable conditions

---

[14] The phrase *Pobre de México, tan lejos de Dios y tan cerca de los Estados Unidos'* [Poor Mexico, so far from God and so close to the United States] is attributed to Mexican president Porfirio Díaz (1830–1915).

[15] An informal group of economic functionaries from the richest twenty-two countries in the world. Created in 1956, the club meets around ten times a year. Since its foundation to 2015, the club had negotiated credits of $580 billion. The Paris Club has concluded 433 negotiations with ninety countries over the last 60 years.

for foreign financial investors. The result was disastrous. In the seven years from 1982 to 1989, Mexican public debt grew from 49% to 78% of the GDP, while inflation went sky-high, investments collapsed and the GDP failed to grow by even a cent.

Since then, the same treatment has been prescribed more than 340 times, always with the same catastrophic results. Every 'rescue plan' with its austerity measures and cuts to public spending has caused economies to collapse, forcing countries to ask for new loans that are granted only with even more draconian conditions imposed by the World Bank and the International Monetary Fund (IMF). If the repeated failure of this 'therapy' in the most diverse countries has not convinced any creditors to change therapy, it is because the primary aim of the prescribed cure is not and never was to alleviate the indebted economy, but instead to impose the neoliberal Word and subject the debtor country to its iron-clad rules. From this point of view, to return to our Voltairean comparison, in order to realize the forced conversion of Planet Earth to the neolib faith, in the wise mix of prayers, spells and arsenic, it is debt that constitutes the poison.

As such, at the end of the 1980s the wind of freedom that had blown so strongly over Africa, Asia and Latin America, encouraging Algeria, Vietnam, Cuba and Angola (to name but a few) to throw off their colonial chains, had died down. By the beginning of the 1990s, the 'debt crisis' had already inspired an endless amount of literature. In 1991, Susan George calculated that between 1982 and 1990, the total flow of money towards developing countries totalled $927 billion, while the cost of servicing those debts by those same countries had reached $1,345 billion, meaning that poor countries had financed rich countries to the tune of $418 billion: 'For purposes of comparison, the US Marshall Plan transferred $14 billion 1948 dollars to war-ravaged Europe, about $70 billion in 1991 dollars. Thus in the eight years from 1982–90 the poor have financed six Marshall Plans for the rich through debt service alone.'[16]

But the real leap of quality in debt technology came with the collapse of the Soviet Union in 1991. Until then, many countries within the US sphere of influence had been sheltered by debt as a weapon of blackmail, because in those countries, a degree of popular consensus was deemed indispensable to neutralize any feared Soviet expansion. States such as South Korea and Italy were laden with debt but never pushed towards insolvency. After 1991, the landscape changed and debt became the tool used to restrain entire populations, not only in developing countries but also those belonging to the OECD and considered 'developed'.

From 1991 onwards, the practice of placing entire nations into receivership was applied not only to those countries of the Fourth and Third World (during the Cold War, communist countries, the Soviet bloc and China, following the Second World), but also to an increasing number of countries in the First World. Whereas previously debt had only been used as a weapon against the destitute of the Earth, it was now pointing at the wealthy too. Citing Wendy Brown, it is through the blackmail of debt that 'both persons and states are construed on the contemporary firm', so that they behave in such a way as to attract investors: 'Any regime pursuing another course faces fiscal crises, downgraded credit, currency or bond ratings, and lost legitimacy at the least, bankruptcy and dissolution at the extreme', just as anyone who does not behave like a capitalist and owner of themselves 'risks impoverishment and a loss

---

[16] Susan George, *The Debt Boomerang: How Third World Debt Harms Us All.* London: Pluto Press, 1992, pp. xvi–xvii. It should be noted how the numbers from back then seem derisory just 30 years later when compared with the debts of industrialized countries. The public debt of Japan alone is \$10,275 billion (of which \$4,250 billion is foreign debt), while Italian foreign debt stands at \$2,444 billion.

of esteem and creditworthiness at the least, survival at the extreme'.[17]

The creditor nations send inspectors to check that debtor nations are conforming to all directives in even the smallest and most insignificant details. For European debtors, the control body is called the Troika (made up of the European Union, the European Central Bank and the International Monetary Fund). To give an idea of just how pervasive the conditions imposed by the Troika are, we can recall how in 2015 Greece was not only forced to deprive its elderly of their pensions, their children of school, their sick of hospital care and essential medicines, but included in the excessive conditions set to renew their credit (i.e., their debt) was the forced deregulation of the shape of loaves, which were no longer allowed to be just the two traditional shapes that had always been sold in the country – one, a kilo and the other, half a kilo – while sandwiches could no longer weigh more than 80 grams.[18]

In short, not only businesses but also sovereign nations (this adjective here sounds almost sarcastic) are subject to benchmarking, used to establish which government is the most diligent and most disciplined when it comes to neolib directives. Before 1991, no European citizen knew what rating agencies were. Now it is part of our received (albeit confused) knowledge that our own lives hang on these agencies, which give us all marks, handing out periodic report cards to businesses, industries, insurance companies and, most importantly, governments. The higher the mark, the lower the supposed risk of investing in that country, that

---

[17] Brown, *Undoing the Demos*, p. 22.

[18] 'Greek bakers rise to reform challenge', *Financial Times*, 15 July 2015, https://www.ft.com/content/832f1e24-2af9-11e5-8613-e7aedbb7bdb7, and Jason Karaian, 'Some of the weirder conditions of Greece's bailout address milk labels, Sunday shopping, and the size of a bread roll', *Quartz*, 14 July 2015, https://qz.com/452265/some-of-the-weirder-conditions-of-the-greece-bailout-deal-address-milk-labels-sunday-shopping-and-the-size-of-a-bread-roll/.

bank, that industry, and so that country, bank or industry is able to ask for loans with lower interest rates. In a world in which everything must become a market, there is also a ratings market, 95% of which is dominated by three agencies: Moody's, Standard & Poor's and Fitch. The first two (the most important) are American, while the third is Anglo-American but US-owned.[19]

We are told the market is always right, that it is omniscient. But it is these very agencies that guide the markets, telling them where to invest, where to write off, where to gamble. It is they who, literally, express the 'the verdict of the markets', compiling report cards for the whole universe. However, their record is anything but rousing, and it is a resounding denial for the dogma that insists on the infallibility of the market, given that these agencies have an irritating tendency to make colossal mistakes, like in 2001 when they continued to advise investors to buy shares in the energy distribution corporation Enron, which collapsed in December of the same year causing the loss of $10 billion, the loss of 29,000 jobs and the total loss of pensions belonging to 20,000 of those. The error was repeated on a macroscopic scale in 2008, when their careless triple AAAs brought the world to the brink of planetary bankruptcy. As Paul Krugman wrote two years later in his column in the *New York Times*, the ratings agencies

---

[19] Much like the single letters traditionally used in a scholastic setting, ratings use three letters differentiated in turn by a + or − for Standard & Poor's and Fitch, and by upper or lower cases with numbers for Moody's. At the top of the rankings are those countries given top marks (there are only nine in the whole world) with a AAA rating, these are then followed by countries with AA+, AA, AA−, A+, A, A−, BBB+, BBB, BBB−, BB+, BB, BB−, B+, B, B−. In 2023, for example, Argentina, Ethiopia and Pakistan were all awarded a rating of CCC−, while Burkina Faso, Congo, El Salvador, Mozambique and Tunisia all received a CCC+. Italy was given a rating of Baa3 by Moody's and BBB by the other two, while the UK was given an AA, an AA− and an Aa3−. Data from: https://tradingeconomics.com/country-list/rating.

bestowed AAA ratings on hundreds of billions of dollars' worth of dubious assets, nearly all of which have since turned out to be toxic waste. And no, that's not hyperbole: of AAA-rated subprime-mortgage-backed securities issued in 2006, 93 percent – 93 percent! – have now been downgraded to junk status. [. . .] The rating agencies began as market researchers, selling assessments of corporate debt to people considering whether to buy that debt. Eventually, however, they morphed into something quite different: companies that were hired by the people selling debt to give that debt a seal of approval.[20]

Here we have the first corollary of the privatization of the world: the extraordinary indulgence shown by the ratings agencies to private corporations, banks and insurance companies, compared to the draconian severity with which they judge states and public companies.

But there is an even more dramatic side to all this. When the agencies downgrade the debt of a state (in the way an officer is downgraded), that state must pay higher interest rates and the money required to service this onerous debt is raised by slashing social services and funds for education, healthcare and pensions, as well as downsizing the number of public employees and their salaries. Ultimately, whether or not I can undergo surgery, you can send your child to school or she can have a decent pension depends entirely on the rating slapped on your country by these three private agencies. Fitch belongs to the media conglomerate Hearst Communications, named after the newspaper magnate William Randolph Hearst (1863–1951), on whom Orson Welles based his 1941 film *Citizen Kane*.[21] Conversely, the two largest shareholders of Standard & Poor's are Vanguard Group (with 8.46% of the

---

[20] Paul Krugman, 'Berating the Raters', *The New York Times*, 25 April 2010, https://www.nytimes.com/2010/04/26/opinion/26krugman.html.

[21] The 1898 telegram sent by Hearst to his illustrator in Cuba has remained legendary: 'You furnish the pictures and I'll furnish the war'.

shares), an investment fund managing assets of $7.2 trillion (the combined GDP of Germany and France) and, with 4.47% of the shares, Black Rock, another investment group managing assets of $10 trillion (the combined GDP of Japan, France and Italy). The third largest shareholder, with 4.39% of the shares, is State Street Global Advisors (Ssga), which manages assets worth $3.48 trillion (more than the GDP of Brazil). This means that we have three of the largest investment funds in the world telling other investors where to invest. Moody's is controlled by Berkshire Hathaway (with 13.5% of shares) and Vanguard (7.57%). The majority shareholder is therefore Berkshire Hathaway, a conglomerate with an annual income of $302 billion and 383,000 employees (as of 2022), with its headquarters in Omaha, Nebraska, and substantially owned by just one person – namely Warren Buffett who owns 38.1% of its share capital and is one of the richest men in the world. In other words: if in Valencia or Thessaloniki or Naples you are unable to receive hospital treatment, it is because some analyst working for Warren Buffett in Omaha, Nebraska, decided so.

This is what the privatization of our lives entails. As such, debt is not only an economic and financial relationship. Debt establishes, even more than economic exploitation, a mode of domination, it defines a power relationship. It is a form of economic servitude with no hope for emancipation. In this way, debt reveals itself to be the most efficient tool for not 'wasting a crisis', to use recessions or pandemics to tighten the grip, to literally discipline governments. With every recession, the debtor states will have to get deeper into debt and see the chance of freeing themselves from the yoke receding forever into the distance.

Italy is a perfect example. In 1992, public debt in Italy was equal to its GDP. Since then, for 28 years the balance of the Italian state has shown an active primary balance (except in 2009, the year of the great crisis, in which there was a primary shortfall of 0.9%). In the last 28 years, the balance has always been active, at times over 6% even. The average active balance is 2.28% (including the year with a shortfall and the one in which it broke even).[22] This means that every year for the last 28 years, the Italian state has given back to its citizens (in services, salaries, healthcare, education, military spending, etc.) 2% less than it has taken from them in taxes. It is clear, then, how over the last 28 years up to the pandemic, Italy has been in a perpetual recession (just as an aside, 1992 was the year following the dissolution of the Soviet Union). Despite this, in the meantime, Italian public debt has risen: while in 1992 it was equal to 100% of the country's GDP, before the 2020 pandemic it had exceeded 130% and now stands at 144%.

This means that the Italian state will never manage to free itself of the debt. In 300 years' time, our grandchildren's grandchildren will not able to build a nursery or a hospital because the debt service will not permit it. As Lazzarato says,

> the debt of today's capitalism is unpayable, unreimbursable, and infinite. The function of credit is expressed still more precisely in the literary, rather than economic, terms of Kafka [Joseph K]. [. . .] The form contemporary debt takes resembles at once an 'apparent settlement' (we go from one debt to another, take out credit and repay it, and so on) and an 'unlimited postponement' in which one is continually indebted [. . .] while the 'spread' informs us of the range of its fluctuations in real time. Variations in public debt in turn drive variations in wages, income, and social services, although always in the same direction – downward. Likewise, debt causes continual

---

[22] The primary balance of the state budget is the difference between how much the state collects and how much it spends, not considering debt servicing (interest payments and principal repayments). Data from Evoluzione del saldo primario italiano, in *Scenarieconomici.it*, 18 April 2017, https://scenariecono mici.it/evoluzione-del-saldo-primario-italiano/.

variations in taxes, but, likewise, always in the same direction – upward.[23]

It is clear, however, that the irrecoverability of the debt depends on power relations: the subject remains subjugated until they re-balance the relationship of power. Debt places its subjects in chains. And it does so in the most efficient way because it is invisible. It has no need to use force to impose measures, to send armies or carry out repressions in order to *compel*. It is the subjects themselves who are forced to carry out self-discipline, to behave as 'good debtors', to remain 'solvent', to repress themselves. The debt creates a servitude whose redemption is set too high to be paid off in a human lifetime nor even in any imaginable historical timeframe. This is why the current capitalist regime has no cyclical form of debt cancellation, like those used in many other societies, for example in the Kingdom of Israel, as the Old Testament established that every 50 years (for the Jubilee) the lands confiscated by creditors had to be restored to the debtors (Leviticus 25:8).[24]

It can be clearly seen that debt is the financial form in which the symbolic violence of dominion is exerted through the double, and opposite, configuration it assumes, when it is not the subjugated states that become indebted, but the dominant one. In dominated states, debt is imposed as a sin which must be atoned for – they have reminded us over and over that in German the word for debt and that for guilt are the same, '*die Schuld*'. An enormous amount of energy has been spent by the media and by technical (or bipartisan, or *Große Koalition*) governments, huge resources have been allocated to 'make the peoples of Europe guilty of a debt they never incurred and

---

[23] Lazzarato, *Governing By Debt*, p. 89.

[24] Land restoration was only valid in the land of Israel and therefore this custom ended with the diaspora.

thus make them responsible for faults they never committed. At the heart of the crisis, technical governments act to build a memory of debt, not of individuals, but of entire peoples'.[25]

What's more, blaming the debtor is rather bizarre: without debtors, creditors would simply not exist, meaning banks would not exist and financial capitalism would fail. To say that capitalism rules through credit (and therefore through debt) and that businesses grow and invest thanks to credit (i.e., debit) is to state the obvious. Getting into debt is encouraged on a global level. The total debt of US companies adds up to $33.93 trillion[26] and businesses often collapse under the unbearable weight of the debt they have accumulated, but no one is casting disdain on them, there is no stigma of being unworthy, unlike what happens with individuals and states. Everything is done to ensure people and governments get into debt before then blaming them for it.

Quite the opposite is the status of debt in the dominant country, i.e. the United States. In 2023, US public debt was huge in absolute terms, standing at $32,039 billion, even if it is slightly less worrying given their GDP, with a debt to GDP ratio of 129%. In this case also, the debt is irredeemable, but for the opposite reason to its European, Asian or 'Third World' subjects: because no one can afford to go to Washington and tell the US, 'Give me back my money'. This is for two reasons: because they don't have the power (military or political) to enforce repayment, and because if the US were to tighten their belts in order to pay back the debt, the global economy would collapse. Not to mention the fact that the American debt is contracted in dollars, i.e. in the American currency which Washington can devalue or revalue against other currencies as they see fit, meaning it can independently establish how much

---

[25] Lazzarato, *Governing By Debt*, p. 42 (translation modified to better adhere to original Italian text).
[26] As of 2022: https://www.statista.com/statistics/1277325/outstanding-corpora te-debt-securities-usa/.

it owes others in their currencies. The US debt therefore takes the form of a tribute (by a different name) that the empire requires of its subjects, or in China's case, as an entrance fee, a tariff the empire demands in order to allow China to participate in the global market and provide access to the American one.[27] As such, the US also uses debt as both a tool and a configuration of domination, only that here it is the debtor that wields the weapon of debt, not the creditor. In Italian financial parlance, bad debts are referred to as 'sufferings', and yet, in the case of the subject, it is the debtor countries that suffer, while in the case of imperial debt, it is the creditors, so again the subjects.

## Financial Corollary

Power relations are, then, structured as an asymmetrical credit/debt relationship, in the sense that the power does not always lie with the creditor. Indeed, as we have seen with the US, the power can lie with the debtor when power allows them to be perpetually insolvent. The credit/debt relationship is a power structure, but in the sense that it acts as a tool of power, it exercises force and is, at the same time, itself the expression of a power relation.

But just as the dominant form of power changes from discipline to control, and does so through the credit/debt relationship, so the driving force moves from manufacturing, to industry, to finance. Not that industry disappears, just like how in the nineteenth and twentieth centuries, the industrial revolution didn't cause the disappearance of agriculture but simply replaced it as the driving, dominant sector of the economy, actually revolutionizing agriculture itself by

---

[27] Richard Vague, 'The Private Debt Crisis', *Democracy. A Journal of Ideas*, no. 42, Autumn 2016, https://democracyjournal.org/magazine/42/the-private-debt-crisis/.

industrializing it. The same thing happens today: industry continues to exist – it actually produces an ever-greater number of goods (just as agriculture produces an amount of food that is infinitely larger than a century ago) – but it is no longer the sector that defines the economy of our time. This sector is now finance, which has in turn financialized industry, just as industry had industrialized agriculture.

Finance is the dominant sector also because it is the one that best matches the digital revolution. There is, in fact, a word that keeps cropping up in various forms in the texts we have drawn on so far: *indifference*. According to Lazzarato:

> Finance and its accounting mechanisms are better expressions of the nature of capital than industrial capital because they are *radically indifferent* to the qualification of production (of automobiles, skills, yogurts, software, subjectivities, gender, etc.). Financial flows are also *indifferent* to the qualification of labor (industrial, cognitive, service, domestic, sexual, media, etc.): all that is relevant to them is drawing from these various forms of production and labor a surplus expressed in abstract quantities of money. This *indifference* asserts itself in a radical way because finance has no other end than the appropriation of monetary surplus regardless of the type of production and labor.[28]

Wendy Brown describes the same reality when talking about best practices and benchmarking:

> A key premise of benchmarking is that best practices can be exported from one industry or sector to another and that some of the most valuable reforms will happen by creatively adapting practices in one field to another. [. . .] The presumed interchangeability of processes and practices across industries

---

[28] Lazzarato, *Governing By Debt*, p. 141 (my italics).

and sectors and the consolidation of best practices out of many different sources have several important implications [. . .] First, in benchmarking, practices are separated from products. Productivity, cost effectiveness, or consumer satisfaction are understood to inhere in practices with little respect to what is being produced, generated, or delivered. This permits private-sector practices to move readily into the public sector; it allows, for example, educational or health care institutions to be transformed by practices developed in the airline or computer industries.[29]

If we put the two quotes together, we understand that best practices are indeed industrial practices, but they are generated by a financial logic that views the extraction of profit in purely monetary terms, regardless of the nature of the product this profit produces.

But this 'radical indifference' to the nature of the product is inherent not only in financial logic, but in the very nature of the digital revolution based on the concept of algorithms. Now, what is the fundamental property of an algorithm? It is to be independent of the object to which it is applied. An algorithm created to minimize journey times (or a combination of journeys) behaves in the same way whether it is applied to delivering pizzas, rationalizing supply logistics for an invading army or speeding up the escape of a group of bank robbers. It is no coincidence that financial speculation is increasingly governed by algorithms that often act independently of the speculators' will.

And it is significant that Shoshana Zuboff also insists on *radical indifference*: according to Zuboff, this new form of power 'cultivates an unusual "way of knowing" that combines the "formal indifference" of the neoliberal worldview with the observational perspective of radical behaviorism [. . .],

---

[29] Brown, *Undoing the Demos*, p. 137.

reduces human experience to measurable observable behavior while remaining steadfastly indifferent to the meaning of that experience. I call this new way of knowing *radical indifference'*. If the ideological style of totalitarianism was 'political religion' says Zuboff, the style of this new power is 'radical indifference'.[30] 'Another way of saying this is that Google is "formally indifferent" to what its users say or do, as long as they say it and do it in ways that Google can capture and convert into data.'[31]

Given that our life's events are raw material 'manufactured', packaged and sold by Google, the indifference to this raw material is the same spoken about by Lazzarato and Brown, in the sense that Google behaves with our exhaust data in the same way finance considers the products from which it extracts profit. As such, the neolib revolution, debt, finance and digital revolution constitute the different tiles of the new configuration of power, a power infinitely greater than that exercised a century ago, albeit in entirely different ways and apparently much more discreet, except when it is called into question: without going back over how Chile was reformed (in the sense of reformatory) in 1973 after having opposed the 'Washington Consensus', it is enough to consider the treatment reserved for Greece and its people in 2015 and the opinion they expressed in a referendum, which was discarded like rubbish.

Here we encounter a first example of unintended consequences, those of any feedback: we will look at others shortly. The magnates that financed the neolib counter-revolution had become wealthy in the most classical sectors of industry: weapons and chemical processes (Olin), electrical components (Bradley), oil and aluminium (Mellon Scaife), ointments (Vicks VapoRub, the Smith Richardsons), oil infrastructure (the

---

[30] Zuboff, *The Age of Surveillance Capitalism*, pp. 376–7, 397.
[31] Shoshana Zuboff, 'Big Other: Surveillance Capitalism and the Prospects of an Information Civilization', *Journal of Information Technology*, vol. 30, 2015, pp. 75–89, p. 79.

Kochs), beer (Coors), but with their financing, they ended up ensuring the passage from industry-dominated capitalism to financially dominated capitalism.

The second observation is that the jeremiads on the 'financialization of the economy', calling for a return to a mythical industrial economy of the past, are entirely useless, lamentable even. As if that were even possible! Finance is simply the current phase of capitalism. Regretting the beautiful industry of yesteryear is like people in the nineteenth century lamenting the dominance of industry over agriculture: a losing game.

The third consequence is that the new structure of dominance, based on control, makes us all anonymous in a different way from that captured by Charlie Chaplin in *Modern Times*, when the crowd leaving the underground in the morning to make their way to work is assimilated with a herd of sheep overflowing from a sheep pen. That was the anonymity of the factory worker, of the office worker, the anonymous individual working on an assembly line or a typing pool. Instead, this new configuration of dominion makes us all '*equivalents without equality*' (Zuboff), reduced to our common denominator of 'behavioural organisms', of debtors atoning for their guilt (*die Schuld*), of interchangeable agents of interchangeable productive processes.

# 10

# And They All Lived Antily Ever After

David Graeber is too naive when he is startled in disbelief by the fact that 'It's [. . .] as if people had been led to believe that the era's technological advances and its greater overall social complexity had had the effect of *reducing* our political, social, and economic possibilities, rather than expanding them'[1]: but of course! We have just seen that the progress in power technologies and the paradigm shift from discipline to control ensure that a greater power is exerted upon us and, therefore, that our personal, individual room for manoeuvre, the space for our own possibilities, contracts like Balzac's wild ass's skin.

At the same time, the very configuration of power has become more blurred, indistinct, as well as more oppressive and more undefined. It had been possible to storm the Bastille and the Winter Palace. Today, however, it would never cross the mind of a revolutionary to attack the European Central Bank building in Frankfurt or, in an outburst of popular rage, devastate the Coca-Coca headquarters in Atlanta or perhaps the Apple campus in Cupertino (the last people to have an idea

---

[1] Graeber, *Debt*, p. 393.

comparable to destroying the Bastille were the Islamists who brought down the Twin Towers of the World Trade Center in New York in 2001, which were to Western capitalism what St. Peter's basilica is to Catholicism), and that is because capitalism is everywhere, *Capitale sive Natura* does not reside in one single place.

This is all true. And yet . . . Our relationship with dominion at the beginning of the industrial revolution was not so idyllic and courteous. Protests were repressed using rifles, if not cannons. We have seen how the workers in Carnegie's steelworks and Rockefeller's miners were still treated at the beginning of twentieth century. The list is infinite, from the Peterloo Massacre (1819) to the repression of the *canuts* (textile workers) in Lyon (1831) and the massacre of Bava Beccaris in Milan (1898).

When fighting the dominant, the dominated can never compete on the terrain of domination itself. Only in particular situations are the subjects able to rip (and at what price!) power from the powerful. But the clash occurs, and has occurred, in many other fields, otherwise nothing would ever change and the dominant of one moment would have maintained their domination forever. We are not talking about the alternation of power between individuals in the same social strata, one dynasty replacing another, the dominance of one geographical area replacing that of another. No. Over the course of history, entire social classes have lost their position in favour of other classes that had, at the beginning, been disadvantaged. Just think of merchants and how many rungs of the social ladder they have been able to climb from the time when they were a subordinate class, brought to their knees by taxes, tariffs and duties, and always at risk of expropriation and requisition. Or, on the contrary, how the castes of priests have lost the outsized power they once held. Not to mention the nosedive taken by the aristocracies and noble classes all over the world.

And we must not forget that even the hyperrealist cynicism of Joseph Stalin would eventually reveal itself to be naïve when, in response to those asking him to give greater consideration to the Catholics, he responded sarcastically: 'The Pope? How many divisions does he have?'. He didn't live long enough to witness the decisive blow Pope John Paul II delivered to the faltering Soviet system in 1980s Poland. It must mean something if even the former US Secretary of the Treasury William Simon, master of ceremonies of the global capitalist empire, stated that 'Ideas are weapons – indeed, the only weapons with which other ideas can be fought'.

Of course, the temptation to allow ourselves to be dazzled, stunned by the outsized power we are facing is enormous, to the extent that many, blinded by capital, have followed the example of Saul of Tarsus on the road to Damascus and converted to neoliberalism (many US neo-cons had started out as Trotskyists, while in Italy, many of those working with Berlusconi came from the ranks of the Italian Socialist Party and the new left). But even for those who have not changed their ways, wallowing in the invincibility of their adversaries is simply an excuse for giving up, for deserting before even enlisting (if we were to use the bellicose metaphor so dear to the counterintelligentsia).

And yet, we have plenty of reasons to fight: the world that neoliberalism promises us and imposes on us is not so wonderful. We are almost tempted to look back fondly on the time of the first industrial revolution, when the bourgeoisie felt the need to promise both themselves and humanity a bright future full of 'magnificent and progressive fate'.[2] Today, no one promises anything anymore. If there is one category missing, it is that of *progress*. There was a time, not too long ago, in

---

[2] This expression, which has since become proverbial in Italian, was coined for ironic effect by the poet Giacomo Leopardi in his 1836 poem, *La ginestra* (*Wild Broom*).

which it was *de rigueur* to criticize the idea of progress and mock 'progressives'. Of course, in many ways that progress did not advance anything, quite the opposite in fact. What was most unbearable about the rhetoric of the time were the 'costs of progress', the idea that there was a 'price to pay' in order to advance, yet mysteriously, it was never those preaching progress that would have to pay but always the other: the 'Third World', the proletarians, the women, the ecosystem. Of course, the progressive lyricism was downright mockery in the mouths of those ruling classes that created the 'late-Victorian holocausts' (as Mike Davis called them) from nowhere, which in Asia, Africa and Latin America in the nineteenth century killed tens of millions of people 'murdered [. . .] by the theological application of the sacred principles of Smith, Bentham and Mill'.[3] This was when the 'Third World' was created, if it is true that 'the mean standard of food consumption in Akbar's empire was appreciably higher than in the India of the early 1960s'.[4]

Many bloody crimes have been carried out in the name of progress, in a variant of what Adorno and Horkheimer called the 'dialectics of Enlightenment'. But what should we say when the same crimes are committed without anyone even bothering to mention progress? The aspiration for a better life, to improve the lot of our children, to send them to school, has been one of the most powerful forces for change in human history. What was the workers' movement demanding if not progress in workers' living conditions? What is wrong with thinking that political action should work to ensure that tomorrow we will all live a little better than we did yesterday? Of course, we need to agree on what 'better' means – whether it is being able to drink Coca-Cola and eat hamburgers or

[3] Mike Davis, *Late Victorian Holocausts: El Niño Famines and the Making of the Third World*. London: Verso, 2001, p. 9.

[4] This estimate is made by Ashok Desai and cited by Mike Davis, *Late Victorian Holocausts*, pp. 285–6.

being more at ease and having more time for ourselves and those dear to us.

When under the yoke of a disciplinary power, the workers could hope to 'break the chains' (as they sang in the choirs of that time). Instead, when on the leash of debt, under continual surveillance, what can the debtor hope for other than not to become insolvent, not to default? Their only, unprecedented hope can be to remain a faithful and punctual debtor for the rest of their lives. They cannot hope to free themselves from the leash, only that it doesn't pull too hard. And indeed, it has been 30 years since anyone was last told: 'if you do what I ask, you will be better off tomorrow'. On the contrary, we are constantly threatened: 'if you don't do what I demand, you will be much worse off', you will fail, you will fall into poverty, you will be abandoned in your old age and you will not be cured when you fall ill. We no longer have 'the carrot and the stick' of disciplinary power (punishments and rewards for production in the factory), all that is left is blackmail – 'like it or lump it': if you don't respect the deadlines, find yourself another job, as told to the delivery drivers, the warehouse workers. Indeed, the ideal work relationship for neoliberalism is that of the Uber driver who exploits themselves all on their own. An admirable example of the self-capitalist.

## The Debt with the Planet, or the Optimal Catastrophe

But if they don't promise us progress, what kind of future does neolib power outline for the human species and the planet? The terrible answer is that there is no future. The future is not contemplated in any way. It is useless, redundant to repeat here the detailed list of environmental disasters that this mode of production and economic system is causing our planet. Not only is there global warming, rising sea levels, the hole in the ozone layer, the desertification of ever-increasing areas of land, cementification, deforestation, atmospheric pollution and the poisoning of the oceans, there is also the accelerated disappearance of living species, to the point people are talking about the sixth mass extinction.

The question everyone is asking: is the industrial revolution responsible for this undeniable, exponential environmental deterioration? Or is it the capitalist market system? Or both? In today's world, there are around 1.49 billion motor vehicles (excluding motorbikes) and in 2019, there were more than 4.7 billion airline passengers on 40 million flights, all figures that are more than 120 times greater than those of the 1950s. Though this is less than the (annual) production of plastic, which has risen from 1.5 million tonnes in 1950 to 397 million in 2021,[5] 260 times greater, while in the meantime, the human population has only tripled, from 2.5 to 7.9 billion people. This means that the number of vehicles and the number of flights have risen more than forty times per capita, while the production of plastic has risen eighty times per capita. Even a child could understand that this increase cannot continue at such a rate and that in 70 years, we will not be able to consume eighty times more plastic per capita than what we consume today (which is already eighty times more than what we consumed in 1950), or have forty times more vehicles per capita and so on. At this rate, by 2090 each of us human beings on Earth, including newborns and the elderly, would consume 2 tonnes of plastic a year and own seven vehicles.

But simply slowing the speed of growth means inverting the acceleration, so, for example, decelerating production and consumption. But capitalism, as Marx described, cannot conceive of a limit for itself. While a blacksmith could once live his whole life in peace, forging and hammering the same

---

[5]  https://www.statista.com/statistics/282732/global-production-of-plastics-since-1950/; in 2018, 359 million tonnes per 7.5 million humans makes 48 kilos of plastic per head.

number of horseshoes without feeling the need to expand his forge, in the capitalist system, anyone who stays the same dies. If a tyre factory's production does not grow, if the market does not expand, if sales do not increase, the entire system of credit/investment/repayment/debt servicing/profit/reinvestment grinds to a halt. Not only does capitalism not conceive of a steady state (despite the fact that all neo-classical economic theory is based on the notion of market equilibrium), but it is also terrorized by the slowing of growth in a non-stationary state.

Capitalism's original problem lies in the fact it is conceived as a system of unlimited expansion, but the Earth is round and finite. By the way, this is the ideological reasoning that drives not only governments but also magnates to relaunch the space race, which is constantly reproposed to us even if it is clearly unworkable. This is not just due to human curiosity, the 'will to know', the fascination of the unknown (even if this is a factor). The idea here is that there is a whole universe out there to be exploited, billions and billions of planets to probe, perforate, colonize, meaning that even if this little original Earth is poisoned and grows uninhabitable, it can be abandoned as unimportant space debris in favour of greener pastures far out in the cosmos. Capitalism cannot help but feel the roundness of our planet as an unbearable cage, a prison it must escape. There are even those who talk about the 'era of multi-planetary capitalism' and this warns us, perhaps too early on, that 'the economic elites of New Space, and the governments that legitimize and arm them, have already definitively taken away our right to free access to outer space in advance, making it clear that we only go out there under the rules of capital'.[6]

It is disturbing to see that human bipeds who had not even stuck their heads out of their own atmosphere and

---

[6] Cobol Pongide, *Marte oltre Marte. L'era del capitalismo multiplanetario.* Rome: DeriveApprodi, 2019, p. 172.

who had taken only cursory steps around their own planet, had already signed treaties on the exploitation of space and the cosmos, codifying a space law in which the principle of *the free exploitation of planets and celestial bodies* (!!!) is sanctioned! This is what we find in the complete title of the document known for brevity's sake as the *Outer Space Treaty*, a document adopted by the United Nations in 1967 (and ratified by 98 states to date, including the US and (at the time) the USSR and undersigned by 27 others), whose complete title is the *Treaty on Principles Governing the Activities of States in the Exploration and Use of Outer Space, including the Moon and Other Celestial Bodies*.[7] Humans were already arguing over who had the right to exploit the galaxy's planets back then!

Neoliberalism has made this logic of unlimited expansionism its own, first and foremost by imposing the dogma of the infallibility of markets. Here, curiously, we encounter a kind of fatalism. If the markets are always right, if we just leave them there will never be any need to worry. This is the 'providential' side of Adam Smith's 'invisible hand'. You can't admit that the market economy produces irreversible environmental damage: it would be blasphemous and would bring down the dogma of infallibility. This is the otherwise inexplicable reason big capital (and all the foundations mentioned so far) are so insistent in their denial of global warming. We innocents wonder, what have they got to lose by admitting it is real? Certainly, in the short term they would lose as they would trade fewer fossil fuels, but in compensation a new market would open up, that of global cooling, and they would earn the same. But no, admitting this would mean recognizing

---

[7] But a special United Nations commission on the topic had already convened in 1959, less than two years after the canine astronaut Laika emitted her first yelp from an artificial satellite orbiting the Earth, and two years before Yuri Gagarin became the first human to follow her into space. See Vegetti, *L'invenzione del globo*, p. 190, note 10, also pp. 80–3.

that the market *needs to be corrected* (sic!), that the market is wrong, that leaving it to its own devices leads us to ruin and extinction.

Only in this way can we understand the fanaticism shown by the Kochs, the Mercatus Center, the George Mason University and all the several other right-wing think tanks when denying something that is plain for all to see and experience. It is interesting that, despite the now 30-year old efforts to find a market solution to our planet's environmental problems, namely through the creation of an environmental market (the market for pollution rights that could be traded like any other obligation), such a market will never see the light of day simply because, in order to respect the rules of this market, states must have the strength and be willing to collect the taxes on pollution, which the tradable permits in effect are. The demonstration that the environment market cannot be entrusted solely to the market is (once again) heresy.[8]

More likely, the market solution to air pollution is the sale of lovely air purifiers for the home (already advertised on TV) and filling the streets and squares of our cities with kiosks selling canisters of pure air, with different qualities of air depending on the size of the customer's wallet, of course. This is not a joke. Air canisters are already on sale. And the Chinese market is particularly promising (this is also part of the 'China model'). Australian entrepreneurs sell pure air from the Yarra Valley for $13.80 (according to the *Sydney Morning Herald*),[9] while the company Vitality sells Canadian air in canisters starting at

---

[8] Equally self-contradictory is the enthusiasm for the green economy as a 'growth' factor: a solution developed by capitalists to tackle the damage created by capitalist development.

[9] Craig Butt, 'Australian Entrepreneurs sell cans of clean Australian air to China', 2 May 2016, https://www.smh.com.au/business/small-business/austr alian-entrepreneurs-sell-cans-of-clean-australian-air-to-china-20160502-goj w1x.html.

8 litres for \$32 (this provides around 160 breaths, as each of us breathes 6 litres of air a minute). Imitators sell canisters of air from the Swiss Alps. An Englishman was the first to coin the expression 'air farming', selling luxury air from the Dorset hills, marketed as Aether, at £80 (\$104) per half litre bottle (580ml): 'There is now luxury air, cold-pressed air, 100% mountain air. There is air canned for the benefit of mothers ("Keep awake and command the household in a natural way.") There is air for work. Air for kids. Air for grandparents.'[10] Perhaps we will see vending machines that dispense air cannisters just like we previously had (free) water fountains and now have ATMs ('money fountains').

An inventive version of this, closer to Ronald Coase's vision, was proposed in 1991 by the rising star of economics, Larry Summers, who was then head economist of the World Bank (and was later Secretary of the Treasury under Bill Clinton and, after that, president of Harvard University), who penned a confidential memorandum in which he proposed installing polluting industries in poor countries:

> 'Dirty' Industries: Just between you and me, shouldn't the World Bank be encouraging MORE migration of the dirty industries to the LDCs [Least Developed Countries]? [. . .] The measurements of the costs of health impairing pollution depends on the foregone earnings from increased morbidity and mortality. From this point of view, a given amount of health impairing pollution should be done in the country with the lowest cost, which will be the country with the lowest wages. I think the economic logic behind dumping a load of toxic waste in the lowest wage country is impeccable and we should face up to that.

---

[10] Alex Moshakis, 'Fresh air for sale', *The Guardian*, 21 January 2018, https://www.theguardian.com/global/2018/jan/21/fresh-air-for-sale.

And this was only one of three arguments in favour of his proposal to alleviate the poverty of developing countries by using them as dustbins for rich countries.[11]

So far we are moving in the classical territory of the relationship between market economy and environmental problems. But Ronald Coase proposed taking into account another factor, namely that the mechanism of supply and demand may perhaps not be infallible, but that in any case, it is self-correcting. As fish in a river increasingly risk extinction, it would be less convenient for the nearby factory to produce the commodities that were causing their disappearance. And this would avoid their extinction. As such, Coase can talk about 'optimal pollution'.

The fact is that from Galileo and Newton to Max Planck and Bohr, science has always aimed to be experimental. And experience tells us that the market economy is extinguishing living species at an alarming rate, annihilating them wholesale: in this respect at least, the market is not correcting itself at all. It is immensely difficult to tackle the problem of irreversibility within economic theory, and this can be seen by the physical metaphor used by neoclassicists – classical mechanics whose equations are symmetrical to time. Statistical thermodynamics would instead seem to be the most suitable model, given that macroeconomic data is the statistical result of single microeconomic behaviours, just as the laws of gas reflect the

---

[11] Larry Summers later defended himself by saying that the intent of the memorandum was a sarcastic response to other World Bank proposals: the fact remains that, whatever his intent, from a purely neolib point of view, his reasoning didn't make the slightest difference. Indeed, it was in these terms that researchers at the Cato Institute (funded by the Koch brothers) defended it 15 years later in the article: Jay Johnson, Gary Pecquet and Leon Taylor, 'Potential Gains from Trade in Dirty Industries: Revisiting Lawrence Summers' Memo', *Cato Journal*, vol. 27, no. 3, Autumn 2007, pp. 397–410. The memorandum text is available online on many sites, such as https://www.uio .no/studier/emner/sv/oekonomi/ECON2920/v20/pensumliste/summers-me mo-1991-%2B-nytimes.pdf.

movements of the molecules from which they are composed. It is the Brownian motion of our billions of individual interests that, if Adam Smith was right, should result in general wellbeing.

But the problem of irreversibility (as in thermodynamics) cannot be incorporated into neo-classical economic theory because addressing this question implies giving direction to the arrow of time; irreversibility would give a one-way direction to time's arrow, which means therefore, at the end of the day, a story. And the entire neolib framework is built on 'a set of philosophical doctrines that [. . .] consists of scientism, behaviorism, operationalism'.[12] The rational decision maker of Becker and Stigler is at all times a *tabula rasa* who weighs up the costs and benefits of their decision today with the same rationality and criteria as yesterday and the day after tomorrow, independent of any historical experience of the past, trauma, exodus or persecution.

Furthermore, there is a difficult relationship between dominant financial capitalism on the one hand and a future on the other. Industrial capitalism takes into account the time it takes to plan and build a factory, to provide it with the necessary infrastructure, procuring the right raw materials and skilled workers, start production, build product distribution networks and therefore it works on a mid- to long-term basis. Instead, when it buys shares in a business, the investment fund demands an immediate return and its investors demand quarterly dividends. The horizon of the investment collapses onto itself, flattened onto the next quarter or next month even. If a business's profitability wanes for a few quarters, immediately start considering whether to dismember it, split it up, sell it in bits and cut costs (redundancies, salary reductions). The financial investor is not interested in whether the business in which it has bought shares produces mobile

---

[12] McCloskey, *The Rhetoric of Economics*, p. 140.

phones or irons or nylon tights. As we have already seen, the investor is characterized by their *indifference* to the specificity of production, hence their lack of long-term interest.

But there are essential investments that must be considered in terms of years if not decades. Building a railway, indeed any major infrastructure (an efficient sewage system or cabling a continent) requires years and cannot yield immediate dividends, hence some of the fascination, mixed with fear and denial, that the Chinese model holds for neolibs. [13] In just a few decades, Chinese state capitalism has managed to provide that immense country with an infrastructure that is unthinkable in the West. They provided it with universities and research institutes that most European countries could only dream of. (The Chinese model is enormously attractive to neolibs for another reason also, but we will return to that.)

The second problem with the relation to the future depends on the debt mentality. Because, when it is used, debt becomes a mental category that shapes all our way of thinking. Even environmental pollution is seen not as damage we inflict on the planet and ourselves, but as a debt we contract with 'nature', debt we cannot or do not want to pay off but – we hope – we can carry, defer, postpone until tomorrow or the day after tomorrow. This view of environmental damage as a debt to pay off in the *future* and never as a tragedy of the *present* explains why such a serious and urgent problem gives rise to movements that are ultimately so weak. This problem touches all of humanity but only a disparate, unarmed (and innocuous) minority are doing anything about it. That this is the case can be shown by proof to the contrary: the environmental problem

---

[13] See the dossier published by *The Economist* on 21 January 2012: 'Emerging-Market Multinationals: The Rise of State Capitalism', https://www.economist .com/leaders/2012/01/21/the-rise-of-state-capitalism. It is worth remembering that *The Economist* was founded in 1848 as the voice of the Mancunian school, hard-core proponent of market freedom, and never, in 185 years, has it ever deviated from that line.

becomes a priority only if and when there is a catastrophe. That is the moment the 'loan' becomes delinquent and the catastrophe becomes the debtor's bankruptcy. Disaster is to environmentalism what revolution is to communism.

## *The Festival of Unintended Consequences*

Erasing the future not only affects the future of our planet and its living species. It also concerns us as people, as individuals of flesh and blood, even if 'there is no such thing as society'. In a world governed by debt, the future is wiped out because it is mortgaged by past debt. If education were defunded in order to repay the debt, entire generations of young people would be unable to attend university or – if by some extraordinary stroke of luck they were able to do so – they would not find adequate employment. More generally, the 'frugality' of the state is merely the prologue to a more drastic diet to be imposed on the whole of society, through which salaries are slowly eroded until they don't even cover the cost of reproduction (the minimum payment threshold that allows the workforce to procreate and raise children). This is why there has been a collapse in the birth rates of all industrialized countries subject to the neolib regime. Entire generations have been – and are still – sacrificed at the altar of neoliberalism. In this case it is literally true that the guilt (*die Schulde* – the debt) falls onto our children, as well as our grand- and great-grandchildren. We might ask ourselves whether we are not perhaps witnessing, in real time, the largest experiment in feedback producing unintended consequences.

Allow me to explain what is meant by feedback: the European colonial powers built empires, Britain conquered India, France conquered Africa. However, today, while there are almost no French people in Africa, there are 7 million first- and second-generation Africans (from the Maghreb and Sub-Saharan

Africa) in France. There are no English people in India, but the UK is home to more than 3 million British people of Indian, Pakistani and Bangladeshi descent. This is feedback.

Just for starters: the entire neolib counter-revolution has been fought to make the state more frugal, to 'starve the beast'. The result, however, is shocking: after 50 years of unbridled neoliberalism, the state is more important than ever. As the *Economist* noted in its dossier, 'the ten biggest oil-and-gas firms, measured by reserves, are all state-owned'.[14] State-owned entities that behave like private businesses, but whose controls remain firmly in political hands. And it is to the state that finance must appeal in order to impose the 'structural reforms' requested by creditors from debtor countries, meaning they are called upon to deprive their own citizens. It is states, not the markets, that manage the recessions, the pandemics, the social crises, and that wage wars. And in this era that insists on the markets' capacity for self-regulation, we constantly feel the urgent need for commercial treaties, each one meticulously codified in thousands of clauses and codicils over thousands of pages in order to 'ensure free competition'.[15]

Moreover, in this era that wholeheartedly worships free trade and the abolition of borders, look what's back? *Trade wars between states.* What is the iron fist of protectionist duties

---

[14] https://www.economist.com/leaders/2012/01/21/the-rise-of-state-capitalism.

[15] To name but a few of the marvellously baroque acronyms of these treaties: we have NAFTA (North America Free Trade Agreement) between the USA, Mexico and Canada; the EACU (Eurasian Custom Union) between Armenia, Belarus, Kazakhstan, Kyrgyzstan and Russia; the RECEP (Regional Comprehensive Economic Partnership) between the ten member states of the Association of Southeast Asian Nations (Brunei, Cambodia, Indonesia, Laos, Malaysia, Myanmar, the Philippines, Singapore, Thailand and Vietnam) and their five FTA (Free Trade Agreement) partners: Australia, China, Japan, New Zealand and South Korea; the CETA (Comprehensive Economic and Trade Agreement) between the European Union and Canada; and the proposed TTIP (Transatlantic Trade and Investment Partnership) between United States and the European Union, blocked in 2019 by Donald Trump, though an attempt was made to resurrect it after the outbreak of war in Ukraine in 2022.

and tariffs launched between the US and China in recent years if not a trade war in the purest mercantile spirit?

In the most advanced evolutionary state of an economic system that is now based on finance and global connectivity, we are back to Colbert, Louis XIV's finance minister and, even further back, to the galleons of the early seventeenth century. In 1614, the governor general of the Dutch East India Company, Jan Pieterszoon Coen, wrote these immortal words from Bantam, Java, to the Heeren XVII (the management board): 'Your Honours should know by experience that trade in Asia must be driven and maintained under the protection and favour of Your Honours' own weapons, and that the weapons must be paid for by the profits from the trade; so that *we cannot carry on trade without war nor war without trade*'.[16]

Furthermore, the neolibs have no problem using the most brutal force to impose their order: the most striking demonstration of this is the Bremer Orders, issued at the beginning of 2004 by the US provisional Coalition Administrator of Iraq, Paul Bremer, which

> mandated selling off several hundred state-run enterprises, permitting full ownership rights of Iraqi businesses by foreign firms and full repatriation of profits to foreign firms, opening Iraq's banks to foreign ownership and control, and eliminating tariffs. [. . .] They outlawed strikes and eliminated the right to unionize in most sectors, mandated a regressive flat tax on income, lowered the corporate rate to a flat 15%, and eliminated taxes on profits repatriated to foreign-owned businesses.[17]

Among the corporations given free access were the agri-food giants who imposed the use of genetically modified seeds (the

---

[16] Cited by Charles Ralph Boxer, *The Dutch Seaborne Empire 1600–1800* (1965). London: Penguin, 1973, p. 107 (my italics). Coen (1587–1629) was the founder of Batavia, modern-day Jakarta.

[17] Brown, *Undoing the Demos*, p. 142 (for all of Bremer's orders, see pp. 142–50).

first sack was given for free) after Iraq's national seed bank (used in times of famine) had been destroyed. The seed bank had been at Abu Ghraib, which was used from that moment on by the US as a prison in which they committed the most atrocious torture.

As advocates of the minimal state, neolibs have a perverse passion for the strong state. They had already demonstrated this with Pinochet in Chile and doubled down in Iraq with Bremer. The strong state has the advantage of 'eliminating the costs of political intermediaries', rendering the electoral process superfluous and therefore saving on the cost of lobbying. This is the second reason for their fascination with the Chinese model: it demonstrates how a capitalist economy can grow vigorously in a total absence of democracy. Until now, the elites had accepted political pluralism and a condition of relative freedom because, according to common belief, this was the regime that guaranteed the most propitious social ecosystem for the capitalist economy. But if now it is clear that capitalism can flourish in a total absence of liberty, the temptation to imitate the Chinese model may well arise.

Neolibs find themselves in the grip of the perversity Hirschman spoke of. Just as Murray and his emulators insisted that all measures to reduce poverty actually increased it, that all efforts to educate increased illiteracy and that all the resources dedicated to improve public health actually reduced life expectancy, we might well point out how the neolibs wanted less state and obtained more state, that they wanted borderless trade and got trade wars.

Not only this. This stronger, more authoritarian state is also sharper-eyed, nosier. The digital-military apparatus leaves us no way out. It is quite ironic that the neolib regimes, the paladins of the private, have completely and definitively suppressed the sphere they should have held dearest: privacy. There is no longer privacy when every email, every tweet or SMS is, in fact, an open postcard; when your television set reports on what you are watching and for how long and how (whether you get up, talk on the phone or aren't paying attention); when your every movement is localized, registered and memorized by your phone; when you are spied on anywhere and at all times by the tools you use, and that you cannot use: you are even under surveillance from the (smart) house you inhabit. We still haven't assessed the long-term effects of the vanishing of privacy for human existence. 'Big Brother' is a reality show in the truest and most perverse sense. It is worth asking what kind of 'private' neoliberals are talking about when they sing the praises of the private over the public. Perhaps they are referring to the etymological origins of the word, which comes from the Latin *'privare'*, to deprive, meaning that private is what lacks something, has had something taken from it.

And again, the German ordo-liberals were obsessed with the idea that in the future, our human society could become a termite's nest, a *Termitenstaat*. In 1944, Wilhelm Röpke wrote:

> We are surely within our rights in speaking of Collectivism as the fundamental and mortal danger of the West and in describing it as nothing less than political and economic tyranny, regimentation, centralization, the despotic organization of every department of life, the destruction of personality, totalitarianism and the rigid mechanization of human society. And we do not doubt that we can count upon general agreement when we say that this resulting *insect state* would not only destroy most institutions and values which comprise a development of three thousand years and which, with a conscious pride, we designate Occidental civilization [. . .] but above all it would take from the life of the individual just that essential purpose which only freedom can bestow.[18]

---

[18] Wilhelm Röpke, *Civitas Humana. A Humane Order of Society*. London: William Hodge, 1948, p. 2 (my italics).

Four years later, the Second World War was over and the man responsible for the German economy, Ludwig Erhard, reiterated: 'Neither anarchy, nor the *Termitenstaat* are forms of life suitable for men.'[19]

The image of collectivist, insectiform communists did not belong solely to the German ordo-liberals but was familiar to all readers of the popular science fiction and fanzines of the time. As they have a complex and articulated social organization that is, however, entirely different from that of humans, ants, bees, termites and all 'swarming' species have been used since the beginning of science fiction as a prototype for aliens, extra-terrestrials, starting with the *Empire of the Ants* (1905) by H.G. Wells. But after the victory of the 1917 October Revolution, ants and termites became an even more useful metaphor for 'collectivism', for situations in which individuals were bound together in such a way that the whole became dominant over its single parts. The anthill therefore became a way of expressing 'the destruction of individual freedom by a collectivist society' (according to the anti-communist propaganda of the time). As such, from the 1920s to the 1970s, in many novels and short stories, giant ants and wasps are the omnipresent prototypes of the threat looming over individual humans, with titles such as *The Green Machine* (1929) by Frank Ridley, *The Demigods* (1939) by Alfred Gordon Bennett, and *The Furies* by Keith Roberts (1966).[20]

The most exemplary novel of the Cold War is, however, *Starship Troopers* by Robert Heinlein (1959), in which free

---

[19] Speech given to the General Assembly of the Scientific Council of Economists (Vollversammlung des Wirtschaftsrates des Vereinigten Wirtschaftsgebietes) held at Frankfurt am Main on 21 April 1948, which can be found at https://www.1000dokumente.de/index.html?c=dokument_de&dokument=0010_erh&object=context&l=de.

[20] We should, however, also mention the counter-current novel *Green Brain* (1966), in which Frank Herbert imagines a multi-species insect colony that evolves to protect the ecological equilibrium of Planet Earth against the short-sighted policies of humans.

and individualist humans fight all out for survival against
arachnoid, collectivist aliens (with no feelings):

> Yes, I agree that the Bugs' planet possibly could have been
> plastered with H-bombs until it was surfaced with radioactive
> glass. But would that have won the war? The Bugs are not like
> us. The Pseudo-Arachnids aren't even like spiders. They are
> arthropods who happen to look like a madman's conception of
> a giant, intelligent spider, but their organization, psychological
> and economic, is more like that of ants or termites; they are
> communal entities, the *ultimate dictatorship of the hive*.
> Blasting the surface of their planet would have killed soldiers
> and workers; it would not have killed the brain caste.[21]

A year earlier, Heinlein had already transposed the syndrome
of mind manipulation by the reds that was so dear to
McCarthyism on to a galactic level with *Methuselah's Children*,
in which alien intelligences manage to take over human minds.
It is now clear why the metaphor of termites was so attractive
to German ordo-liberals.

There is a double irony in this fascination with swarming
insects. The first: ants really are a very good model for the
human brain, structured by a process of self-organization
similar to that of termites' nests or beehives, according to
Douglas R. Hofstadter's famous 'Aunt Hillary' dialogue,[22]
which would contradict Erhard's arrogance. The second irony
lies in the features Röpke found odious and which pushed him
to assimilate collectivism with the *Termitenstaat*:

> If we now hear that to organize society in a socialist fashion
> and with a planned economy, is to shape it scientifically, that

[21] Robert Heinlein, *Starship Troopers* (1958). London: Hodder, 2015, pp. 140–1
(my italics).
[22] Douglas R. Hofstadter, *Gödel, Escher, Bach: an Eternal Golden Braid* (1979).
New York: Basic Books, 2008.

means: vitamins, microscopes, logarithms, slide rules, atomic fission, psychoanalysis, physiology, mathematical statistics, hormones. [. . .] In this conception of the world men occupy a rank not higher than that of the dogs on which the Russian physiologist Pavlov carried out his famous experiments with the 'conditioned reflexes', and the social question now becomes a kind of bacillus which only has to be discovered by employing the 'exact' methods of mathematical statistics – the method of 'multiple correlation', of the elasticity coefficients of demand and supply and so forth, and then, at a scientific world congress – the more participants, the better – the appropriate panacea is found. *Men are categorized and directed in every situation and in every stage of their development by means of checks and counter-checks according to highly elaborated testing procedures; the predictability of their opinions is thoroughly investigated in order to deduce from it forecasts of their future conduct, and finally 'scientific' methods are worked out for forming and shaping man according to an image which in turn is prescribed by 'science'.*[23]

It is extraordinary! It is as if Röpke were describing word for word the mechanisms spoken about in great detail by Shoshana Zuboff, with the harvesting of data by Google, Facebook and co. in order to design frameworks that forecast behaviour and, ultimately, shape it. Moreover, who has contributed most to mathematizing the economy – with 'the method of "multiple correlation," of the elasticity coefficients of demand'[24] – if not neo-classical economists? So here we have yet another unintended consequence: in its furious battle against the *Termitenstaat*, neoliberalism has led us to all become termites, at least in Röpke's meaning of the term. And who knows whether

---

[23] Wilhelm Röpke, *The Social Crisis of Our Time*. Chicago, IL: University of Chicago Press, 1950, pp. 157–8 (my italics).
[24] Ibid., p. 169.

the internet and new means of communication, increasingly incorporated into our lives and persons, are not contributing to making the human species more swarm-like? (Or to use Marx's phrase from his famous *Fragment on Machines*, do they not feed the 'general intellect'?)[25] Just as digital surveillance replicates to the nth power the Big Brother George Orwell so feared in communist societies, in the same way the social organization that emerges from the neolib counter-revolution causes the *Termitenstaat* so abhorred by Cold War ideologues to pale in comparison.

In conclusion, each unintended consequence is more paradoxical than the last. And it is in the name of freedom that they have rendered freedom a precious commodity. Without privacy, under continuous surveillance and tied to debt, what kind of freedom are we left with? That thrilling liberty to choose between Pepsi and Coke, between Burger King and McDonalds. In the society they imagine for us, the only idea of freedom we are allowed is the freedom of the menu: the most painful, most hard-won freedom is being able to, having to choose between a grilled sea bass and a filet mignon (as long as you can afford it). A menu, therefore, or rather, a salad bar, where you are free to decide which ingredients (radishes, tomatoes, lettuce, sweetcorn) to put on your plate and how much. But of course you could never choose an ingredient that is missing from the buffet. This idea of freedom satisfies

---

[25] 'Nature builds no machines, no locomotives, railways, electric telegraphs, self-acting mules etc. These are products of human industry; natural material transformed into organs of the human will over nature, or of human participation in nature. They are organs of the human brain, created by the human hand; the power of knowledge, objectified. The development of fixed capital indicates to what degree general social knowledge has become a direct force of production, and to what degree, hence, the conditions of the process of social life itself have come under the control of the general intellect and been transformed in accordance with it.' Karl Marx, *The Grundrisse*. New York: Harper & Row, 1971, p. 143 (the 'Fragment on Machines' can also be found online at: https://thenewobjectivity.com/pdf/marx.pdf).

the ironic thesis of atomic physicist Leó Szilárd (1898–1964): 'But even when things were at their worst the majority of Americans were free to say what they thought for the simple reason that they never thought what they were not free to say.'[26]

Naturally, the selection is much broader the more you are able to pay. Freedom does not mean being free *from* money, but being free *through the use of* money. Take that freedom whose lack has been considered the most oppressive form of totalitarianism – freedom of movement. It is interesting to see how this has changed over time. Forty years ago, I went to the train station and bought a ticket: but what would I buy? *Any* journey from point X (Berlin) to point Y (Athens) in whichever class (second). I would look at the timetable and see that there were two trains, one in the morning and one in the evening, and I could choose either or, if I arrived too late for one, I could take the other. This meant that I did not have to plan my future down to the smallest of details. Today, if I go to the station and buy a ticket, what do I buy? I buy *that* journey, and just that specific one, at that precise time. If I arrive late, the ticket is no longer valid (unless I buy an open ticket which is much, much more expensive) and I cannot get on the next train unless I pay a small fortune, even if that train is practically empty. This means that the freedom of changing your mind ('I will take the next train') is systematically discouraged and, above all, has a price. I am pushed, forced almost, to plan out my life months in advance: the earlier I plan, the less I will pay for my air ticket, train ticket, hotel room. I am obliged to make myself predictable, to ensure that the powers of control and surveillance not only know what I am doing now, but that they know in advance what I will do in the ever more distant future.

[26] Helen S. Hawkins, G. Allen Greb and Gertrud Weiss Szilárd (eds.), *Toward a Livable World: Leo Szilárd and the Crusade for Nuclear Arms Control* (Collected Works of Leo Szilárd, Vol. III). Cambridge, MA: MIT Press, 1987, p. 164.

I remember what a Russian physicist who emigrated to Cornell University told me in 1992, just after the collapse of the USSR: 'In the Soviet Union we said that our economy was planned, but I never learned what planning was until I arrived in the US. At home, we would go to someone's house and ask them, "shall we dine together?"' Here in the US, you call a month in advance to fix an appointment: real planning out of life is what you have here in the US.'

Graeber was right when he said that 'economic freedom, for most of us, was reduced to the right to buy a small piece of one's own permanent subordination'.[27]

[27] Graeber, *Debt*, p. 383.

# 11

# Social Pornography

B ut what sort of hell do they want us to live in? One wonders what would happen if all their aspirations, all their ideals were realized and they made us frolic in the paradise that they imagine for themselves and us. A polluted world submerged in plastic, with cities flooded by ocean water due to the ice that has melted because of global warming, metropolises poisoned by particulates and smog in which you can only survive by buying new canisters of pure air. A world in which almost no one pays their taxes except to fund the army and the police (though these might also be farmed out to contractors). A society in which the few that have must defend themselves against the many who do not, locking themselves in gated communities, defended by vigilantes, barbed wire and rottweilers.

Thirty years ago, we Europeans travelling through the Indian sub-continent were shocked by the abominable poverty that existed alongside the mansions of the powerful, by those dying of hunger on the pavement outside the jewellery stores of Bombay or Karachi. We asked ourselves how the wealthy of these places could live without seeing what was all around them. Now we are the ones who have become blind and this spectacle has become a familiar sight in the richest metropolises of 'advanced economies', with tent cities in Paris springing up in the hallowed avenues of French fashion's *dernier cri*. Because if we don't pay our taxes, we do not end up like Sweden but like Pakistan. Or like Brazil, where I had a taste of the future when, from the street, I could see well-off families spending their afternoons in their verandas closed off by railing, literally 'behind bars', prisoners of themselves and their own fear for the society that they, in theory, dominate.

From this perspective, life expectancy would diminish drastically given that only a few would be able to afford medical care, and as such, in the future, for the majority of humans, what Thomas Hobbes (1588–1679) wrote, concerning the early days of humanity, would become a reality: the state where there are 'no Arts; no Letters; no Society; and which is worst of all, continual fear, and danger of violent death; And the life of man, solitary, poor, nasty, brutish, and short'.[1] A world that would put into practice, even partially, Nozick's affirmation that 'taxation of earnings from labor is on a par with forced labor',[2] could not, indeed, *must not* guarantee universal public education to all of its citizens (also because citizens belong to a state, and in this world there are no states), and as such, the majority of subjects will either not get an education at all or they will go to a makeshift school thanks to vouchers (which we can assume will not be generous, given that 'the beast has been starved'). In this society reduced to rabble, to lowlife, the master feels entitled to claim the right of rebellion of the powerful against the masses. What's more, they are already doing

---

[1] Thomas Hobbes, *Leviathan: Or the Matter, Forme and Power of a Commonwealth, Ecclesiastic and Civil* (1651), https://www.globalgreyebooks.com/leviathan-ebook.html#downloads, 2019, p. 103. Usually only the final words of this text are cited, but when considered in its entirety, it shows that the wild state described by Hobbes corresponds to the future state hoped for by Margaret Thatcher: 'There is no such thing as society.'

[2] Nozick, *Anarchy, State, and Utopia*, p. 169.

so, given that a 2016 article published in the highly authoritative *Foreign Policy* magazine was titled: 'It's Time for the Elites to Rise Up Against the Ignorant Masses.'[3] It is worth noting that this magazine was founded in 1970 by that same Samuel Huntington we have met several times on our journey.

The people are therefore reduced to *plebs*, to <u>that</u> *multitude* Rousseau compares to *society*:

> There will always be a great difference between subduing a multitude and ruling a society. Even if scattered individuals were successively enslaved by one man, however numerous they might be, I still see no more than a master and his slaves, and certainly not a people and its ruler; I see what may be termed an aggregation, but not an association; there is as yet neither public good nor body politic.[4]

Since it is a vision of the world in which 'there are no values, only value' (Lazzarato), the only standard is cash profit. In this future they promise us, the verb 'to sell oneself' is no longer indecorous, it is nothing to be ashamed of, it is in fact a commendable business, a deserving propensity to put one's human capital to profit, to the point that the perspective outlined by Jean-Claude Michéa is not so paradoxical:

> In Germany [. . .] some female workers dismissed by Capital understandably found themselves being offered places as escorts in the new Eros Centers by the local placement agency as part of their redeployment. This way of resolving the problem of youth unemployment, however, tackles only one of its aspects. If [. . .] prostitution is a job like any other, and

---

[3] James Traub, 'It's Time for the Elites to Rise Up Against the Ignorant Masses', *Foreign Policy*, 28 June 2016, https://foreignpolicy.com/2016/06/28/its-time-for-the-elites-to-rise-up-against-ignorant-masses-trump-2016-brexit/.

[4] Jean-Jacques Rousseau, *Discourse on Political Economy and The Social Contract*. Oxford: Oxford University Press, 1994, p. 53.

if the role of School is always to prepare the youth for their future employment, then it is logically inevitable that public education would take on, from secondary school, the training of those students who wish to pursue this future profession (the creation of sector diplomas and appropriate options; a development not only of the programme, but of the theoretical and practical content of exams destined to test the acquired skills; and finally the creation of a faculty and an inspection body to bring to life this eminently modern project).[5]

Due to the growing cost of university fees in the UK (£9,250 a year for public universities, much more for private ones), what Michéa proposed on a whim in 2007 has become a reality:

> The University of Leicester, Newcastle University, Manchester University all offer advice and safeguarding resources to their students who are sex workers. [. . .] [In 2020] the University of Leicester produced a landmark resource aimed to provide guidance to students engaging in sex work. [. . .] For students there is a guide on the legalities of sex work and tips for students to keep themselves safe if they are engaging in sex work.[6]

Quite frankly, these neolibs nurture an unbridled passion for slavery. Nozick had already insisted, we have seen, that 'a free system will allow [an individual] to sell himself into slavery'.[7] Posner had argued in favour of a free baby market. By the same token, it is perfectly legitimate to sell one's own kidney, testicle (why not two? After all, you can still live when

---

[5] Jean-Claude Michéa, *L'empire du moindre mal. Essai sur la civilisation libérale* [*The Empire of the Lesser Evil. Essay on Liberal Civilisation*] (2007). Paris: Flammarion, 2010, pp. 60–1.

[6] https://thetab.com/uk/2021/09/20/thousands-of-students-are-sex-workers -universities-need-to-do-more-to-protect-them-222364.

[7] Nozick, *Anarchy, State, and Utopia*, p. 331.

castrated, the eunuchs have known this for millennia), or even an eye (why not two? You can still live if you're blind). Without going quite to these lengths, what are the various Amazon, Uber, takeaway riders if not modern slaves? Once again, 30 years ago, on the sub-continent, we were disgusted by the spectacle of gaunt human beings forced like oxen, or mules, to pull other human beings just like them along on a cart: the rickshaws. Today, we see the same job carried out by muscular lads from the hyper-fed West. When will we return to the bed carriers of Ancient Rome, not out of necessity but as a status symbol?

The fascination slavery holds for these cantors of freedom is enigmatic, and not just for those afflicted by subliminal racism, like Posner was, who tried 'only' to avoid white couples being 'saddled' with adoptive children of colour. Robert William Fogel (1926–2013) was certainly not one of these. He was the child of Jewish immigrants from Odessa (Ukraine), a communist until the age of 22 when (1948) he married Enid Cassandra Morgan, an Afro-American activist, who was his wife for 45 years. At that time, inter-racial weddings were punished with imprisonment in certain states and viewed dimly in all others. A disciple of Stigler and professor of economic history in Chicago, he was awarded the Nobel prize in 1993 for imposing *cliometrics* (Clio was the muse of history for the Greeks) on existing historiography, which is to history what Law and Economics is to law.

Fogel became famous in 1974 when he rehabilitated (in an economic sense) the slavery-based economy of the confederate states before the civil war (1861–1865). He argued that agriculture in the South was more efficient (by a third) than agriculture in the North and that plantations practised a division of labour akin to an assembly line which guaranteed economies of scale ('the ultimate objective of slave management was the creation of a highly disciplined, highly specialized, and well-coordinated labor force').

In Fogel's reconstruction, the black slaves of the South had an average life span longer than in many European countries, even the most advanced ones at that time; they lived in houses no less dilapidated than those in the North, they probably had a better diet. The interesting point is that all of this research was aimed at uprooting the racism that was strong even in the abolitionists when they accused slavery with being responsible for the supposed cultural and psychological under-development of black people ('the innate inferiority of the Negro race was said to manifest itself in laziness, limited intellectual capacity, a childlike simplicity, docility, sensuousness, and tempestuousness').[8]

Accused of having rehabilitated (in all senses) slavery, 15 years later Fogel responded, insisting that the reason for rejecting slavery was its 'moral horror': 'Although the slave system was horribly retrogressive in its social, political, and ideological aspects, it was quite advanced by the standards of the time in its technology and economic organization.' 'The case for abolition of slavery [. . .] thus appears to turn on issues of morality and equity rather than on the inability of a slave system to yield a high rate of economic growth.' 'The first, and overarching, count in the new indictment is that slavery permitted one group of people to exercise unrestrained personal domination over another group of people.'[9]

This argument is very close to that of 'heart to the left and wallet to the right' that was very fashionable among those doing penance for having belonged to the workers' movement.

[8] Robert William Fogel and Stanley L. Engerman, *Time on the Cross: The Economics of American Negro Slavery.* New York: Norton, 1974, pp. 203, 216. On the life expectancies of slaves, see pp. 125–6; on their food and lodgings, pp. 109–16.

[9] Robert William Fogel, *Without Consent or Contract: The Rise and Fall of American Slavery* (1989). New York: Norton, 1994: the three quotes can be found respectively on pp. 10, 391 and 394.

An aggravating factor was that the author of these sentences was one of Stigler's disciples, the guru of the economy as a new 'imperial science', which would submit every single aspect of human life (including the moral) to its specific rationality: if the economy can explain any choice (even those that are apparently irrational only because their rationality is concealed – we will come back to this shortly), then it makes no sense to say that a social system is efficient and economically profitable but morally reprehensible, given that even a moral choice can be described in terms of some kind of profit. Ultimately, already in 1944 in his fantastic essay on the 'negro problem' in the US, Swedish economist Gunnar Myrdal had recognized (as Fogel himself reminds us) the economic advantages of slavery: 'This fundamental unity of interest between capital and labor – as labor was *capital* – constituted a main point in the pro-slavery theory.'[10] Only Myrdal was not a neoliberal, he did not believe that everything that is human can be explained using specific market-economic terms.

With his lifelong dedication to the theme of slavery, Fogel shows a disconnect between his moral considerations and his cliometrics: by no means accidentally, at the end of his life he wrote a book in which he magnified the role of religion in the great egalitarian and civil movements of American history, which he believed always come from a religious awakening. In this book he offers an optimistic and generally positive impression of the religious fundamentalism of televangelists and the moral majority of the post-war era.[11]

Even in Fogel there is an excessive fascination with the slavery system that is hard to understand. He himself provides us with a clue when he writes:

---

[10] Gunnar Myrdal, *An American Dilemma: The Negro Problem and Modern Democracy*. New York: Harper & Row, 1944, p. 261.

[11] The book in question is *The Fourth Great Awakening & the Future of Egalitarianism*. Chicago, IL: University of Chicago Press, 2002.

Nobody doubts that human beings were a form of capital in slave society. Slaves who were traded commanded prices as specific and well-defined as those on land; buildings, or machines. Since prices of slaves varied by age, health, skill level, and geographic location, it is clear that the vocational training of slaves or their relocation from one region to another were just as much forms of investment as the erection of a building or extension of a fence. [. . .] What made the application of the concept of human capital to free societies seem odd is that free people are not traded in well-defined markets and hence do not command market prices. [. . .] (Legal recognition of the fact that free people continue to have capital values takes place whenever courts grant cash awards to the widows of men killed in industrial accidents. The amount of such an award usually turns on a debate regarding the capital value of the deceased at the time of his death.) Viewed in this light, the crucial differ-ence between slave and free society rests not *on the existence* of property rights in man, in human capital, but on who may hold the title to such property rights. Under freedom, each person holds title, more or less, to his own human capital. [. . .] In slave societies, however, a large number of individuals were permanently deprived of the title to their own human capital.[12]

We finally have a historian who clarifies for us the origin of that concept used so brilliantly and nonchalantly by Becker, and which Foucault took as self-evident: 'human capital'. This idea can only come from slavery, as it is with slavery that the enslaved human being is reduced to economic capital in the true sense (they can be bought and sold, they can be invested in to make them more profitable, and above all, socially, they are nothing but 'immobilized' walking capital). Primordial slavery is to the neolibs the equivalent of the original bartering system for Adam Smith. This is the origin of the theory that explains

---

[12] Fogel and Engerman, *Time on the Cross*, p. 233.

why procreating a child can be compared to buying a domestic appliance, a commodity with a long duration that is, at the same time, a capital good. And it explains, for the most part at least, the fascination that slavery holds for neolibs. It is the economic system in which their idea of the free market, of competition and of human capital is realized in its purest form: that of slavers and their trade.

For me, this short circuit between the neolib conceptual revolution and slavery has been a real revelation that has clarified an undefined sensation, a vague discomfort that gripped me the more I studied their texts. There is not one that provides a response that gives you hope, that gives you a reason for a more human, less polluted, less Hobbesian world. Instead, they are all imbued with an underlying nihilism like those magnates that make money while poisoning the air that they too will have to breathe one day. Perhaps this was why Posner loves Nietzsche so much.

Or perhaps there is a less noble aspect, such as a *theoretical pornography*. This is not my phrase; it was expressed with bare-faced candour by Charles Murray, author of *Losing Ground* and *The Bell Curve*, in a long conversation with a *New York Times* correspondent during a boozy flight. The correspondent writes:

Murray's persona in print is that of the burdened researcher coming to his disturbing conclusions with the utmost regret; but at the moment, he seems to be having the time of his life. 'It really is social science pornography,' he says. Social science pornography. The phrase may explain more about Murray's influence than he intended [. . .]. Much of that influence has stemmed from his ability to express, through seemingly dispassionate analysis, many people's hidden suspicions about race, class and sex. His writings comprise a kind of Michelin guide to the American underpsyche. The phenomenon is one that he himself has acknowledged, at least inadvertently. 'Why can a publisher sell it?' he asked in the proposal for *Losing Ground*. 'Because a huge number of well-meaning whites fear that they are closet racists, and this book tells them they are not. It's going to make them feel better about things they already think but do not know how to say'.[13]

The notion of sociological pornography conveys how the idea of a free buying and selling of children, or of children as fridges, or of asking how many crimes can go unpunished titillates the readers, jolting their sensibilities with the shiver of scandal.

---

[13] Jason Deparle, 'Daring Research or "Social Science Pornography?": Charles Murray', *The New York Times Magazine*, 9 October 1994, https://www.nyt imes.com/1994/10/09/magazine/daring-research-or-social-science-pornogra phy-charles-murray.html.

# 12

# The Circular Thought of the Economic Circuit

The power of the neolib discourse is such that no one questions it, no one challenges its coherence, let alone its categories. Even Foucault, who got us used to being so suspicious of the concepts he grappled with (just think of how he delved into the idea of madness), suddenly takes such enigmatic terms as *competition* for granted, as if they were fact: what relationship is there between *competition* and *war*? The cutting affirmation cited above by the governor of the Dutch East India Company, Jan Pieterszoon Coen, in 1614 should have raised one or two doubts for him about the philosophical crush he had developed on neoliberalism: there is no trade without war, nor war without trade. In war as in *competition*, there is a winner and a loser, and in both, the outcome of the 'competition' is to do away with (away from the market) the adversary (the competitor). While war eventually ends, because one of the two contenders has lost, in neo-classical theory, competition should survive competition itself, competition should be the stationary state, the condition for balance in the economy. This is a conceptual contradiction, and we can see with our own eyes that this is not the case. There are not legions of search engines competing fairly among themselves:

in each market there is only one. Google in the West, Baidu in China, Yandex in Russia. Nor are there multitudes of competitors in e-commerce, but Amazon in the West and Alibaba in China. Again, with social media there is always a dominant group in each market: Facebook/Meta in the West, VKontakte in Russia, Qzone in China, and so on. And when there are not monopolies, there are oligopolies (and it is here that the 'revolutionary contribution' by Henry Manne comes to our aid, in which he states, contrary to common sense, that mergers between companies do not hurt competition, and that competition survives even under a monopolistic or oligopolistic regime).

Nor does Foucault go rummaging in that opaque concept referred to by economists of the neo-classical school as *utility*, from which the 'utility function' is derived that led to the mathematical formalism used and abused by the Chicago School. Having been a theoretical physicist in my youth, I do not share the reverential fear philosophers hold for formulas of differential analysis. Equations are often a powerful rhetorical tool used by modern economists to provoke unease. That numbers have a fascinating power has been known since ancient times: the aura of numbers released itself in the kabbalah. Only rarely are numbers interrogated in a linguistic or rhetorical way: 'What is a number? Is it a word like any other, an integral part of language? Or is it a purely scientific object of an extra-linguistic nature?'.[1] Advertising makes full use of the rhetoric of numbers, as we see in the playful advert for shoes: 'Buy one, get one free', based on the double meaning of a pair of shoes, or '99 euros for 99 meals', based on the same number applied to different objects and so on. Most importantly, a number offers us an 'exact' determination that neutralizes any further

---

[1] Jacques Durand, 'Rhétorique du nombre' [*The Rhetoric of Numbers*], *Communications*, no. 16, 1970, pp. 125–32, p. 125, https://www.persee.fr/doc/comm_0588-8018_1970_num_16_1_1231.

questioning: you can object to 'dozens of infections' in a region, but not to '47 infections'. The precise figure, therefore, offers a factual immediacy purified of any opinion.

It might shock us, but less than a century ago economics did not make great use of mathematics: in half a century, everything had changed. In 1985, Deirdre McCloskey was already writing how:

> Especially since the 1930s economists of all schools have become enchanted by the new and scientific way of talking. Most journals of economics nowadays look like journals of applied mathematics or theoretical statistics. The *American Economic Review* of the early 1930s, by contrast, contained hardly an equation; assumptions were not formalized; the graphs were plots of series, [. . .] [while], of the 159 full-length papers published in the *American Economic Review* during 1981, 1982, and 1983, only 6 used words alone and only 4 added to their words tabular statistics alone.[2]

But what strikes you the most (in a negative sense) is how carelessly economists handle differential calculation. Strangely, no mathematician has sifted through the economists' use of it. It is from the differential rhetoric that economic ideology gains its non-ideological appearance. Mathematics functions here as a tool to obscure the highly questionable conclusions reached through a specific approach to the economics. Mathematics is the short circuit used to elevate economics to scientific status. And yet many sciences have made incredible progress in understanding the world around us without the use of mathematics; just look at anatomy, botany or zoology.

In economics, mathematical modelling is of course highly useful, indispensable in fact, as it is in all fields that are *in and of themselves* numerical, such as the stock or derivatives

---

[2] McCloskey, *The Rhetoric of Economics*, pp. 3–4.

market and more generally in all areas of finance dealing with 'calculable' objects and in which von Neumann and Morgenstern's game theory obviously plays a decisive role. But applying these models to eminently multi-factorial situations, which are therefore not linear, verges on charlatanism, particularly if you think that we have not even yet solved the conceptually simple equation of the movement of three bodies attracting one another with a gravitational force.

It is not just Deirdre McCloskey and I who have noticed the purely rhetorical, promotional use of mathematics and quantitative models in economics. It was also noticed by Ronald Coase, considered to be the father of Law and Economics, whose view of his own discipline was perhaps also influenced by the 1958/9 academic year he spent at Stanford with Thomas Kuhn, the philosopher of science who connected scientific revolutions to the consensus that theories obtain from scientists. According to Coase, in the choice between competing economic theories, quantitative studies

> perform a function similar to that of advertising and other promotional activities in the normal products market. They do not aim simply at enlarging the understanding of those who believe in the theory but also at attracting those who do not believe in it and at preventing the defection of existing believers. These studies demonstrate the power of the theory, and the definiteness of quantitative studies enables them to make their point in a particularly persuasive form. What we are dealing with is a competitive process in which purveyors of the various theories attempt to sell their wares.[3]

It is interesting that Coase uses the neolib *perspective* (reducing everything real to a metaphor for the market) in order to

---

[3] Ronald H. Coase, *How Should Economists Choose?* Washington, DC: American Enterprise Institute, 1982, p. 17, available at, https://www.aei.org/wp-content/uploads/2016/03/NutterLectures03.pdf

question the neolib method, i.e. the mathematical metaphor. Furthermore, the overwhelming majority of equations displayed by economists are there to be written and not to be solved, much less calculated. Further demonstration of their prevalently ornamental function.

Coase also makes clear a feeling we all had when reading the works of the Chicago School, those written by the Stiglers, Beckers and Posners, and that is, that whatever subject they are dealing with, and whatever problem they are tackling, we are always reading essentially the same article, repeated over and over in the same way. It doesn't matter whether you are talking about Beethoven's *Clair de Lune* or a can of tinned meat, the procedure remains exactly the same. It may well be highly interesting to pinpoint what the sonata and the tinned meat have in common, but after a while you would also like to know what sets them apart. Indeed, as Coase says:

> It seems to me that when you get to [Stigler's] later work, say with Becker, you know what the conclusion is going to be before you start the argument. In a sense, you're assembling arguments to support a conclusion. I mean, that may be unkind and untrue but it's an impression. And it's even more so in the work of Richard Posner. Have you read any of that? It seems to me that the plot is always the same, and characters stay fixed.[4]

The impression of reading a story that is always the same is due, in reality, to the circular structure of their concepts, to take for a demonstration what is only a description.

[4] Freedman Craig, *The Way Things Work: The Empirical Bent of Economists – Ronald Coase on George Stigler*, cited by Steven G. Medema in 'Embracing at Arm's Length: Ronald Coase's Uneasy Relationship with the Chicago School', *Oxford Economic Papers*, vol. 72, no. 4, October 2020, pp. 1072–90, https://doi.org/10.1093/oep/gpaa011. Medema's article demonstrates the various substantial points of disagreement between Coase and the exponents of the Chicago School, who could argue about everything except the identity of their enemy.

## The Rotten Kid Theorem and Other Tautologies

Let's begin with the concept of 'utility'. According to one dictionary,

> utility represents the satisfaction or pleasure that consumers receive for consuming a good or service. Utility function measures consumers' preferences for a set of goods and services. [...] but calculating the benefit or satisfaction that consumers receive is abstract and difficult to pinpoint. As a result, economists measure utility in terms of revealed preferences by observing consumers' choices. [...] In economics, the utility function measures the welfare or satisfaction of a consumer as a function of the consumption of real goods, such as food or clothing.[5]

Even Ronald Coase was sceptical about the usefulness of the concept utility, finding it 'rather sterile': 'To say that people maximize utility tells us nothing about the purposes for which they engage in economic activity and leaves us without any insight into why people do what they do.'[6]

The most devastating critique of this notion of 'utility' comes, however, from the great economist Joan Robinson (1903–1983): '*Utility* is a metaphysical concept of impregnable circularity; *utility* is the quality in commodities that makes individuals want to buy them, and the fact that individuals want to buy commodities shows that they have *utility*.'[7]

---

[5] Andriy Blokhin, 'Utility Function Definition, Example, and Calculation', *Investopedia*, 5 August 2019, https://www.investopedia.com/ask/answers/072 915/what-utility-function-and-how-it-calculated.asp.

[6] Ronald H. Coase, 'Economics and Contiguous Disciplines', *The Journal of Legal Studies*, vol. 7, no. 2, June 1978, pp. 201–11, p. 208.

[7] Joan Robinson, *Economic Philosophy*. Harmondsworth: Penguin Books, 1962, p. 48, available at: https://web.archive.org/web/20160221095721/http://diga mo.free.fr/ecophilo.pdf.

The circularity of this kind of reasoning frontally engages the entire epistemological 'imperialism' of the economics in those fields Coase referred to as 'contiguous disciplines': 'Utility theory seems more likely to handicap than to aid economists in their work with contiguous disciplines.'[8] When Becker says that a mother sacrifices herself because she gains a 'psychic income' from doing so, what does this statement tell us? Nothing, because, if the mother does not sacrifice herself, we say it is because she gains nothing from doing so. The action we must explain becomes the demonstration of the cause that should produce it: the psychic income is 'demonstrated' by the mother's sacrifice. This reasoning does not allow us to predict anything, because we must already know in advance whether the mother considers her sacrifice a (psychic) income or not: we only have verification after the fact. As Brian Barry wrote, 'the constant danger of "economic" theories is that they can *come to "explain" everything merely by redescribing it. They then fail to be any use in predicting that one thing will happen* rather than another.'[9]

It is a tautological thought, therefore. Though tautologies can be powerful, as Barry himself recognizes: studying the justice system from the perspective of how much it costs to run and enforce surely throws new light on the attitude of police forces and explains the otherwise inexplicable behaviour that sees certain crimes go unpunished: 'the police just watched'.

But only to a certain point.

Rational choice arguments tend to become less persuasive and less useful as the real goals of actors become more idiosyncratic. Thus, rational choice arguments do a good job of explaining why most members of the US Congress cater to the interests of

---

[8] Coase, 'Economics and Contiguous Disciplines', p. 208.
[9] Brian Barry, *Sociologists, Economists and Democracy*. Chicago, IL: University of Chicago Press, 1970, p. 33 (my italics).

their constituents; but they would not, in my view, do a good job of explaining why a few Russian intellectuals joined Lenin in his apparently hopeless struggle to overthrow the czar. [. . .] The ability of the analyst to attribute plausible goals to actors a priori thus limits the domain within which rational choice arguments are useful. [. . .] The person who, for instance, gives all his or her possessions to a religious cult can be said to be rationally pursuing the goal of self-abnegation. But when goals are directly inferred from observed behaviour, the arguments slide from 'creative tautology', to use Brian Barry's phrase, into mere tautology.[10]

The world champion of tautology is without doubt Gary Becker, who beat the record with his *Rotten Kid Theorem*. This theorem states that 'Each beneficiary [of the benevolence of an altruistic family], no matter how selfish, maximizes the family income of his benefactor and thereby internalizes all effects of his actions on other beneficiaries'.[11] To put it bluntly, it is worth receiving a gift from your family if your family is rich, and therefore it is worth behaving accordingly. Or, to put it brutally, it is worth it even for a rotten kid to treat their own parents well and behave in a way that does not lead them to ruin.

That the theorem is then reduced down to a shopping list is made clear by the following statement:

> The Rotten Kid Theorem can explain why a parent delays some contributions until later stages of his lifetime: he wants to provide his children with a long-run incentive to consider the interests of the whole family. Indeed, he might retain some contributions until after he dies so that he can have the last

---

[10] Barbara Geddes, *Paradigms and Sand Castles: Theory Building and Research Design in Comparative Politics*. Ann Arbor, MI: University of Michigan Press, 2003, pp. 180–1.

[11] Becker, *A Treatise on the Family*, p. 288.

word. [. . .] This analysis can explain why altruistic parents leave bequests to their children even when the taxes on gifts *inter vivos* are lower than the taxes on bequests.[12]

Even those of us who have not received the Nobel prize in economics can suppose that a parent would prefer not to give away all their money immediately so that the child continues to treat them well in order not to lose their inheritance.

Actually, beyond tautology, here we have also a paralogism. It consists in using the word 'utility' or 'advantage', in a specifically monetary sense (prices in money, costs, profits) – a sense in which it can be added, subtracted, multiplied and divided – but then extending its meaning to all fields of human activity before eventually cartwheeling back and applying to this generalized meaning the rules (and operations) that only work in a monetary sense. First, we are utilitarians talking about economic utility, then we are utilitarians saying that every human action must have some kind of utility (things are done for *a* reason) and finally, this last utility is described in purely monetary terms.

As such, the attack on this vision of the world is not necessarily an attack on utilitarianism or rationalism (in his own way even good old Hegel said that 'the real is rational'). What should be attacked is the peculiar reduction of utilitarianism to a specific subset of it: that of monetary exchange. From a certain point of view, we could say that even psychoanalysis implements a form of utilitarianism when it studies actions that yield no advantage on a conscious level, instead leading to sometimes extreme disadvantages (otherwise it would make no sense to study them) and therefore assumes that these conscious disadvantages are balanced by (or are the price to pay for) advantages on an unconscious level: if there were an arithmetic of the 'psychic advantages', the unconscious would

[12] Ibid., p. 293.

serve to 'square the books' that do not add up on a conscious level. Just as 'dark matter' (which we can never 'see' with any instrument) must constitute 90% of the mass of the entire universe in order for the cosmological model of the Big Bang to work (from a purely rhetorical point of view, the use of *darkness* as a metaphor is interesting in both cases).

The problem with any rationalism is to ask how wide the domain is to which that concept of reason applies. Even Marx was a rationalist, but the 'self-fulfilment' of all political action would be difficult to express using the 'utility function' of rational choice theorists.

Not every rationalism is a fish market: I'll give you a bream, you give me three prawns. Biology offers us an extraordinary example of how every different organizational level implies different logics and concepts. The logic of quantum physics works for electrons and can be described using Schrödinger's equation. But for a macromolecule, it would be useless (as well as impossible) to describe it using the same equations and the same magnitudes. Nor does it make sense to describe the action of muscle fibres or cartilage in terms of molecular dynamics. Not because Schrödinger's equation stops being valid, but because it becomes unusable, as well as incalculable, at higher levels of organization and exchange. All living beings are made up of atoms (and, before that, protons, neutrons, electrons), but flowers emit scents that bees perceive and we use words other humans understand: just you try describing that in terms of electromagnetic waves or elementary particles! Biologist François Jacob (1920–2013) wrote that

> Every object that biology studies is a system of systems. Being part of a higher-order system itself, it sometimes obeys rules that cannot be deduced simply by analysing it. This means that each level of organization must be considered with reference to the adjacent levels. It is impossible to understand how a television set works without first knowing how transistors

work and then something about the relations between transmitters and receivers. At every level of integration, some new characteristics come to light.[13]

As such, physical or biological metaphors applied to the social sciences are laughable. Like social Darwinism, the theory tacitly underlying all theories of competition: the survival of species as the victorious competition in the market of nature. Jacob, again, told me: 'The concepts that function on one level do not function on a higher or lower level of integration [. . .] there is no particular reason why Darwinism − a mechanism that functions on the basis of reproduction and errors of reproduction, sex, death − would work on such a different level, that of social integration.'[14]

Even if the logic of bartering were enough to explain all the variants and nuances of the interaction between two single humans (and this is in no way the case), adopting the same model to describe the workings of social interactions woven by millions of humans simultaneously is unthinkable. We would end up trapped in the mercantile metaphor, exporting the concepts from one field to another in a way that makes no sense.

## The Ideological Entrepreneur and Other Anachronisms

We sometimes read phrases without questioning them. When neolibs tell us that every individual is the entrepreneur of himself and that their own Self should be understood as

---

[13] François Jacob, *The Logic of Life. A History of Heredity.* New York: Pantheon Books, 1982, p. 307.

[14] Marco d'Eramo, 'La logica del vivente vent'anni dopo. Intervista a François Jacob' [The Logic of Life Twenty Years On. Interview with François Jacob], in AA.VV., *Dalle forze ai codici [From Forces to Codes]*. Rome: manifestolibri, 1992, pp. 49–63, pp. 61–2.

an enterprise, very few people ask what they actually mean. Foucault remarked in passing: 'A whole history could be written of these economic, historical, and social notions of the entrepreneur and the enterprise, with the derivation of one from the other from the end of the nineteenth to the middle of the twentieth century'[15] (and beyond, it is worth adding). But this is one of those observations that Foucault makes in passing, without really delving into the concept. A little like when he interrogates the 'new governmentality of the [political] party' 'which appeared in Europe at the end of the nineteenth century'.[16] But again these are fleeting thoughts that are flushed out by the main argument. It is not our aim here to carry out the research Foucault had hoped for, albeit vaguely. It is possible, however, to tease out a few consequences from the thesis by which 'every human being is the entrepreneur of themselves'. It is worth reasoning here in medieval Aristotelian terms: if everyone is an entrepreneur of themselves, this means that something called 'entrepreneurship' is intrinsic to the very condition of humanity, like how the rose is defined by its 'roseness' and the tiger by its 'tigerness' (the modern translation of the scholastic theory of substance would say that the tiger is a tiger because 'tigerness' 'is contained in its DNA').

This means that entrepreneurship is a universal part (a predicate) of being human. And that therefore 'entrepreneuring' is not only an economic action by which someone undertakes a business, a company (an enterprise in the modern sense), but that every human takes on (in a modern sense) an undertaking (in the ancient sense, like the undertakings of the heroes). Conversely, any human activity becomes an 'entrepreneurial' act. I am not talking here about the glorification

---

[15] Foucault, *The Birth of Biopolitics*, p. 160.
[16] Ibid., p. 197: 'In any case this is what I may try to show you next year, if I still have these ideas in mind', but his ideas clearly changed and the statement remained as is.

of the entrepreneur and their assimilation with other heroes and demigods of human history. In 1913, Werner Sombart was already attributing superhuman qualities to the entrepreneur: 'The successful undertaker must be a trinity composed of (1) conqueror, (2) organizer, and (3) trader'. 'But he must be a conqueror also in his ability to take high risks, and to stake his all in order to achieve greatly. In this he is akin to the gambler. Sum it all up, and what is his mental outfit? Intellectual elasticity, mental energy, and intensity and constancy of will.'[17]

In 1942 Schumpeter hails the entrepreneur as the demiurge of technological innovation, comparing them to medieval knights, even if he does so in order to predict their end as a social figure, just like the feudal cavalry was replaced by the bourgeois infantry:

> the role [...] of the capitalist entrepreneur [...] though less glamorous than that of medieval warlords, great or small, also is or was just another form of individual leadership acting by virtue of personal force and personal responsibility for success. His position, like that of warrior classes, is threatened as soon as this function in the social process loses its importance, and no less if this is due to the cessation of the social needs it served than if those needs are being served by other, more impersonal, methods.[18]

The perspective taken by Sombart and Schumpeter belonged to tradition: it attributed to the new figure of the entrepreneur qualities that in previous eras had been manifested in other fields, such as commanding armies or ruling states; it drew

---

[17] Werner Sombart, *The Quintessence of Capitalism: A Study of the History and Psychology of the Modern Business Man* (1913). New York: E.P. Dutton and Co., 1915, pp. 52, 53, 54 (Conqueror, Organizer, Trader).

[18] Joseph A. Schumpeter, *Capitalism, Socialism and Democracy.* London: Allen and Unwin, 1976 [1942], p. 133.

parallels between the entrepreneur and the warlord, the statesman, the prophet. We have seen this procedure in the post-mortem apotheosis of the Apple founder, Steve Jobs (1955–2011).

Neolib ideology, instead, requires an inversion of this perspective; it demands that the old qualities that were manifested previously in other fields now be subsumed into the modern category of entrepreneurship. It therefore requires a literal operation of conceptual anachronism. It is the Assyrian warlord of the second millennium BCE, the Athenian statesman from the fifth century BCE, the Bedouin prophet of the seventh century CE and the Mongol conqueror of the thirteenth century who are all assimilated into the Anglo-American entrepreneur of the twentieth century. This macroscopic anachronism has been committed by a school of history (!!!!), more precisely by the cliometric school we encountered with Robert Fogel. The most illuminating example of this is provided by Douglass North (1920–2015), who was awarded the Nobel prize in economics for historical research alongside Fogel. As a historian, North was profoundly unsatisfied by neolib anthropology – which he shared nevertheless (he founded a journal with Ronald Coase) – because this approach could in no way resolve either the problem of the state or that of institutions more broadly (Where do they come from? What need is there for them if the market is enough?) or the problem of long-term changes. For neoliberalism, preferences and tastes are fixed facts, and if they vary, they only do so on a whim, because of fashion, because some prices fall and some others rise, but they never consider changes to be long term. How, then, do you explain that an entire civilization stopped being cannibalistic? Or that only after several centuries paedophilia stopped being a socially acceptable behaviour?

More generally, North recognized that its epistemological imperialism, of which Becker is the Kipling, runs into serious aporias. If it is true that only what risks being punished is a crime, what is stopping someone from taking a wallet they find on the street, even if no one is there to claim it? If the problem of the law is how much it costs to enforce it, then

> the costs of maintenance of an existing order are inversely related to the perceived legitimacy of the existing system. To the extent that the participants believe the system fair, the costs of enforcing the rules and property rights are enormously reduced by the simple fact that the individuals will not disobey the rules or violate property rights even when a private cost/benefit calculus would make such action worthwhile. If everyone believes in the sanctity of a person's home, houses will remain unlocked while vacant without fear of vandalism or burglary. If a beautiful countryside is considered a public 'good,' individuals will not litter.[19]

This leads North to re-evaluate the role of ideology in shaping human history. 'Facts do not explain the world around us; explanation requires theory – not necessarily conscious, explicit theory but nevertheless theory.' Hence the importance of ideology:

> Ideology is an economizing device by which individuals come to terms with their environment and are provided with a world view so that the decision-making process is simplified. Ideology is inextricably interwoven with moral and ethical judgments about the fairness of the world the individual perceives. This situation clearly implies a notion of possible alternatives – competing rationalizations or ideologies. [. . .] Individuals alter their ideological perspectives when their experiences are inconsistent with their ideology.[20]

[19] Douglass C. North, *Structure and Change in Economic History*. New York: W.W. Norton & Co., 1981, p. 53.
[20] Ibid., pp. 48–9.

North's is therefore a worthy effort. He wants to break the asphyxiating tautological game imposed by the Beckers and the Stiglers:

> Competing rationalizations of the world around us have been the basic ingredient of history since long before Pericles' rhetoric was decisive in his struggle with Cimon for the support of Athenian citizens. This ingredient has dominated historical conflict ever since. Becker and Stigler, however, would ignore Christ, Mohammed, Marx, and – in 1980 – Khomeini, not to mention the thousands of other sources of ideology in history.

Only at this point is his neolib imprinting revealed, and so how does North resolve the problem? Like this: 'Ideologies can develop without the guidance of intellectuals [. . .] but they do so only exceptionally. I do not propose to analyze the reward system that produces what I call the *intellectual entrepreneurs of ideology*; however, entrepreneurs spring up whenever there develop contrasting views of the world around us as a result of differential experiences.'[21]

*Et voilà*, out of the hat comes the rabbit, the *ideological entrepreneur* who reconciles the intellectual universe of neoliberalism with the extraneous intrusion of something such as ideology, which – through this new ad-hoc figure – is thus led back to the logic of entrepreneurship and commercial rationality.

The problem is that in North, the ideological entrepreneur plays the same role as the *deus ex machina* which, in Greek tragedy, appears when the reasoning encounters a difficulty with no easy out. 'Beyond noting that the ideological entrepreneur works to change minds and, in so doing, changes institutions, North does not really develop the concept of the ideological entrepreneur. He does not fully describe the

---

[21] Ibid., p. 51 (my italics).

mechanism through which his ideological entrepreneur brings about institutional change', writes one of his admirers from the Mercatus Center (the one financed by the Koch brothers at the George Mason University).[22]

The problem is not that the concept is insufficiently developed, but the concept itself. As is clear from the lines above, for North, Christ, Mohammed, Marx and Khomeini are all ideological entrepreneurs. Added to the list are 'such persons as Rabbi Akiba ben Joseph and his pupil Rabbi Meier', as well as 'Saul of Tarsus, who was perhaps the decisive influence in the spread of Christianity', an influence 'replete with actions based on ideological conviction'.[23]

But how? Jesus Christ, director general of the Chamber of Commerce, sector 'young entrepreneurs of ideology'; Mohammed floated on the stock market; Marx calculating the quarterly dividends of Communism Ltd.; Saul of Tarsus as the precursor to William Hearst and Rupert Murdoch. And why not Siddhartha patenting the lotus position, and perhaps Buddha charging an entrance fee to Nirvana? Here we find ourselves in the territory of pure anachronism. It is as if Herodotus were considered a professional special correspondent.

Of course, ideological entrepreneurs exist, we have encountered them repeatedly in this book and have done nothing but narrate their 'entrepreneurial' successes: William Simon, Anthony Fisher, Michael Joyce, James Piereson, Richard Fink, to name but a few. But they were intellectual entrepreneurs, or rather, *ideological managers*, in the sense that they managed economic capital in order to produce ideas and import them to the market. It is no coincidence that Richard Fink defined a strategy for 'manufacturing and selling' ideas

---

[22] Virgil Henry Storr, 'North's Underdeveloped Ideological Entrepreneur', in Emily Chamlee-Wright (ed.), *The Annual Proceedings of the Wealth and Well-Being of Nations, vol. 1, 2008–2009*, pp. 99–115, available at: https://papers.ssrn.com/sol3/papers.cfm?abstract_id=1738823.

[23] North, *Structure and Change in Economic History*, p. 121.

in exquisitely industrial-commercial terms. But for the Finks and Pieresons, the emphasis is on the term 'entrepreneur', while 'ideological' refers only to the sector, such as 'textile entrepreneur' or 'technological entrepreneur'. 'Ideological' is the adjective to the noun 'entrepreneur'. And, in fact, think tanks are to all intents and purposes 'ideological businesses'. The way in which North applies it, however, to characters such as Christ, Khomeini or Marx, 'entrepreneur' is adjectivized, it is the predicate, while 'ideological' is elevated to noun and the correct expression would be 'entrepreneurial ideologue'.

But why should entrepreneurship limit itself to ideology? Entrepreneurship, like any attribute of the human substance, could be predicated for intellectuals and artists. Hence why we find books on the 'musician as entrepreneur'.[24]

Of course, music was the show business of times gone by, but that does not mean that Beethoven saw himself as an entrepreneur or behaved as such. Why not write 'poet as entrepreneur'? Catullus and Keats could be referred to as wise innovators (despite dying extremely young), while Poe the penniless and the suicidal Virginia Woolf would be truly excellent examples of artistic entrepreneurship.

The perversion (here it is truly the case) is such that we find essays that ask the question: 'Is Marquis de Sade an entrepreneur?',[25] in which the authors jump through hoops to state that Sade was an 'institutional entrepreneur', or actually wasn't, but they use him to demonstrate the 'Sadian' excesses today's conception of entrepreneurial freedom can fall foul of.

Once again, we sail in a sea of metaphors. And one of the problems with metaphors is that it is incredibly difficult to keep them under control, with one leading to another, becoming

---

[24] William Weber (ed.), *The Musician as Entrepreneur, 1700–1914*. Bloomington, IN: Indiana University Press, 2004.

[25] Campbell Jones and André Spicer, 'Is the Marquis de Sade an entrepreneur?', in Daniel Hjorth and Chris Steyaert (eds.), *The Politics and Aesthetics of Entrepreneurship*. Cheltenham: Edward Elgar, 2009, pp. 131–47.

more and more addictive. And so we have two other researchers of the Mercatus Center who coined the (fairly bizarre) concept of ideological psychic capital, by stating the obvious in saying 'The entrepreneur reaps greater psychic returns from spreading or implementing his ideology than do others who have made no such investment', before then concluding that 'The supply of ideological entrepreneurs is relatively inelastic.'[26]

---

[26] The two researchers, Paul Dragos Aligica and Cameron Harwick, published this article online despite saying they did not want to be quoted. I respect their wishes and will provide only a site where it can be read: http://www.thephilant hropicenterprise.org/wp-content/uploads/2014/10/Aligica-Harwick-Working -Paper-TPE-2014.pdf.

# 13

# The Game is Rigged. However . . .

et's start off by debunking the myth that an effective
counter-offensive against the conservative revolution
can be financed and fed by 'liberal' foundations or a
hypothetical 'left wing of capital'. As if capital had two teams
and one, the ultra-conservative, had found an infallible winning formula, a little like how a witty journalist from the *New
York Times* wrote: 'Feeling outmatched in the war of ideas,
liberal groups have spent years studying conservative foundations the way Pepsi studies Coke, searching for trade secrets.'
To the extent that Democrat strategist, Rob Stein, said of these
foundations (as if referring to an adversary at the stadium):
'The right has done a marvelous job, [. . .] "They are strategic,
coordinated, disciplined and well financed. And they're well
within their rights in a democracy to have done what they've
done".'[1]

Far-right foundations have ripped the liberal ones to shreds,
not because they had more money or access to the most
intelligent minds, but because of the fundamental asymmetry

---

[1] Rob Stein, cited in Deparle, 'Goals Reached, Donor on Right Closes Up Shop',
*The New York Times*, 29 May 2005.

that in a capitalist regime unbalances left and right with respect to a hypothetical centre. The asymmetry lies in the fact that the extreme right does not question (or threaten) the capitalist order, capitalism as a system, while the left, even the moderate left, calls it into question (the reason for which, when the chips are down, capital will always prefer a fascist solution to a socialist one, not because of some inherent malignancy but because of a simple will to survive). This means that there are alt-right capitalist foundations but none on the 'alt-left'. At the level of great fortunes (which we are talking about), 'class traitors' have been incredibly rare.

The game is, therefore, rigged. The words of banker Enrico Cuccia in reference to publicly traded companies is also valid for politics: 'shares should be weighed, not simply counted': alt-right foundations 'weigh more' even if they are numerically (or economically) inferior, because they spread an extreme message with an almost ferocious determination, a message that is utopian even (or dystopian if you prefer) of out-and-out radical capitalism, while the 'left-wing', liberal or progressive foundations necessarily have a moderate message that inherently proposes a compromise between capital and labour. Essentially, you cannot ask a capitalist, no matter how well-intentioned they may be, to kill themselves as a capitalist. For this reason, the letter written by Henry Ford II in 1977 announcing his resignation from the Ford Foundation board sounds almost pathetic. He had been a member of the foundation's board since its creation in 1936 by his grandfather Henry and his father Edsel. In the 1970s the foundation was considered the liberal foundation *par excellence* and, as such, was the nemesis of the Olins, Kochs, Mellons and Coors. The letter reads:

> The foundation exists and thrives on the fruits of our economic system. The dividends of competitive enterprise make it all possible. A significant portion of the abundance created by US

business enables the foundation and like institutions to carry on their work. In effect, the foundation is a creature of capitalism – a statement that I'm sure would be shocking to many professional staff people in the field of philanthropy. It is hard to discern recognition of this fact in anything the foundation does. It is even more difficult to find an understanding of this in many of the institutions, particularly the universities, that are the beneficiaries of the foundation's grant programs. I am not playing the role of the hard-headed tycoon who thinks all philanthropoids are socialists and all university professors are Communists. I'm just suggesting to the trustees and the staff that the system that makes the foundation possible very probably is worth preserving. Perhaps it is time for the trustees and staff to examine the question of our obligations to our economic system and to consider how the foundation, as one of the system's most prominent offspring, might act most wisely to strengthen and improve its progenitor.[2]

Ford's letter clearly explains the inevitable, incurable imbalance between the foundations on the far-right and those on the centre-left. And how, as such, we cannot expect redemption from the 'left wing of capital'.

Even if the game is rigged, we have to play it, otherwise the masters of the Earth win hand after hand without us even realizing, as we have seen up until now. And it is not due to a lack of will. I must just say that I have never heard a more stupid phrase than that once so popular in the workers' movement: 'pessimism of the intellect, optimism of the will', which Antonio Gramsci attributes to Romain Rolland and makes his own. If intellect tells you to be pessimistic and you insist on being optimistic, then you're a fool and deserve to lose. It pairs well with other profundities worthy of being included in the Dictionary of 'received notions' in which Flaubert's Bouvard

---

[2] Cited by Miller, *Strategic Investment in Ideas*, pp. 11–12.

and Pécuchet find so much glee. Take the phrase 'wallet on the right, heart on the left': it is clear, when put in these terms, that the wallet will always win (this is the reason why all objections to neoliberalism that focus their attack on the idea of *homo oeconomicus* are inherently weak and stand to fail). If there is no optimism of intellect (like that of Marx), then you might as well wave the white flag and hope for (unlikely) clemency to be shown by the winners.

But is there space for an optimism of intellect? In my opinion, there is. To be clear: the nightmarish future, even the destruction of the future itself, that the neolibs are shaping impacts not only us human bipeds, but all living beings on this planet. The inconsistency, the circularity, the theoretical somersaults of their doctrine, the 'pornography' of their social concepts is not enough. At the end of the day, for almost 2,000 years, we Westerners have managed to wage lethal wars over important issues such as the 'pre-destination of grace', to massacre humans because they did not want to admit that a glass of wine was 'transubstantiated' into the blood of Christ, to burn thousands of women because they dared, as we all are well aware, to fly on broomsticks at night. So, there is no reason to rule out equally irrational beliefs, such as markets being phoenixes that are born, regulated and regenerated all by themselves, and that, as such, human coexistence is founded on competition (meaning being together is based on warring with one another) lasting for centuries or millennia if those subjected allow this to happen without ever reacting to stop these oddities ordering their lives.

No. The reason for optimism lies in the fact that we do not take ourselves seriously enough; we are victims of Groucho Marx syndrome, the comedian who would refuse to join any club that would have him as a member due to his incredibly low self-esteem. We value our ideas and our past much less than our enemies do, as has emerged very clearly in everything I have written here. Lewis Powell's

famous Memorandum already explicitly exhorted that the
lessons of the workers' movement be learnt and, in practice, he was proposing the creation of a Leninist party for
businessmen. And remember Michael Joyce who directed
first the Olin Foundation and then the Bradley Foundation?
According to Forbes, as I have cited previously, 'Joyce was
inspired by Antonio Gramsci. He wanted to effect radical
transformation' not by Adam Smith or Benjamin Constant,
but by the man who wrote the *Prison Notebooks*. And all the
think tanks of the conservative right that have plagiarized
the concepts of 'hegemony' and 'ideology', have they not
used the notion of class struggle to their own advantage? In
short, the billionaires' counterintelligentsia has learnt a great
deal from their adversaries. Just think of what the historian
commissioned by David Koch to compile a confidential history of his brother's political activity said about Charles:
'[He] was not going to be satisfied with being the Engels or
even the Marx of the libertarian revolution. *He wanted to be
the Lenin.*'[3]

All of these capitalists and cantors of capitalism who dream
of being the Engels, Marx, Gramsci or Lenin of capital are
impressive.

It is not just a vague inspiration; these are not just models to
imitate. These are real tactics to be learnt, strategies to reclaim,
a choice of objectives to be assimilated. We will start with the
most successful ideological counter-revolution forged by the
foundations: Law and Economics.

There is a precise historical reason why these ultra-conservative billionaires decided to finance this legal discipline in
such a wholesale fashion. And the reason is that the left, the
progressives, the liberals had taught the right how decisive the

---

[3] The historian is Clayton Coppin and his research was commissioned in 2002
and completed under the title *Stealth: The History of Charles Koch's Political
Activities* (note just how many disparate contexts in which we find the adjective
stealth). The phrase is cited by Mayer, *Dark Money*, p. 66 (my italics).

judiciary could be in political battles. The events are now too distant (between 49 and 75 years ago at the time of writing) and we no longer remember them, or we no longer recognize them, but almost all the victories won by the civil rights struggle in the 1960s were undoubtedly due to the pressure applied by movements, to the heroism and the activists' spirit of sacrifice, but they were sanctioned, consolidated and rendered long-lasting not by the legislative acts of Congress but by Supreme Court rulings, by judicial acts. To mention but a few:

- *Shelley v. Kraemer* (1948): this ruling made all 'racially restrictive clauses' in housing contracts illegal, 'clauses' that limited the right to own houses to whites, excluding all other races;
- *Brown v. Board of Education* (1954): with this ruling the Court prohibited racial segregation in public schools;
- *Bailey v. Patterson* (1962) outlawed racial segregation on public transport within state lines and between single states;
- *Loving v. Virginia* (1967) declared the state laws prohibiting inter-racial marriages to be unconstitutional;
- *Jones v. H. Mayer Co.* (1968), on the exclusion of all racial discrimination in the sale or location of property;
- *Griggs v. Duke Power Co.* (1971): in this case, the Court ruled that certain educational prerequisites and IQ tests used by employers in order to exclude African-American candidates had no bearing on their ability to do the job and were prohibited;
- *Roe v. Wade* (1973) established the fundamental right of American women to choose whether or not they wanted an abortion and declared unconstitutional Texas's ban on abortion;
- *Lau v. Nichols* (1974): the Court found a city's school system's inability to provide English language teaching to Chinese students to be 'illegal discrimination'.

On one hand, when we look at all these rulings side by side, we realize just how ferocious racial segregation was in the US, where there were states in which black people could not get on the same buses as white people, marry white people, buy houses in the same area or study in the same schools. I remember the photo of a toilet in Koinonia, in deepest Georgia: written on one large urinal was 'whites' and written on another, smaller urinal was the word 'negros'. Or the silhouette of a hand stretching out its index finger, which read 'negro entrance'.[4] This was the society that the John Birch Society longed for, supported by the billionaires who financed the neolib counter-revolution.

On the other hand, in all cases, except *Jones v. H. Mayer Co.*, in which the Court declared constitutional a law that had already been ratified, these historic anti-segregationist rulings were autonomous decisions taken by the highest body of the US judiciary. Civil rights were literally extra-parliamentary victories, both because these rules were not adopted either by parliamentary initiative or decisions made by Congress, and because they were adopted thanks to the application of external pressure on institutions, by 'movements' and by public opinion.

Neolib strategists had therefore seen at their own cost the importance of the judicial apparatus (especially where Common law rules, so where law is not passed on penal or civil codes but on an accumulation of a body of rulings) and had first-hand experience of just how important ideological orientation was in the magistrates' ruling, particularly when it came to those nominated for life (like federal or Supreme Court judges) and, as such, independent from the logic of interest groups to be kept happy in order to ensure re-election. Indeed, the decisions taken by the magistrates had convinced

---

[4] Marco d'Eramo, *Via dal vento. Viaggio nel profondo sud degli Stati Uniti [Away From the Wind. A Journey Through The Deep South of the United States]*. Rome: manifestolibri, 2004, pp. 75–6.

a neolib historian of economy such as Douglass North to claim
the importance of ideology in economic analysis:

> The clearest instance of the dominant role of ideology is the
> case of the independent judiciary. Judges with lifetime tenure
> are relatively immune from interest group pressure. It is true
> that their initial appointment may reflect such pressure [. . .]
> but their subsequent decisions over a wide range of policies
> reflect their own convictions of the 'public good'. Efforts
> to explain the independent judiciary in an interest group
> perspective are simply unconvincing.[5]

And so, this brings us to the second front on which neolibs
have learnt from their enemies: the crucial importance of
ideology. It is incredible how much they have learnt about
this subject. Remember the extraordinary relevance the
marine corps attribute to this concept, which has become a
swearword for conformists and progressives from well-to-do
quarters. Even Fogel, the historian who had re-evaluated the
slave economy, when talking about the image of black people
held by racist abolitionists, was shocked by 'this exceptional
demonstration of the power of ideology to obliterate reality'.[6]
Even Douglass North had to invent the strange notion of
'ideological entrepreneur' in order to incorporate ideology into
the neolib universe, to appropriate it and use it.

Most noteworthy of what the neolibs have learnt,
assimilated and finally put into practice is the idea that society
is governed by a perpetual class struggle, a war between the
dominant and the dominated. This is demonstrated by all the
bellicose metaphors this book has reported in abundance in
their most minute details, even providing academies with
'beachheads'. It brings to mind the seventeenth-century

---

[5] North, *Structure and Change in Economic History*, pp. 56–7.
[6] Fogel and Engerman, *Time on the Cross*, p. 215.

libertines who considered the art of power to have always been founded on a colossal deceit by the dominant classes. As such, in the last 50 years, just as the dominant formalized and unleashed class struggle against the dominated, one of the tools of this fight consisted in convincing subjects that there was no struggle, that class was a whimsical invention of some extremist and that, even if it had existed once upon a time, it was now extinct, swept away by history and all that remained was a legendary, omni-comprehensive, vague and fluctuating 'middle class' and at most, an underclass of the 'undeserving poor'.

Whilst they were organizing the 'war of ideas', their adversaries, none the wiser, wallowed (we wallowed) in the happy illusion of a society without class or conflicts of interest, clouded by the image of a system-country, of Italy Ltd (or France Ltd or UK Ltd, etc.), of a harmony of interests, of us 'all rowing in the same direction', while the winners of the war accumulated and continue to accumulate immeasurable riches and powers.

Because one of the most exhilarating, and most tragic, characteristics of the interminable litany on the 'growth of inequality' is its total disconnect from the problem of dominance. Incidentally, it is important to note that 'dominion' and 'power' are two different concepts: 'dominion' also has the verb 'dominate' with a past participle 'dominated', while the verb 'to power' has a very different meaning from the noun 'power' and 'powered' doesn't mean 'subject to a power'. So, while all dominions imply power, not all powers imply dominance: a traffic warden giving me a ticket exercises a power over me but has no dominion. Foucault focuses entirely on power, but never considers dominion, and one of the weaknesses of his approach lies precisely in the complete lack of the dimension of domination from his analysis of power devices and, therefore, on a macroscopic level, the absence of the problem of empire.

We all know that society is becoming increasingly unequal, that ten people in the world possess a wealth equivalent to that held by half the human race. It has even become rather chic to cite the works of Thomas Piketty on the subject: but all of that is irrelevant. 'We are unequal, so what?' Inequality has become such an obvious, predictable fact that it is exempt from any interrogation as to why; it is like saying that in Sicily there is the mafia, that in California there are earthquakes, in Russia there are oligarchs and in the Caribbean there are hurricanes. Inequality now appears like a natural phenomenon, already transformed from a contingency into an inevitability.

# 14

# Time to Learn from Your Enemies

Just as the dominant have learnt so much from the dominated, it is timely and urgent that we in turn learn from them. We have surveyed here how they conducted their victorious counter-revolution; we have surveyed here the battlefields they marked out one after another – ideology, taxation, justice, education and debt – which now have to be ours.

First and foremost, they taught us that ideology plays a decisive role; the first objective has to be to restore the dignity of doing ideological battle, the centrality of which was somehow lost in the face of the seemingly implacable logic of the dominated. 'Ideas are weapons – indeed, the only weapons with which other ideas can be fought', as William Simon put it. Von Hayek is surely right on one score, when he says that during the era in which they possessed hegemony, leftist parties 'regularly and successfully acted as if they understood the key position of the intellectuals. Whether by design or driven by the force of circumstances, they have always directed their main effort toward gaining the support of this "elite"'.[1]

---

[1] Friedrich von Hayek, *The Intellectuals and Socialism* (1949), in George B. de Huszar (ed.), *The Intellectuals: A Controversial Portrait*. Glencoe, IL: The Free Press, 1960, pp. 371–84, p. 372.

By intellectuals von Hayek intended 'secondhand dealers in ideas', a group that

> does not consist only of journalists, teachers, ministers, lecturers, publicists, radio commentators [as von Hayek wrote in 1949], writers of fiction, cartoonists, and artists – all of whom may be masters of the technique of conveying ideas but are usually amateurs so far as the substance of what they convey is concerned. The class also includes many professional men and technicians, such as scientists and doctors, who through their habitual intercourse with the printed word become carriers of new ideas outside their own fields and who, because of their expert knowledge on their own subjects, are listened to with respect on most others. There is little that the ordinary man of today learns about events or ideas except through the medium of this class.[2]

Today, however, the paradox we face is not von Hayek's, namely, that the spokespeople of the 'masses' achieve hegemony by getting the 'elite' on their side. At the time von Hayek wrote these words, the left was electorally over-represented among people in the lowest income brackets, with little or no capital or higher education. Over the past 70 years, the electoral base of the left has substantially changed, so that today the left is over-represented among the highly educated who, even if they have relatively low levels of wealth in terms of property, have mid to high incomes, whereas it is under-represented among those with very low incomes and minimal education. To use

---

[2] Ibid. Von Hayek is probably basing this on the 'two-step flow' theory, developed at that time by Paul Lazarsfeld to explain why workers reading right-wing tabloids voted for left-wing parties. According to this theory, this occurred because the communication regarding political themes came from 'local opinion leaders' who mediated the information received from (left-wing) newspapers. Working-class voters placed greater trust in these leaders on a number of issues than in the tabloids they read (today, social media influencers and followers offer this same configuration but with more steps, a kind of multi-step flow theory).

the words of Piketty, who carried out one of the most recent important inquiries into this paradox, today the left represents the 'brahmins' whereas the right represents the 'merchants'.[3] This evolution has had a collateral effect, which, Piketty perhaps does not sufficiently underscore, namely that this population, or 'plebs', with low income and educational levels, is no longer represented by any political force on either the traditional right or the traditional left. If they were in ancient Rome, they would have had the ear of 'tribunes of the plebs'. In today's world, they don't even have that voice.

At the same time, the left doesn't give the intellectuals, its most over-represented constituency, sufficient social and political due. Paradoxically, to use Piketty's dichotomy once more, intellectuals are held to be more important by the merchants (as the Olins, the Kochs, the Bradleys, the Mellon Scaifes, the Coors and so on have shown us throughout this book), while the merchants' money holds an irresistible fascination for left-wing intellectuals. The issue is further confused by the fact that today's intellectuals, all substantially conservative, and conformist to (in the sense that they want to conform to) neoliberalism, view themselves as being on the left precisely because of the neolib ideological counter-revolution, which, by cancelling out the categories of 'labour' and 'exploitation', has caused the battle lines to disappear, immersing us in a kind of social jam. Perhaps this is also due to the fact that the ideological defeat is so enormous that it is no longer known what is actually meant by the word 'left', even if I stubbornly continue to maintain that, as far as I am concerned, 'being on the left' always and only means 'being on the side of the dominated against the dominant (and against dominion itself)'.

---

[3] Thomas Piketty, *Brahmin Left vs Merchant Right: Rising Inequality and the Changing Structure of Political Conflict (Evidence from France, Britain and the US, 1948–2017)*, WID.world Working Paper Series 2018/7. EHESS and Paris School of Economics, March 2018, available at: http://piketty.pse.ens.fr/files /Piketty2018.pdf.

But the role of ideology, as General Petraeus explained, is fundamental to reconstituting this distinction of who is on which side and against whom, creating the us/them dichotomy. It is fundamental to our awareness that we are not all on the same side, that we are not all capitalists of our own human capital, but that some people are our adversaries and we are the adversaries of others. And this was *exactly* what they have taught us over the last 50 years with their language of war. How is it possible that it takes a general of the marines to remind us that 'insurrection has been the approach most frequently used by the weak against the strong'?[4]

The first step in re-legitimizing the conflicts, the 'insurrections' ('turmoils' as Machiavelli would have called them) is the fight against euphemisms. The euphemism is not just hypocrisy, it is a technology of power, a technique for command. It is a form of denial, the discourse that 'says what it says only in a form that tends to show that it is not saying it'.[5] Similarly, there are modes of domination in which power can only be exercised in a way that appears that it is *not* being exercised at all. George Orwell illustrated this brilliantly when, in his novel *1984*, he invented 'newspeak', in which the ministry for war was called the 'Ministry of Peace', that for repression, the 'Ministry of Love', and that for the manipulation of the news and disinformation, 'Ministry of Truth'. In doing this, Orwell summed up how the aim of political language 'is designed to make lies sound truthful and murder respectable'.[6]

---

[4] Petraeus and Ames, *FM-324*, i-9.

[5] Pierre Bourdieu, 'Les modes de domination', *Actes de la Recherche en Sciences Sociales*, vol. 2, no. 2–3, June 1976, pp. 122–32. This article is drawn on in English in the section 'Modes of domination' in the book *Outline of a Theory of Practice*, Cambridge: Cambridge University Press, 1977, p. 194.

[6] George Orwell, 'Politics and the English Language', *Horizons*, April 1946, available at: https://www.orwell.ru/library/essays/politics/english/e_polit. The novel *Nineteen Eighty-Four* (1949) is available in many editions, such as Penguin Classics, London, 2004.

Today, we might not have the Ministry of Peace, but we certainly have a large number of delightful 'humanitarian wars', which kill for philanthropy, torture out of brotherly love, starve out of compassion (*oh, compassionate conservatism!*). A splendid example of the newspeak used today is the word 'reform'. Once upon a time, reform referred to something that improved the human state; today reform is a threat. Children are told 'If you don't stop being naughty, I'll issue a reform'. The masses, however, as soon as they hear anyone mention pension reform, know that they are going to be left without a penny in their old age; welfare reform means the progressive abolition of social protections; healthcare reform means we will die without receiving treatment. If you meet a 'reformist' on the street, you'd better cross to the other side. In the same way, in the 'pluralist' West there is a society in which everyone has the same opinions, one where *you must* (1) accept the dogma of the free market; (2) have no thoughts or intentions that are not moderate; (3) be unconditionally pro-American and denounce even the most minimal hints of anti-Americanism.

Indeed, we find the ultimate euphemism in the US's implementation of their own empire. In fact, euphemism is the form of empire they have imposed on the world. Firstly, because it is an empire that refuses to be named as such, just as the bourgeoisie never wanted to be named, being, according to Barthes, 'ex-nominated'. The empire is hidden even from its own citizens: 'Most Americans do not recognize – or do not want to recognize – that the United States dominates the world through its military power. Due to government secrecy, they are often ignorant of the fact that their government garrisons the globe. They do not realize that a vast network of American military bases on every continent except Antarctica actually constitutes a new form of empire.'[7] There must be

---

[7] These are the opening words of the book by Chalmers Johnson, *The Sorrows of Empire: Militarism, Secrecy, and the End of the Republic*. New York: Metropolitan, 2004.

a reason they don't understand. In the past, when a state maintained military bases in other countries, it was said that they were 'occupying' those countries; today it is 'defending' them (this euphemistic evolution had already begun with those empires described as 'protecting' their colonies, which they called, precisely, 'protectorates'). And there are as many as 80 countries 'defended' by the United States, ruled over through the use of around 800 bases.[8] The states that are defended, protected, looked after, spoon-fed are not 'subjects' like in the old empires, but 'allies'. This linguistic expedient had already been used by the ancient Romans who, in battle, always deployed the 'cavalry of the federates' in their flanks, so a cavalry of allies (in reality, tributaries) who were bound to Rome by an 'alliance', a *foedus*. The ambiguous nature of this alliance comes from the fact that it is from *foedus* that we get 'feud', the feudal system and vassalage. Once, subjects paid tributes to the empire; now they 'lend' money that will never be paid back by buying their federal bonds.

I am not saying that the US empire is the worst. Indeed, throughout history other empires have been much more bloody, more oppressive, more brutal, even more short-sighted and rough than that of the US (relatively speaking, of course). I am simply saying that theirs is an empire, and that when we reason on the relations of dominion found on our planet, including those exerted on each of us personally, we must not remove the fact we are the subjects of an empire. To use the language of the neolibs, we must insert this data into the equation of the utility function.

The very role played by foundations belongs to this process of euphemization. The word 'foundation' is itself reassuring, bringing to mind the foundations of a building, the birth of something stable (the foundation of Rome), it connotes a

---

[8] Alice Slater, 'The US has Military Bases in 80 Countries. All of Them Must Close', *The Nation*, 24 January 2018, https://www.thenation.com/article/arch ive/the-us-has-military-bases-in-172-countries-all-of-them-must-close/.

benevolent trans-temporal apoliticism. The word foundation makes us think of everything except the source of finance for an extreme and partisan ideological apparatus. It sounds like a contradiction in terms that this philanthropic entity might dedicate itself to the dismantling of protections for those most in need.

The fight against euphemism might seem marginal in the ideological clash, but in reality, it is the only conceptual weapon we have for revealing, for lifting the veils from, reality. What did the great subversive thinkers do if not unmask euphemisms? Machiavelli's power in demonstrating the morality of politics has nothing to do with the politics of morality; and for centuries, no establishments of any colour or regime forgave him for having revealed their dirty little secret to the masses. The power of Mandeville who shows how collective economy has a different (if not opposite) logic to the domestic economy and that the wealth of nations comes not from virtues but 'vices' (and one of these vices will be raised by Adam Smith as the driving force behind human wellbeing: interest, or rather, egoism). Marx's breakthrough comes when he places man 'back on his own feet' by stating that it is our material life that shapes our ideas, not the contrary.

As such, unlike Wendy Brown and many others, accusing the neolib of having reduced human beings to *homo oeconomicus* is, in my opinion, a very weak criticism that does not hit the mark and is nothing more than a more elaborate variation of the trite 'wallet to the right, heart to the left'. In order to convince them, it's enough to consider Marxist materialism. This had been an incredibly liberating theoretical force, precisely because it revealed the 'low interests' that lay behind 'noble sentiments'. And not only that. As we have seen, tautologies also help us discover aspects of reality that have been hidden from us. Up to a certain point, even the comparison of a child to a fridge can be demystifying. The problem arises when the child is nothing more than a fridge. On the contrary, neolib ideology becomes unbearably saccharine when it turns a migrant who has drowned in the Mediterranean into a 'capitalist of themselves who has failed in their investment', an underpaid delivery driver into a 'self-entrepreneur' and a poisoner of nature as an 'optimal polluter'.

Perhaps it is time to react to this denial of the real, and unmask the economic euphemism. They have convinced us that wealth should not be redistributed and that it is right that corporations be registered in tax havens, that billionaires shouldn't pay tax, as Warren Buffett with his ineffable candour (and whose wealth in 2023 was valued at around $117.7 billion, give or take ten billion depending on stock market fluctuations)[9] recognized, stating that he belonged to an income tax bracket that meant he paid less than half that of his secretaries.[10]

But all of this leads back to the issue of public and universal education. Without this, as Rousseau told us, there are no citizens, only servants. Without this, there is no people but only plebe, and without this, you are not ruling a society but subduing a multitude. The entire neolib offensive of the last 50 years has been fought, as Friedman said, to demolish 'the nationalization of the education industry', in order to achieve a society of semi-illiterate people in thrall to Big Brother, X Factor, China's (or Britain's, or Italia's) Got Talent and Survivor.

Manipulating people is very simple when they are not educated, though nothing can act as a universal vaccine against such things. The Germans were receiving a good collective education when they allowed themselves to be seduced by Nazism. Of course, a collectivity without historical memory

---

[9] The World Real Time Billionaires. 2023 List, *Forbes*, https://www.forbes.com/real-time-billionaires/#50028a1b3d78

[10] Conor Clarke, 'Why Buffett pays less than his secretary', *The Atlantic*, 18 March 2009. https://www.theatlantic.com/politics/archive/2009/03/why-buffett-pays-less-than-his-secretary/1616/.

is thrown around like reeds in a typhoon by the enormous powers that dominate us.

A public, universal and free education is the prerequisite for the indispensable and overwhelmingly immense task of making people politically literate once more. They convinced us that 'revolting is unjust', that the revolutionaries of all eras were nothing more the progenitors of monstrous tyrants. This is an operation that has been running since the rewriting of the 1789 French Revolution, in which we remember the aristocrats killed by the Jacobin Terror but no one remembers the even more bloody attacks of the Thermidorians, the so-called 'White Terror'. Stalin and his regime manipulated the photos of the October Revolution, slowly removing Trotsky, Bukharin and the other reprobates from the stage from which they would watch the Red Army parades. The revisionists of the French Revolution carried out similar censorship, making monsters of Marat, Saint-Just and Robespierre, and honouring the Thermidorian Abbot Sieyès who, together with Fouché, organized a *coup d'état* on Brumaire 18th 1798, bringing Napoleon Bonaparte to power.

So many historiographers dream of an idyllic world in which we would reach the same social progress achieved through revolution but 'without its excesses'. They are forgetting that, if today we are not serfs of the glebe, not illiterate, if there is a minimum of democracy, we owe that to revolution, the French Revolution first and foremost.

Revisionists forget that one of their legends, considered to be the leader of modern moderate liberalism, Benjamin Constant (1767–1830), was already warning in 1797 against wanting to reinstate the *ancien régime* and their privileges at all costs:

> When a revolution conducted beyond its limits stops, it is immediately returned to its limits. But this is not enough. It retreats as much as it had advanced. Moderation ends, reactions begin. There are two kinds of reaction: those exerted upon

men and those whose object is the ideas [. . .] The reactions against men perpetuate revolutions, because they perpetuate the very oppression that causes them. The reactions against ideas make revolutions fruitless because they restore abuses. The former beat individuals to death; the latter stupefies an entire species.[11]

To show just how much we have retreated, consider this prediction by Constant: 'Slavery, feudalism, these are not the causes of war. Superstition of the religious kind is on the defensive almost everywhere. If inheritance divides us, it is because the princes that exclude it have not yet grasped that it is theirs. In a century's time they will talk of inheritance in the same way we talk of slavery'.[12]

It is wonderful to see how extremist the moderates were two centuries ago. They assumed superstition to have been swept away, unaware that two centuries later, horoscopes, recipes for miraculous potions and appointments for satanic rites would be travelling down the optic fibres of computer networks. They considered inheritance such an aberration that they believed it would disappear just like slavery. To be fair, Warren Buffett also thought this, saying that abolishing inheritance tax to favour heirs would be a 'terrible mistake': 'the equivalent of "choosing the 2020 Olympic team by picking the eldest sons of the gold-medal winners in the 2000 Olympics"'.[13]

At the end of this meandering journey to the depths of the neolib counter-revolution, through the twists and turns of the revolt of the dominant against the dominated, of the war those

---

[11] Benjamin Constant, *Political Writings*, Cambridge University Press, Cambridge, 1988 Des réactions politiques (1797), in *De la force du gouvernment actuel de la France et de la nécessité de s'y rallier. Des réactions politiques. Des effets de la terreur*, Flammarion, Paris, 1988, pp. 91–159.

[12] Ibid., p. 151.

[13] David Cay Johnston, 'Dozens of the Wealthy Join to Fight Estate Tax Repeal', *The New York Times*, 13 February 2001, https://www.nytimes.com/2001/02/13 /politics/dozens-of-the-wealthy-join-to-fight-estate-tax-repeal.html.

on top have unleashed on those below, it is time to remember that nothing good has ever come from a society without conflict, without struggle, without insurrection, without a revolt by the dominated against the dominant, of the 'ignoble' against the 'noble' to use the words of Niccolò Macchiavelli, the first, and one of the only, philosophers in history to have judged revolutions positively: 'If we consider the goal of the nobles and that of the common people, we shall see in the former a strong desire to dominate and in the latter only the desire not to be dominated.' Hence why 'The desires of free peoples are rarely harmful to liberty, because they arise either from oppression or from the suspicion that they will be oppressed.' As such, the Florentine secretary could state:

> I say that those who condemn the tumults between the nobles and the plebs, appear to me to blame those things that were the chief causes for keeping Rome free, and that they paid more attention to the noises and shouts that arose in those tumults than to the good effects they brought forth, and that they did not consider that in every Republic there are two different viewpoints, that of the People and that of the Nobles; and that all the laws that are made in favor of liberty result from their disunion [. . .] Nor is it possible therefore to judge these tumults harmful, nor divisive to a Republic, which in so great a time sent into exile [. . .] where there are so many examples of virtue, for good examples result from good education, good education from good laws. And good laws from those tumults which many inconsiderably condemn; for he who examines well the result of these will not find that they have brought forth any exile or violence prejudicial to the common good, but laws and institutions in benefit of public liberty.[14]

---

[14] Niccolò Machiavelli, *Discourses on Livy*, citations are taken respectively from Book 1 chapter 5 and chapter 4. Available in English at https://library.um.edu .mo/ebooks/b13625184.pdf.

Macchiavelli said it: 'good laws arise from tumults'. The work ahead of us that is necessary to convince our fellow human bipeds of this truth is immense, titanic and terrifying indeed. But let's not forget that in 1947, the founders of neoliberalism had to meet almost in secret, they seemed to be preaching in the wilderness, just as we are now. However, they believed so deeply in their own ideas, persisted so tenaciously, that they finally won. Remember it took 30 years for the school of Law and Economics to 'rapidly move from insurgency to hegemony'.[15]

Of course, I will not live another 30 years, but, unlike the neolibs, I do not believe that the world or the human species ends with me.

There are so many friends who have helped me in the most varied of ways, but I cannot go without thanking Daniella Ambrosino, Daniele Barbieri, Camilla Cottafavi, Victoria De Grazia, Lia Forti, Marina Forti, Mariagrazia Giannichedda, Corinne Lucas Fiorato, Giuseppe Mascoli, Anna Nadotti, the Nnoberavez family, Gabriella Paolucci, Jaime Riera, Livio Sansone and Matteo Vegetti.

An appreciative thought also goes to Marcello De Cecco, dear departed friend, whose economic ideas continue to guide me through the fog of modern times.

---

[15] Teles, *The Rise of the Conservative Legal Movement*, p. 216.

# Postscript:
# In the Name of the Father, the Son and the Bank Account

The phrase 'If you want to feed your soul, ours is a great menu' stands out from an advert displayed inside the carriage of a New York subway train. With this genius turn of phrase, the advert for a religious sect combines two of American society's deepest-held passions: on one hand, an inexorable collective bulimia that has a breakdown if it hasn't got something on hand to chew, swallow, ingest, on the sidewalk, in an elevator, in the car, in bed, at the cinema; and on the other, an extremely intense religious vocation that dates back to the very origins of the nation, to those pilgrim Fathers of the Mayflower who landed there in 1620 to practise their own puritan extremism.

At the same time, this advert reminds us of a mystery, because it reconciles materialism, the carnality of US culture and the ascetism of its own foundation in that oxymoron that sees the verb 'to feed' used with an object such as 'the soul'.

That same mystery needs to be clarified for the reactionary counter-revolution, a mystery that I have left for last because it does not affect its planetary framework, but only its American variant, that of both North and South America. In Latin America and Germanic America, but not in Europe, the counterintelligence of the neolib ideology has joined forces, entwined itself and melded with the most conservative Christianity. It can be seen in the United States under Donald Trump and Brazil under Jair Bolsonaro. And yet, the neo-liberal ideology makes a point of disregarding morality as a method and as a perspective, deifying personal egoism and even subjecting the concept of justice to the measure of how much it would cost to enforce. It doesn't recoil from the prospect of either slavery or the buying and selling of children. Despite this, these very billionaires and their foundations which sponsor capitalism in its rawest forms, who push for world globalization, are financing and supporting an identitarian religion aimed at maintaining traditions. The inverted nature of this relationship is also a mystery: how can these Christians who should practise poverty and privilege the concept of 'love thy neighbour as thyself' support the ideology of personal interest, of egoism?

This question was asked by Wendy Brown after a massive number of votes from conservative Christians secured the re-election of George Bush Jr. for his second mandate:

> How does a rationality that is expressly amoral at the level of both ends and means (neoliberalism) intersect with one that is expressly moral and regulatory (neoconservatism)? How does a project that empties the world of meaning, that cheapens and deracinates life and openly exploits desire, intersect one centered on fixing and enforcing meanings, conserving certain ways of life, and repressing and regulating desire? How does support for governance modeled on the firm and a normative social fabric of self-interest marry or jostle against support for governance modeled on church authority and a normative social fabric of self-sacrifice and long-term filial loyalty, the very fabric shredded by unbridled capitalism?[1]

---

[1] Wendy Brown, 'American Nightmare', p. 692.

One response is that the neoliberals are simply using religion. As the first one to revisit Polybius in Christian Europe,[2] Niccolò Machiavelli stated that religion was introduced into human societies as a governance tool: 'Whoever considers well the Roman histories sees how much religion served to command armies, to animate the plebs, to keep men good, to bring shame to the wicked.' But going further than Polybius, Machiavelli says that in order to introduce religion to Rome, Numa Pompilius 'pretended to have close relationship with a nymph', meaning he *pretended* to have received the divine Word: 'the religion introduced by Numa was among the principal reasons for the happiness of that city, because it produced good institutions, the good institutions created good fortune, and from good fortune arose the happy successes of their undertakings. Just as the observance of divine worship is the cause of the greatness of republics, so the disregard of divine worship is the cause of their ruin'.[3]

In doing so, Machiavelli began the libertine tradition that says religion is nothing more than a pretence, a necessary deception for disciplining the plebs (*instrumentum regni*). A tradition that coagulated around the theme of the 'three imposters', by which Moses, Jesus and Mohammed were seen as three imposters who, like Numa Pompilius, pretended to

---

[2] According to Polybius (206–124 BC): 'I believe that it is the very thing which among other peoples is an object of reproach, I mean superstition, which maintains the cohesion of the Roman State: [. . .] a fact which will surprise many. My own opinion at least is that they have adopted this course for the sake of the common people. It is a course which perhaps would not have been necessary had it been possible to form a state composed of wise men, but as every multitude is fickle, full of lawless desires, unreasoned passion, and violent anger, the multitude must be held in by invisible terrors and suchlike pageantry. For this reason, I do not think that the ancients acted rashly and at haphazard in introducing among the people notions concerning the gods and beliefs in the terrors of hell, but that the moderns are most rash and foolish in banishing such beliefs.' *Histories*, Book VI, chap. 56. Available at: http://penelo pe.uchicago.edu/Thayer/E/Roman/Texts/Polybius/6*.html.

[3] Machiavelli, *Discourses on Livy*, Book 1, chapter 11, pp. 51–2.

receive the word of God in order to discipline the masses: 'that neither God, nor the Devil, nor Paradise, nor Hell, nor the Soul, are such as religion has represented them to be, and as most reverend divines have maintained. These latter sell their fables for truths, being people of bad faith who abuse the credulity of the ignorant by making them believe whatever they please'.[4]

The title of a text by the Heritage Foundation seems to prove the libertines right: *Why Religion Matters: The Impact of Religious Practice on Social Stability.*[5] Its key points, indicated in the summary, are: '1. Religious practice appears to have enormous potential for addressing today's social problems' and '2. Strong and repeated evidence indicates that the regular practice of religion has beneficial effects.' The author lists the following beneficial effects:

> The strength of the family unit is intertwined with the practice of religion. [. . .] Regular church attendance, for example, is particularly instrumental in helping young people to escape the poverty of inner-city life; [. . .] Regular religious practice generally inoculates individuals against a host of social problems, including suicide, drug abuse, out-of-wedlock births, crime, and divorce. The regular practice of religion also encourages such beneficial effects on mental health as less depression (a modern epidemic), more self-esteem, and greater family and marital happiness.[6]

In short, to use Polybius' words, religion is needed to 'maintain the cohesion of the state'.

---

[4] *Treatise of the Three Imposters*. New York: The Mantle, 2015 [1719]. Also available at: https://www.gutenberg.org/files/50534/50534-h/50534-h.htm.

[5] Patrick Fagan, *Why Religion Matters: The Impact of Religious Practice on Social Stability*, report published on 25 January 1996 on the foundation's website: https://www.heritage.org/civil-society/report/why-religion-matters-the-impact-religious-practice-social-stability.

[6] Ibid.

In this sense, the 'libertine' use of religion knows no political bounds. From Eisenhower onwards, all American presidents have participated at least once during their mandate in the National Prayer Breakfast, organized every year by a very discreet association known as 'The Family', through their Fellowship Foundation created in 1953. That year, the official theme of the inaugural breakfast was 'Government under God'. All of Hillary Clinton (2010), Donald Trump (who went four times in 4 years) and Joe Biden (2023) have attended. This 'religious' breakfast, in which 3,800 (paying) guests from more than 130 countries visit Washington to take part,[7] is sponsored by Congress. The 'Family' is surrounded by the most varied conspiracy theories, due to the strict secrecy maintained regarding the names of its associates. What we do know is that during the Cold War, the Fellowship forged relationships in the 1960s between the US government and the Brazilian dictator general Artur da Costa e Silva and Indonesian dictator Suharto, held a secret meeting between Sadat and Begin at the 1978 National Prayer Breakfast, organized meetings in the 1980s between the US government and El Salvadorean former general Carlos Eugenio Vides Casanova, who was invited to a Prayer Breakfast in 1984 before being condemned for the torture of thousands of citizens during the 1980s in a Florida courtroom in 2004. Also invited on that occasion was Honduran general Gustavo Álvarez Martínez who, linked to both the CIA and the death squads, would later become an Evangelical missionary before being assassinated in 1989.[8]

Experience, however, tells us that the hypothesis of cynicism – i.e., that the powerful are cynically exploiting the superstitions of the masses – may well be true, but that this is too gracious,

---

[7] Kenneth P. Vogel and Elizabeth Dias, 'At Prayer Breakfast, Guests Seek Access to a Different Higher Power', *The New York Times*, 28 July 2018, https://www.nytimes.com/2018/07/27/us/politics/national-prayer-breakfast.html

[8] Jeff Sharlet, 'Jesus Plus Nothing: Undercover among America's secret theocrats', *Harper's Magazine*, March 2003, pp. 53–64.

because those same powerful individuals (politicians or billionaires) ultimately end up believing the very superstitions
they set out to exploit. And not only this. The thesis formulated
by Machiavelli and the libertines can be applied to all rulers of
any leaning, just as the Prayer Breakfasts in Washington are
bipartisan. But as we can clearly see from the phenomenon
of Pentecostalism in Latin America, there is a specificity in
the relationship between conservative Christianity and neolib
extremism that is anything but bipartisan.

This is obviously not the first time that capitalism and
Christianity have joined forces. In 1905, Max Weber was
already clearly elucidating how the protestant work ethic had
shaped the spirit of capitalism. And yet, he too could not help
but be shocked by this: 'It is precisely this however that seems
so incomprehensible and puzzling, so sordid and contempt-
ible, to precapitalist man. For anyone to make the purpose of
his life's work exclusively the idea of eventually going to one's
grave laden with a heavy weight of money and goods seems to
him the product of perverse instinct, of the *auri sacra fames*.'[9]

But once again, this is more a question of mental attitude
than a political position. At exactly the same time in which
the German sociologist was investigating the connections
between Calvinist work ethic and the spirit of capitalism, in the
United States a version of the Bible prevailed that was moving
in precisely that direction: the Scofield Reference Bible. Cyrus
Ingerson Scofield (1843–1921) was like a character from a
spaghetti western. Originally from Tennessee, a heavy drinker
with marriage problems from an early age, the scandal-ridden
Scofield fought for the confederates in the war of secession,
worked as a lawyer and hunted native Americans in Kansas,
the state from which he was forced to flee (abandoning his
wife and two children) because he was accused of stealing the

---

[9] Max Weber, *The Protestant Ethic and The Spirit of Capitalism*. New York:
Penguin Books, 2002, p. 24.

political contributions made by his former business partner. Imprisoned in St. Louis in 1879 for counterfeiting and fraud, he was 'born again' in prison and became one of the fathers of modern US fundamentalism, devoting himself to a crusade against anarchists, communists and socialists. The definitive version of his annotated Bible was published by the Oxford Press in 1916, selling two million copies in less than 2 years (a new edition in 1967 sold more than 2.5 million copies).[10]

Scofield was one of the first to practise arbitrary selectivity over which Bible passages to interpret and which to ignore: that the world was created exactly 4,004 years before the birth of Christ should be taken to the letter (from which we get all the creationist texts that are still all the rage in the United States), while instead the Sermon on the Mount should be understood only as a metaphor. According to Scofield's Bible, the metaphor of 'Blessed are the poor in spirit, for theirs is the kingdom of heaven' (Matthew 5:3) [. . .]. 'But woe to you who are rich, for you have already received your comfort [. . .] Woe to you who laugh now, for you will mourn and weep' (Luke 6:24–25) will only happen in the millennium before the Rapture, and so until that distant future is upon us, not only is pursuing riches not a sin, but is a kind of duty for any good Christian.

This thesis has been expressed with even more apodictic strength in the *Acres of Diamonds* sermon given for the first time in 1869 by the Baptist pastor, founder and first rector of Philadelphia's Temple University, Russell Herman Conwell (1843–1925), and repeated by its author another 6,152 times throughout the world. Conwell is categorical: 'I say that you ought to get rich, and it is your duty to get rich.'

Money is power, and you ought to be reasonably ambitious to have it. You ought because you can do more good with it than

---

[10] Paul Boyer, *When Time Shall Be No More: Prophecy Belief in Modern American Culture*. Cambridge, MA: Harvard University Press, 1992, pp. 97–8.

you could without it. Money printed your Bible, money builds your churches, money sends your missionaries, and money pays your preachers, and you would not have many of them, either, if you did not pay them. I am always willing that my church should raise my salary, because the church that pays the largest salary always raises it the easiest. [. . .]. The man who gets the largest salary can do the most good with the power that is furnished to him.

And so, the reverend repeats: 'I say, then, that you ought to have money.'[11] No matter how brazen this peremptory order to get rich may appear, its logic starts to make sense when Conwell begins praising the Rockefellers, Carnegies and Astors, the potential supporters of the university he would go on to found in 1884: 'Why is it Mr. Carnegie is criticized so sharply by an envious world? Because he has gotten more than we have.'

But all becomes clear when Conwell launches an attack on the trade unions, first because they lump all jobs in together, placing on the same level those in well-paid jobs and those paid poverty wages, the skilled and unskilled, and, most of all, because the trade unions dare to criticize the 'oppressive rich': 'He is an enemy to his country who sets capital against labor or labor against capital.'[12] What the reverend really cannot stomach is 'the war between capital and work': class struggle.

Since the nineteenth century, the big capitalists and the conservative wing of Christianity have been united against a common enemy: the workers' movement, atheist and

---

[11] Russell H. Conwell, *Acres of Diamonds*. New York: Harper & Brothers, 1915, pp. 18 and 20. This sermon is available online on several websites, including Internet Archive.

[12] The versions of the sermon differ slightly. These final lines I have taken from the online version provided by Temple University: https://www.temple.edu /about/history-traditions/acres-diamonds. However, in the version published by Harper, neither Rockefeller nor the trade unions are cited, while Carnegie is named in another context.

anti-capitalist socialism. Once more, 'the enemy of my enemy is my friend'. This is why the relationship between big capital and conservative Christianity grows even closer, more intimate when, in the 1930s, both capitalists and Christians find themselves opposed to Roosevelt's New Deal, at a time when the workers' movement claimed significant victories as a result of the Great Depression. Let's not forget that after 1929, big capital had some very bad press. The suffering of millions of people without homes or jobs was attributed to the detestable greed shown by the magnates of industry and finance. Capitalism had been discredited by its failures, and Franklin Delano Roosevelt used an abundance of religious quotations and paraphrased rulings by the Social Gospel – the religious wing of the progressive movement – at the beginning of the twentieth century. It was then that the employers' associations turned to preachers to defend capitalism 'from state interference': corporate titans enlisted conservative clergymen in an effort to promote new political arguments embodied in the phrase 'freedom under God'. To the point that at the 1940 Convention of the National Association of Manufacturers, where speeches were given by the CEOs of General Motors, Standard Oil, General Electric, Mutual Life, Sears and Roebuck (as well as the head of the FBI, J. Edgar Hoover), the speech that won the most applause was that given by reverend James W. Fifield Jr. (1899–1977), known as 'the Millionaires' apostle', in which he attacked 'the New Deal's "encroachment upon our American freedoms"', and 'the menace of autocracy approaching through bureaucracy': 'these titans of industry had been told, time and time again, that they were to blame for the nations downfall. Fifield, in contrast, insisted that they were the source of its salvation'.[13]

---

[13] Kevin M. Kruse, *One Nation Under God: How Corporate America Invented Christian America*. New York: Basic Books, 2015, pp. xiv, 7.

The bridge between the Gospel and capitalism was individualism. For these preachers, the salvation of the soul is individual, people only ever save themselves and, therefore, any salvation ethic must lean on that of individualism, and so, on capitalism. As such, when the Cold War broke out after the Second World War, with a clear communist enemy (Soviet Satan), the Christian-business machine was already well oiled and ready to fully utilize new technology: namely, television.

The father of modern conservative religious integralism is Billy Graham (1918–2018) who, at the end of the 1940s, launched his 'crusades' in various US cities and was made famous thanks to being publicly supported by the newspapers of magnate Randolph Hearst. His Evangelical Foreign Missions Association was an effective tool during the Cold War. Graham founded the largest evangelical newspaper 'Christianity Today' as well as the Urban Missionary Conferences, and was one of president Richard Nixon's closest confidantes.

The John Birch Society (named after a pastor killed in China in 1945) was also founded under the Eisenhower presidency. This is the same society that was financed by Fred Koch (from the Kansas oil family) and Harry Bradley (from the Bradley family who owned a company in Wisconsin), two families whose foundations played a leading role in the story we have just told. The Bradley and Koch families were bigoted from the start (just like the Coors, the beer dynasty that is another sizeable financier of right-wing culture), and the history of their financing of religious extremists intermingles with that of their donations to reactionary research centres. From the outset, the John Birch Society has been a hotbed of antisemitic, racist and paranoid anti-communist fanatics, to the point that they accused president Dwight D. Eisenhower and the head of the CIA, Allen Dulles, of being communist spies, and insisted for decades that John Rockefeller was a member of the mysterious masonic sect, the Illuminati. The John Birch Society reached its pinnacle in 1964 with Barry Goldwater's presidential candidacy for the Republican Party, but his defeat also marked the organization's decline as it was increasingly discredited by its own paranoia.

Despite this, many leaders of the conservative Christian revolution that brought Ronald Reagan to power came from its ranks in the 1970s. Reagan was the first presidential candidate to insist that the acceptance speech at his party's convention end with the words 'God bless America!', a phrase that no candidate has dared since omit.[14]

It is from the John Birch Society that Tim LaHaye (1926–2016) came, his series of *Left Behind* novels sold 80 million copies (not by coincidence, in these novels the Antichrist is a man who resembles Robert Redford, has the terrible affliction of being a 'polyglot' and is the Secretary General of the UN). These books have been made into both films and TV series.

Don't forget that in the long hours spent driving during a typical day in America, it is nigh on impossible not to hear radio sermons. Nor can you channel hop while watching TV without coming across one televangelist after another. Television was the medium of choice for spreading the message of Christian conservatives, to the point where the role of the televangelist has become proverbial. In 1960, Pat Robertson (1930–2023) founded the Christian Broadcasting Network (CBN), which immediately became the front line in the culture wars, being broadcast in more than 200 countries and in 70 languages. His programme, the 700 Club, is watched by a million people. Robertson also founded International Family Entertainment Inc., a satellite channel with 63 million subscribers, sold to Fox Kids Worldwide in 1997 for $1.9 million. Robertson also founded Regent University, Operation Blessing International Relief, Development Corporation and the American Center for Law and Justice.

14 Ibid., p. 274.

Another televangelist, the Baptist preacher Jerry Falwell (1933–2007), founded Moral Majority in 1979 (which he led until 1987), a movement that was anti-abortion, anti-gay, anti-feminist and creationist. It was against the SALT negotiations with the USSR, in favour of media censorship and decisive in bringing Reagan to the White House in 1980. In 1989, Moral Majority was dissolved and absorbed into Robertson's Christian Coalition.

The end of the Cold War and the events of 9/11 led Christian conservatives to change tack. They had always been anti-Semites, but whereas previously this had been directed at Jews, from this point on it was aimed firmly at Arabs. Robertson was convinced Islam was a religion that wished to destroy all others. For former president of the Southern Baptist Convention, Jerry Vines, Mohammed was a 'paedophile possessed by the devil' while Franklin Graham (son and heir of Billy) branded Islam 'a very evil and wicked religion'. In January 2001, Franklin Graham gave an introductory speech before Bush's swearing in at the White House. And Donald Trump had supported the fake news that Barack Obama was actually a Muslim who had frequented madrassas (one survey suggested 80% of US citizens believe that Obama was born in America, but only 39% know he is Christian and 29% believe him to be Muslim).[15]

It remains a mystery, however, as to why the big capitalists have such unbridled passion for fundamentalists (the US is much more relaxed with Begin than with Rabin, with the fundamentalist Zia-ul-Haq over the secular Gandhis). The most profound reason is the very one that shocked Wendy Brown: no society can base itself on a 'rationality that is expressly amoral at the level of both ends and means (neoliberalism)', on 'a project that empties the world of meaning, that cheapens

---

[15] D'Angelo Gore, 'Eight Years of Trolling Obama', FactCheck.Org, posted on 19 January 2017, https://www.factcheck.org/2017/01/eight-years-of-trolling -obama/.

and deracinates life and openly exploits desire'. In short, a society cannot be held up by pure competition. The German ordo-liberals of the Freiburg School were also aware of this:

> we have no intention to demand more from competition than it can give. It is a means of establishing order and exercising control in the narrow sphere of a market economy based on the division of labor, but not a principle on which a whole society can be built. From a sociological and moral point of view, it is even dangerous because it tends more to dissolve than to unite. If competition is not to degenerate, its premise will be a correspondingly sound political and moral framework.[16]

The more amoral and antisocial the market and competition, the more an extra-economic social glue is needed. We were already given reason to suspect this by a gross neolib incongruence when they stated (as Friedman and Thatcher did) that the basic unit of the economy is both the individual and the family. But the family can only be considered a unit if the bonds that unite it are not solely those of the market (no matter what Gary Becker says), otherwise the family is broken up into the individuals of which it is composed and is not an economic unit. The basic unit cannot be the individual and the family, it must be one or the other.

As such, the more globalized capital becomes, cut loose from countries, traditions, history and now purely behavioural, the more it needs something that reconstitutes those countries, traditions and history. The varyingly veiled racist sympathies of all neolibs knit the flesh, blood and bodies to a theory and practice that is increasingly bloodless and immaterial, symbolized by ultra-fast stock trading now uncoupled from

---

[16] Wilhelm Röpke, *The Social Crisis of Our Time*, p. 181, can be downloaded from the website of the von Mises Institute: https://mises.org/library/social-crisis-our-time.

any human protagonist and managed by computers. One of the most important reasons Occupy Wall Street ran out of steam is because Wall Street is no longer on Wall Street. Technically, it no longer exists as the New York Stock Exchange is – physically at least – an immense series of servers and computers stacked up in gigantic refrigerated hangars in Mahwah, New Jersey.[17]

If this hypothesis is true, if, that is, globalist cosmopolitism needs territorial localism, then identitarian and nationalist movements are nothing more than the other side of globalization: one cannot be without the other, just as fundamentalism is a product, a creature of modern secularism.

Talking of fundamentalism, another perhaps decisive reason for the reciprocal fascination between conservative Christianity and neoliberalism is that the free market is a real faith, with its missionaries, apostles, temples (banks) and Mega-Churches (the mega-banks that are 'too big to fail'). We believe in the free market and its invisible hand in the same way we believe in the Holy Trinity or in the humanity and divinity of Jesus. And we have already seen that human capital is the modern equivalent of a soul.

Moreover, I am by no means the first to note the religious dimension of capitalism. Karl Marx was the first to do so with his extremely famous passage on 'the mystery of commodities' and its fetishism:

> to find an analogy we must take flight into the misty realm of religion. There the products of the human brain appear as autonomous figures endowed with a life of their own, which enter into relations both with each other and with the human race. So it is in the world of commodities with the products of men's hands. I call this the fetishism which attaches itself to the products of labour as soon as they are produced as

---

[17] Alexandre Laumonier, 6/5. Brussels: Éditions Zones sensibles, 2013.

commodities, and is therefore inseparable from the production of commodities.[18]

And we have already come across Marx's comparison of 'lack of faith in the national debt' with 'the sin against the Holy Ghost, for which there is no forgiveness'.[19]

Ernst Bloch was even more explicit with his belief that Calvinism had introduced 'the elements of a new "religion": capitalism as religion and church of Mammon'.[20] In that same year, Benjamin wrote a famous fragment titled *Capitalism As Religion* and it begins like this: 'A religion may be discerned in capitalism – that is to say, capitalism serves essentially to allay the same anxieties, torments, and disturbances to which the so-called religions offered answers.' Benjamin says that the religious structure of capitalism is 'not merely, as Weber believes, as a formation conditioned by religion, but as an essentially religious phenomenon': 'capitalism is a purely cultic religion, perhaps the most extreme that ever existed. In capitalism, things have no meaning only in their relationship to the cult'; 'the cult makes guilt pervasive. Capitalism is probably the first instance of a cult that creates guilt, not atonement'.[21]

But the situation changed when, by applying the doctrine of rational choices developed in the 1960s to the realm of faith, economists began to use the metaphor of the market in the religious sphere, producing an 'economy of religion' (we have already met Rodney Stark). At that point, religious scholars reciprocated and an inverse field of studies was founded, in the sense that they began to search for what can be understood about the market by considering it using the same categories

---

[18] Marx, *Capital*, p. 165.
[19] Ibid., p. 919.
[20] Ernst Bloch, *Thomas Müntzer als Theologe der Revolution* (1921). Frankfurt am Main: Suhrkamp, 1977.
[21] Walter Benjamin, *Capitalism as Religion* [Fragment, 1921], available at: https://cominsitu.wordpress.com/2018/06/08/capitalism-as-religion-benjamin-1921/

as religion.[22] Harvey Cox wrote a book called *Market as God* (Cox always uses a capital M for market 'to signify both the mystery that enshrouds it and the reverence it inspires in its adepts').[23]

> The phrase 'religion of the market' is not just a figure of speech. Faith in the workings of markets actually takes the form of a functioning religion, complete with its own priests and rituals, its own doctrines and theologies, its own saints and prophets, and its own zeal to bring its gospel to the whole world and win converts everywhere. The fact that acolytes of the market faith do not formally acknowledge it as a religion does not change this reality.[24]

We might add that the god-market is now an Aristotelian God, given that, for Aristotle, the pure act is 'the thought that thinks itself', and for neolib capitalism 'the market sells itself on the market'. Up until the end of the last century, all stock exchanges including the London Stock Exchange, Wall Street and the Chicago Mercantile Exchange had to be neutral, belonging to no one. But in 1998, financial markets could be transformed 'into commercial businesses like any other, with shareholders that receive dividends depending on how well society performs. The most paradoxical aspect was that a market could in turn introduce itself to the market and be floated'.[25] Wall Street stocks are quoted, sold and bought in Wall Street: it is the market that sells the market, the thought that thinks the thought.

[22] Andrew M. McKinnon, 'Ideology and the Market Metaphor in Rational Choice Theory of Religion: A Rhetorical Critique of "Religious Economies"', *Critical Sociology*, vol. 39, no. 4, 2013, pp. 529–43.

[23] Harvey Cox, *The Market as God*. Cambridge, MA: Harvard University Press, 2016, p. 8.

[24] Ibid., p. 6.

[25] Laumonier, *6/5*, p. 57 (my italics).

Like the ancient gods and the Jewish Jehovah, the Market
too is an irascible god, punitive and changeable:

> In days of old, seers entered a trance state and then informed
> anxious seekers what kind of mood the gods were in, and
> whether this was an auspicious time to begin a journey, get
> married, or start a war [. . .] Today, The Market's fickle will is
> clarified by daily reports from Wall Street and other sensory
> organs of finance. Thus we can learn on a day-to-day basis that
> The Market is 'apprehensive,' 'relieved,' 'nervous,' or even at
> times 'jubilant.' On the basis of this revelation, awed devotees
> make critical decisions about whether to buy or sell. Like one
> of the devouring gods of old, The Market – aptly embodied
> in a bull or a bear[26] – must be fed and kept happy under all
> circumstances'. [. . .] The diviners and seers of The Market's
> moods are the financial consultants and CEOs of major
> investment houses. They are the high priests of its mysteries.
> To act against their admonitions is to risk ex-communication
> and possibly damnation. If, for example, any government's
> policy vexes The Market, those responsible for the irreverence
> will be made to suffer.[27]

As in all religions, that of the Market also has heresies that
must be punished, not with fire but with debt:

> The troubles with countries from Japan to Greece, I recognized
> the Market's votaries to be arguing, derive from their heretical
> straying from free-market orthodoxy – they are practitioners of
> 'crony capitalism,' or 'ethno-capitalism' or 'statist capitalism'.
> Like those of ancient Arians or medieval Albigensians, their

---

[26] In market terms, a 'Bull' speculator acts when securities are on the rise, while
a 'Bear' speculator acts when securities fall: the former buys hoping to sell at
a higher price, while the latter sells hoping to be able to buy back at a lower
price.

[27] Cox, *The Market as God*, pp. 16–17.

theories are all deviations from the one true faith – in other words, heresies. In the Great Recession of 2007–2009, I saw the kind of crisis that shakes the foundations of belief. But faith is strengthened by adversity, and the market religion emerged buttressed and renewed from its trial by financial heterodoxies.[28]

There is one more detail I'd like to add: there is a reason that Jehovah is a quick-tempered and cruel god, and it is provided by Friedrich Nietzsche in a much-studied passage from *Genealogy of Morals*. His reason is that 'The feeling of "ought," of personal obligation [. . .] has had, as we saw, its origin in the oldest and most original personal relationship that there is, the relationship between buyer and seller, creditor and debtor.' 'Whence is it that this ancient deep-rooted and now perhaps ineradicable idea has drawn its strength, this idea of an equivalency between injury and pain? [. . .] in the contractual relationship between creditor and debtor.' It is these relationships that give rise (in the case of insolvency) to the need for the debtor to atone, and therefore 'the creditor is granted by way of repayment and compensation a certain sensation of satisfaction – the satisfaction of being able to vent, without any trouble, his power on one who is powerless, the delight of', '*de faire le mal pour le plaisir de le faire*', doing evil for evil's sake, 'the joy in sheer violence [. . .] Thanks to the "punishment" of the debtor, the creditor participates in the rights of the masters. At last he too, for once in a way, attains the edifying consciousness of being able to despise and ill-treat a creature – as an "inferior" [. . .] The compensation consequently consists in a claim on cruelty and a right to draw thereon.'[29]

---

[28] Ibid., pp. 6–7.
[29] Friedrich Nietzsche, *The Genealogy of Morals: A Polemic* (1887), available at: https://www.gutenberg.org/files/52319/52319-h/52319-h.htm, citations from chapters 8, 4 and 5, respectively.

How can we help but think of what the Troika of creditors imposed on Greece the debtor when we read these phrases? Did their use of a diktat to decree even the shape of bread loaves not perhaps give them 'the satisfaction of being able to vent, without any trouble, his power on one who is [in this case, a country] powerless'? Did the supposedly 'frugal' nations of Northern Europe not finally reach 'the edifying consciousness of being able to despise and ill-treat' those Greek layabouts as 'inferior'?

But there is another detail shared by capital and the gods spoken about by Nietzsche, and it is the 'inexpiability', 'impossibility of paying the penalty' of debt to both capital and the gods.[30] The theologian Cox also probes into the relationship between old religions and the new faith in the market, coming to the conclusion that the most probable solution is that the ancient gods will submit to the new divinity and live in its shadow, just as identities can flourish in the globalizing shadow of capital: 'it seemed highly unlikely that traditional religions would rise to the occasion and challenge the doctrines of the new dispensation. Most of them seemed content to become its acolytes or to be absorbed into its pantheon, much as the old Nordic deities, after putting up a game fight, eventually settled for a diminished but secure status as Christian saints'.[31]

But perhaps Cox's more consequence-laden observation is made when he says that the Market is a demanding god: 'So the Market God needs to transform people from what they once were into people prepared to receive and act on its message. They have to be born again. They have to be reconfigured.'[32]

'Born again' is an expression that perhaps has little significance in Europe but is highly relevant in the United States (for example, president George W. Bush proclaimed

---

[30] Ibid., chapters 20, 21.
[31] Cox, *The Market as God*, p. 20.
[32] Ibid., p. 193.

himself proud to be 'born again'). It means being reborn to a new life after experiencing God. And the decisive rational maximizer, the choice and use of means to reach the aims theorized by Gary Becker is essentially the person *born again* to a capitalist life.

It is on this terrain of faith that the great 'secular' centres for study, Washington's conservative think tanks, connect with the possessed Pentecostal mystics. As a member of the conservative Ludwig von Mises Institute said in 1980: 'Our people deal in absolutes.'[33]

[33] Lewis H. Lapham, 'Tentacles of Rage: The Republican Propaganda Mill, A Brief History', *Harper's Magazine*, September 2004, pp. 31–41, p. 41.

# Bibliography

Anonymous, *Treatise of the Three Imposters*. New York: The Mantle, 2015 [1719]. Also available at: https://www.gutenberg.org/files/50 534/50534-h/50534-h.htm.

Althusser, Louis, 'Ideology and Ideological State Apparatuses (Notes Towards an Investigation)', in *On Ideology*. London: Verso, 2008.

Anderson, Perry, 'Renewals', *New Left Review*, no. 1, January–February 2000, pp. 5–24.

Aristotle, *Politics*, Book V (trans. Benjamin Jowett). Oxford: Clarendon Press, 1885. Available at: https://www.files.ethz.ch/isn /125519/5013_Aristotle_Politics.pdf.

Arriagada Herrera, Genaro and Carol Graham, 'Chile: Sustaining Adjustment during Democratic Transition', in Stephan Haggard and Steven B. Webb (eds.), *Voting for Reform: Democracy, Political Liberalization, and Economic Adjustment*. New York: Oxford University Press for the World Bank, 1994, pp. 242–89.

Austen-Smith, David and Jeffrey Banks, 'Elections, Coalitions, and Legislative Outcomes', *American Political Science Review*, vol. 82, no. 2, 1988, pp. 405–22.

Barkan, Joanne, 'Plutocrats at Work: How Big Philanthropy Undermines Democracy', *Dissent*, Autumn 2013.

Barry, Brian, *Sociologists, Economists and Democracy*. Chicago, IL: University of Chicago Press, 1970.

Barthes, Roland, *Mythologies*. London: Vintage Books, 2000.

Baum, Sandy, *The Evolution of Student Debt in the U.S.: An Overview*. The Urban Institute, George Washington University, October 2013.

Becker, Gary, 'Crime and Punishment: An Economic Approach', *Journal of Political Economy*, vol. 76, no. 2, March–April 1968, pp. 169–217.

Becker, Gary, *A Treatise on the Family* (1981). Cambridge, MA: Harvard University Press, 1991.

Benjamin, Walter, *Capitalism as Religion* [Fragment, 1921], available at: https://cominsitu.wordpress.com/2018/06/08/capitalism-as-re ligion-benjamin-1921/.

Bloch, Ernst, *Thomas Müntzer als Theologe der Revolution* (1921). Frankfurt am Main: Suhrkamp, 1977.

Bloom, Allan, 'Our Listless Universities', *The National Review*, 10 December 1982.

Bonney, Richard, *False Prophets: The 'Clash of Civilization' and the War on Terror*. Oxford: Peter Lang, 2008.

Bourdieu, Pierre, 'Les modes de domination', *Actes de la Recherche en Sciences Sociales*, vol. 2, no. 2–3, June 1976, pp. 122–32. See also *Outline of a Theory of Practice*. Cambridge: Cambridge University Press, 1977.

Bourdieu, Pierre, *Masculine Domination*. Stanford, CA: Stanford University Press, 2001.

Bourdieu, Pierre, *Practical Reason. On the Theory of Action*. Cambridge: Polity, 2001.

Boxer, Charles Ralph, *The Dutch Seaborne Empire 1600–1800* (1965). London: Penguin, 1973.

Boyer, Paul, *When Time Shall Be No More: Prophecy Belief in Modern American Culture*. Cambridge, MA: Harvard University Press, 1992.

Brown, Wendy, 'American Nightmare: Neoliberalism, Neo-conservatism, and De-Democratization', *Political Theory*, vol. 34, no. 6, December 2006, pp. 690–714.

Brown, Wendy, *Undoing the Demos: Neoliberalism's Stealth Revolution*. New York: Zone Books, 2015.

Canfora, Luciano, *Critica della retorica democratica [Critique of Democratic Rhetoric]*. Rome-Bari: Laterza, 2011.

Carnegie, Andrew, *The Gospel of Wealth and Other Writings*. New York: Penguin Classics, 2006.

CEPS (Centre for European Political Studies) Task Force Report, *Benchmarking in the EU: Lessons from the EU Emissions Trading System for the Global Climate Change Agenda*. Brussels, 2010.

Coase, Ronald H., 'The Nature of the Firm', *Economica*, vol. 4, no. 16, November 1937, pp. 386–405.

Coase, Ronald H., 'The Problem of Social Cost', *Journal of Law and Economics*, vol. 3, October 1960, pp. 1–44. Reprinted in Ronald H. Coase, *The Firm, the Market, and the Law*. Chicago, IL: University of Chicago Press, 1988, pp. 95–156.

Coase, Ronald H., 'Economics and Contiguous Disciplines', *The Journal of Legal Studies*, vol. 7, no. 2, June 1978, pp. 201–11.

Coase, Ronald H., *How Should Economists Choose?*, Washington, DC: American Enterprise Institute, 1982, available at: https://www.aei.org/wp-content/uploads/2016/03/NutterLectures03.pdf.

Constant, Benjamin, 'Des réactions politiques' (1797), in *De la force du government actuel de la France et de la nécessité de s'y rallier. Des réactions politiques. Des effets de la terreur*, Paris: Flammarion, 1988, pp. 91–159.

Conwell, Russell H., *Acres of Diamonds*. New York: Harper & Brothers, 1915, available at: https://web.archive.org/web/2013010 1215120/http://www.temple.edu/about/history/acres-diamonds.

Cox, Harvey, *The Market as God*. Cambridge, MA: Harvard University Press, 2016.

Davis, Mike, *Late Victorian Holocausts: El Niño Famines and the Making of the Third World*. London: Verso, 2001.

Debord, Guy, *The Society of the Spectacle*. Critical Editions, 2021.

Deleuze, Gilles, *Postscript on the Societies of Control* (1990), available at: https://theanarchistlibrary.org/library/gilles-deleuze-postscript-on-the-societies-of-control.

Deleuze, Gilles and Félix Guattari, *Anti-Oedipus. Capitalism and Schizophrenia*. Minneapolis, MN: University of Minnesota Press, 2000.

Deloitte ArtTactic, Art & Finance Report 2017, https://www2.delo itte.com/content/dam/Deloitte/at/Documents/finance/art-and-fi nance-report-2017.pdf.

d'Eramo, Marco, *La logica del vivente vent'anni dopo. Intervista a François Jacob [The Logic of Life Twenty Years On. Interview with François Jacob]*, in AA.VV., *Dalle forze ai codici [From Forces to Codes]*. Rome: manifestolibri, 1992, pp. 49–63.

d'Eramo, Marco, *The Pig and the Skyscraper. Chicago: A History of Our Future*. London: Verso, 2002.

d'Eramo, Marco, *Via dal vento. Viaggio nel profondo sud degli Stati Uniti [Away From the Wind. A Journey Through The Deep South of the United States]*. Rome: manifestolibri, 2004.

Dobkin Hall, Peter, 'Philanthropy, the Nonprofit Sector & the Democratic Dilemma', *Daedalus*, vol. 142, no. 2, Spring 2013, pp. 139–58.

Durand, Jacques, 'Rhétorique du nombre' [The Rhetoric of Numbers], *Communications*, no. 16, 1970, pp. 125–32.

Fagan, Patrick, *Why Religion Matters: The Impact of Religious Practice on Social Stability*, 25 January 1996, https://www.heritage.org/ci vil-society/report/why-religion-matters-the-impact-religious-pr actice-social-stability.

Fink, Richard, 'From Ideas to Action: The Role of Universities, Think Tanks and Activist Groups', *Philanthropy*, vol. 10, no. 1, Winter 1996.

Fisher, Mark, *Capitalist Realism: Is There No Alternative?* Winchester: Zero Books, 2009.

Fogel, Robert William, *Without Consent or Contract: The Rise and Fall of American Slavery* (1989). New York: Norton, 1994.

Fogel, Robert William and Stanley L. Engerman, *Time on the Cross: The Economics of American Negro Slavery*. New York: Norton, 1974.

Foucault, Michel, *The Birth of Biopolitics: Lectures at the Collège de France, 1978–1979*. New York: Picador, 2010. French original: *Naissance de la biopolitique. Cours au Collège de France, 1978–1979*. Paris: Gallimard-Seuil, 2004.

Foucault, Michel (ed.), *I, Pierre Rivière, having slit the throats of my mother, my sister and my brother: a Case of Parricide in the 19th Century*. Lincoln, NE: University of Nebraska Press, 1982.

Fox Piven, Frances and Richard A. Cloward, *Why Americans Still Don't Vote: And Why Politicians Want It That Way*. New York: Pantheon Books, 1988.

Friedman, Milton, 'The Role of Government in Education', in Robert A. Solo (ed.), *Economics and the Public Interest*. New Brunswick, NJ: Rutgers University Press, 1955, pp. 123–44, available at: https://la.utexas.edu/users/hcleaver/330T/350kPEEFriedmanRo leOfGovttable.pdf.

Friedman, Milton, 'The Case for the Negative Income Tax', *National Review*, 7 March 1967, pp. 239–41.

Friedman, Milton, *The Optimum Quantity of Money, and Other Essays*. London: Macmillan, 1969.

Friedman, Milton, *Capitalism and Freedom* (1962). Chicago, IL: University of Chicago Press, 2002.

*G20/OECD Principles of Corporate Governance*. Paris: OECD Publishing, 2015.

Geddes, Barbara, *Paradigms and Sand Castles: Theory Building and Research Design in Comparative Politics*. Ann Arbor, MI: University of Michigan Press, 2003.

George, Susan, *The Debt Boomerang: How Third World Debt Harms Us All*. London: Pluto Press, 1992.

Graeber, David, *Debt: The First 5,000 Years* (2011). London: Melvin House, 2014.

Harberger, Arnold C., 'Secrets of Success: A Handful of Heroes', *The American Economic Review*, vol. 83, no. 2, May 1993, pp. 343–50.

Hayek, Friedrich August von, *The Road to Serfdom* (1944) (The Reader's Digest condensed version as it appeared in April 1945). London: Institute of Economic Affairs, 2001.

Hayek, Friedrich August von, 'The Intellectuals and Socialism' (1949), in George B. de Huszar (ed.), *The Intellectuals: A Controversial Portrait*. Glencoe, IL: The Free Press, 1960, pp. 371–84.

Hayek, Friedrich August von, *The Mirage of Social Justice: Law, Legislation and Liberty vol. 2*. Chicago, IL: University of Chicago Press, 1976.

Hawkins, Helen S., G. Allen Greb and Gertrud Weiss Szilárd (eds.), *Toward a Livable World: Leo Szilárd and the Crusade for Nuclear Arms Control* (Collected Works of Leo Szilárd, vol. III). Cambridge, MA: MIT Press, 1987.

Heinlein, Robert, *Starship Troopers* (1958). London: Hodder, 2015.

Hirschman, Albert Otto, *The Rhetoric of Reaction: Perversity, Futility, Jeopardy*. Cambridge, MA: The Belknap Press of Harvard University, 1991.

Hobbes, Thomas, *Leviathan: Or the Matter, Form and Power of a Commonwealth, Ecclesiastic and Civil* (1651), available at: https://www.globalgreyebooks.com/leviathan-ebook.html#downloads.

Hofstadter, Douglas R., *Gödel, Escher, Bach: An Eternal Golden Braid* (1979). New York: Basic Books, 2008.

Hume, David, 'On the First Principles of Government', *Essays and Treatises on Several Subjects*, 1758 edition, in *Political Essays*, Cambridge: Cambridge University Press, 1994.

Jackson, Kenneth T., *Crabgrass Frontier: The Suburbanization of the United States*. New York: Oxford University Press, 1985.

Jacob, François, *The Logic of Life. A History of Heredity*. New York: Pantheon Books, 1982.

Johnson, Chalmers, *The Sorrows of Empire: Militarism, Secrecy, and the End of the Republic*. New York: Metropolitan, 2004.

Kitch, Edmund W., 'The Fire of Truth: A Remembrance of Law and Economics at Chicago, 1932–1970', *Journal of Law and Economics*, vol. 26, April 1983, pp. 163–234.

Kolbert, Elizabeth, 'Gospels of Giving for the New Gilded Age', *The New Yorker*, 28 August 2018.

Kruse, Kevin M., *One Nation Under God: How Corporate America Invented Christian America*. New York: Basic Books, 2015.

La Boétie, Étienne de, *The Politics of Obedience: The Discourse of Voluntary Servitude* (1554), available at: http://www.public-libra ry.uk/ebooks/16/4

Landes, Elisabeth M. and Richard A. Posner, 'The Economics of the Baby Shortage', *Journal of Legal Studies*, vol. 7, no. 2, 1978, pp. 323–48.

Lapham, Lewis H., 'Tentacles of Rage: The Republican Propaganda Mill, A Brief History', *Harper's Magazine*, September 2004, pp. 31–41.

Laumonier, Alexandre, *6/5*, Brussels: Éditions Zones sensibles, 2013.

Lavinas, Lena, '21st Century Welfare', *New Left Review*, no. 84, November–December 2013, pp. 5–40.

Lazzarato, Maurizio, *Governing By Debt*. South Pasadena, CA: Semiotext(e), 2015.

Lippmann, Walter, 'A Theory about Corruption', *Vanity Fair*, November 1930, pp. 61, 90.

Machiavelli, Niccolò, *Discourses on Livy*. Oxford: Oxford University Press, 2008.

Macpherson, C.B., *The Political Theory of Possessive Individualism: Hobbes to Locke*. Oxford: Oxford University Press, 1962.

Manne, Henry, 'Mergers and the Market for Corporate Control', *Journal of Political Economy*, vol. 73, no. 2, April 1965, pp. 110–20.

Marx, Karl, 'Class Struggle in France: 1848–1850', in Karl Marx and Friedrich Engels, *Selected Works in Three Volumes. Vol. 1*. Moscow: Progress Publishers, 1973.

Marx, Karl, *The Grundrisse*. New York: Harper & Row, 1971.

Marx, Karl, *Capital. A Critique of Political Economy. Volume 1*. London: Penguin Classics, 1976.

Mayer, Jane, 'How Right-Wing Billionaires Infiltrated Higher Education', *The Chronicle Review*, 12 February 2016.

Mayer, Jane, *Dark Money: The Hidden History of the Billionaires Behind the Rise of the Radical Right* (2016). New York: Penguin Random House, 2017.

Mayer, Jane, 'One Koch Brother Forces the Other Out of the Family Business', *The New Yorker*, 8 June 2018.

McCloskey, Deirdre, *The Rhetoric of Economics* (1985). Madison, WI: University of Wisconsin Press, 1998.

McGann, James G., *2017 Global Go To Think Tank Index Report*. Think Tanks and Civil Societies Program (TTCSP), University of Pennsylvania 2018, available at: https://repository.upenn.edu/th ink_tanks/13.

McKinnon, Andrew M., 'Ideology and the Market Metaphor in Rational Choice Theory of Religion: A Rhetorical Critique of "Religious Economies"', *Critical Sociology*, vol. 39, no. 4, 2013, pp. 529–43.

Medema, Steven G., 'Embracing at Arm's Length: Ronald Coase's Uneasy Relationship with the Chicago School', 29 July 2019, available at: http://dx.doi.org/10.2139/ssrn.3428759.

Michael, Robert T. and Gary S. Becker, 'On the New Theory of Consumer Behavior', *Swedish Journal of Economics*, vol. 75. no. 4, December 1973, pp. 378–96.

Michéa, Jean-Claude, *L'empire du moindre mal. Essai sur la civilisation libérale [The Empire of the Lesser Evil. Essay on Liberal Civilisation]* (2007). Paris: Flammarion, 2010.

Miller, John J., *Strategic Investment in Ideas: How Two Foundations Reshaped America*. Washington, DC: Philanthropy Roundtable, 2003.

Miller, John J., *A Gift of Freedom: How the John Olin Foundation Changed America*. New York: W.W. Norton & Co., 2009.

Mirowski, Philip and Dieter Plehwe (eds.), *The Road from Mont Pelerin: The Making of the Neoliberal Thought Collective*. Cambridge, MA: Harvard University Press, 2009.

Murray, Charles, *Losing Ground: American Social Policy 1950–1980*. New York: Basic Books, 1984.

Myrdal, Gunnar, *An American Dilemma: The Negro Problem and Modern Democracy*. New York: Harper & Row, 1944.

Nietzsche, Friedrich, *The Genealogy of Morals: A Polemic* (1887). London: Penguin Classics, 2013, available at: https://www.guten berg.org/files/52319/52319-h/52319-h.htm.

North, Douglass C., *Structure and Change in Economic History*. New York: W.W. Norton & Co., 1981.

Nozick, Robert, *Anarchy, State, and Utopia*. Oxford: Blackwell, 1974.

OECD, 'Dépenses de santé en proportion du PIB', in *Health at a Glance 2017: OECD Indicators*. Paris: OECD Publishing, 2017, available at: https://www.oecd-ilibrary.org/docserver/health_glan ce-2017-45-fr.pdf.

Orwell, George, 'Politics and the English Language', *Horizons*, April 1946, available at: https://www.orwell.ru/library/essays/politics /english/e_polit.

Orwell, George, *Nineteen Eighty-Four* (1949). London: Penguin Classics, 2004.

Paine, Thomas, *Common Sense; Addressed to the Inhabitants of America, on the following interesting Subjects. i. Of the Origin and Design of Government in general, with concise Remarks on the English Constitution. ii. Of Monarchy and Hereditary Succession. iii: Thoughts on the present State of American Affairs. iv. Of the Present Ability of America, with some miscellaneous Reflections. Written by an Englishman* (Printed, and Sold, by R. Bell, in Third-Street, Philadelphia, 1776), available at: loc.gov/item/2006681076.

Pope Paul VI (Giovanni Battista Montini), *Gaudium et spes, Pastoral Constitution*, 7 December 1965, https://www.vatican.va/archive /hist_councils/ii_vatican_council/documents/vat-ii_const_19651 207_gaudium-et-spes_it.html.

Petraeus, D.H. and James Ames, *The U.S. Army/Marine Corps Counterinsurgency Field Manual*. Chicago, IL: University of Chicago Press, 2007. Alternatively, *FM-324: Counterinsurgency* can be downloaded from https://fas.org/irp/doddir/army/fm3-24 fd.pdf.

Phillips-Fein, Kim, *Invisible Hands: The Making of the Conservative Movement from the New Deal to Reagan*. New York: Norton, 2009.

Piereson, James, 'Planting the Seeds of Liberty', *Philanthropy*, May– June 2005.

Piketty, Thomas, *Brahmin Left vs Merchant Right: Rising Inequality and the Changing Structure of Political Conflict (Evidence from*

*France, Britain and the US, 1948–2017)*, WID.world Working Paper Series 2018/7. EHESS and Paris School of Economics, March 2018, available at: http://piketty.pse.ens.fr/files/Piketty2018.pdf.

Plato, *The Republic*, 338c–339a. Cambridge: Cambridge University Press, 2000.

Pongide, Cobol, *Marte oltre Marte. L'era del capitalismo multiplanetario*. Rome: DeriveApprodi, 2019.

Posner, Richard A., 'The Regulation of the Market in Adoptions', *Boston University Law Review*, vol. 67, 1987, pp. 59–72.

Powell, Lewis F., *Attack on American Free Enterprise System*. Confidential Memorandum to the US Chamber of Commerce, 23 August 1971, available at: https://www.historyisaweapon.com/defcon1/powellmemo.html.

Radden Keefe, Patrick, 'The Family That Built an Empire of Pain', *The New Yorker*, 30 October 2017.

Reich, Rob, *Just Giving: Why Philanthropy Is Failing Democracy and How It Can Do Better*. Princeton, NJ: Princeton University Press, 2018.

Riker, William H., *The Theory of Political Coalitions*. New Haven, CT: Yale University Press, 1962.

Riker, William H., 'The Political Psychology of Rational Choice Theory', *Political Psychology*, vol. 16, no. 1, 1995, pp. 23–44.

Robinson, Joan, *Economic Philosophy*. Harmondsworth: Penguin Books, 1962, available at: https://web.archive.org/web/20160221095721/http://digamo.free.fr/ecophilo.pdf.

Romano, Roberta, 'After the Revolution in Corporate Law', *Journal of Legal Education*, vol. 55, no. 3, 2005, pp. 342–59.

Roncaglia, Alessandro, *L'età della disgregazione. Storia del pensiero economico contemporaneo [The Age of Disgregation. History of contemporary Economic Thought]*. Rome-Bari: Laterza, 2019.

Röpke, Wilhelm, *Civitas Humana. A Humane Order of Society*. London: William Hodge, 1948.

Röpke, Wilhelm, *The Social Crisis of Our Time*. Chicago, IL: University of Chicago Press, 1950, available at: https://mises.org/library/social-crisis-our-time.

Rousseau, Jean-Jacques, *Discourse on Political Economy* (1755), available at: https://www.files.ethz.ch/isn/125495/5020_Rousseau _A_Discourse_on_Political_Economy.pdf

Rousseau, Jean-Jacques, *Discourse on Political Economy and The Social Contract.* Oxford: Oxford University Press, 1994.

Sassen, Saskia, *Territory, Authority, Rights: From Medieval to Global Assemblages* (2006). Princeton, NJ: Princeton University Press, 2008.

Savage, John, 'The John Birch Society is Back', *Politico*, 16 June 2017.

Scalia, Antonin, 'The Two Faces of Federalism', *Harvard Journal of Law and Public Policy*, vol. 6, no. 1, 1982, pp. 19–22.

Schor, Juliet B., *The Overspent American: Why We Want What We Don't Need.* New York: Harper, 1999.

Schultz, Theodore W., *Investment in Human Capital: The Role of Education and of Research.* New York: Free Press, 1971.

Schumpeter, Joseph A., *Capitalism, Socialism and Democracy.* London: Allen and Unwin, 1976.

Sharlet, Jeff, 'Jesus Plus Nothing: Undercover among America's Secret Theocrats', *Harper's Magazine*, March 2003, pp. 53–64.

Sjaastad, Larry A., 'The Costs and Returns of Human Migration', in *Investment in Human Beings, Journal of Political Economy*, vol. 70, no. 5, part 2, 1962, pp. 80–93.

Smith, Adam, *An Inquiry into the Nature and Causes of the Wealth of Nations* (1776), available at: http://geolib.com/smith.adam/wo n1-02.html.

Sombart, Werner, *The Quintessence of Capitalism: A Study of the History and Psychology of the Modern Business Man* (1913). New York: E.P. Dutton and Co., 1915.

Stark, Rodney and Roger Finke, *Acts of Faith: Explaining the Human Side of Religion.* Berkeley, CA: University of California Press, 2000.

Steiner, Jürg, 'Rational Choice Theories and Politics: A Research Agenda and a Moral Question', *PS: Political Science & Politics*, vol. 23, no. 1, March 1990, pp. 46–50.

Stigler, George J., 'The Optimum Enforcement of Laws', *Journal of Political Economy*, vol. 78, no. 3, May–June 1970, pp. 526–36.

Stigler, George J., 'Economics – The Imperial Science?', *Scandinavian Journal of Economics*, vol. 86, no. 3, 1984, pp. 301–13.

Stoléru, Lionel, *Vaincre la pauvreté dans les pays riches [Vanquishing Poverty in Rich Countries]*. Paris: Flammarion, 1977.

Storr, Virgil Henry, 'North's Underdeveloped Ideological Entrepreneur', in Emily Chamlee-Wright (ed.), *The Annual Proceedings of the Wealth and Well-Being of Nations, vol. 1, 2008–2009*, pp. 99–115, available at: https://papers.ssrn.com/sol3/papers.cfm?abstract_id=1738823.

Teles, Steven M., *The Rise of the Conservative Legal Movement*. Princeton, NJ: Princeton University Press, 2010.

Traub, James, 'It's Time for the Elites to Rise Up Against the Ignorant Masses', *Foreign Policy*, 28 June 2016, https://foreignpolicy.com/2016/06/28/its-time-for-the-elites-to-rise-up-against-ignorant-masses-trump-2016-brexit/.

Vague, Richard, 'The Private Debt Crisis', *Democracy. A Journal of Ideas*, no. 42, Autumn 2016.

Vegetti, Matteo, *L'invenzione del globo. Spazio, potere, comunicazione nell'epoca dell'aria [The Invention of the Globe. Space, Power, Communication in the Age of Air]*. Turin: Einaudi, 2017.

Weber, Max, *The Protestant Ethic and The Spirit of Capitalism*. New York: Penguin Books, 2002.

Zinn, Howard, *A People's History of the United States: 1492–Present* (1980). New York: HarperCollins, 1999.

Zuboff, Shoshana, 'A Digital Declaration', *Die Frankfurter Allgemeine Zeitung Feuilleton*, 15 September 2014, available at: https://opencuny.org/pnmarchive/files/2019/01/Zuboff-Digital-Declaration.pdf.

Zuboff, Shoshana, 'Big Other: Surveillance Capitalism and the Prospects of an Information Civilization', *Journal of Information Technology*, vol. 30, 2015, pp. 75–89.

Zuboff, Shoshana, *The Age of Surveillance Capitalism: The Fight for a Human Future at the New Frontier of Power*. London: Profile Books, 2019.

# Index

n denotes entries in notes

AAA ratings 148–9
abortion 64
absolute poverty 68
Abu Ghraib (Iraq) 175
*Acres of Diamonds* sermon 240–1
Adam Smith Institute 18
Adolph Coors Foundation 10
adoption system 61, 62, 64–5, 66
Adorno, Theodor 162
affirmative action 47
Africa 37, 100, 145, 162
air canisters 167–8, 183
'air farming' 168
air pollution 167
airline passengers, increase in
    number of 164
Akiba ben Joseph, Rabbi 209
Alabama 81
Alcoa (aluminium) 8
Algeria, independence 145
algorithms and finance 156

Alibaba 194
    marquis of 130
Aligica, Paul Dragos 211n
Alito, Samuel 117
Allegheny Foundation 8
Allende, Salvador 25
Althusser, Louis 2, 19
altruism 114–15
Amalgamated Association of
    Iron and Steel Workers 80
Amazon 133, 187, 194
    landgrave of 110
American Civil Liberties Union
    81
American Enterprise
    Association 21
American Enterprise Institute
    17, 19, 21–2, 43, 196n
American Express 139
American Federation of Labor
    (AFL) 81

Americans for Prosperity
    Foundation 12
American Prosecutors Research
    Institute 12
Ames, General James 1, 2n, 225n
Amoco 15
Amway 15
Anachronisms 203–9
*ancien régime* 230–1
Anderson, Perry 29
Angola, independence of 145
Antichrist 244
ants 176–9
Appalachia 82
Apple 159, 206
Argentina 25, 148n
Aristotle vii–viii, 54, 132, 249
Arizona 21
Armenia 173n
Aron, Raymond 118n
Ashcroft, John 58
Asia 145, 162, 174
Asimov, Isaac 87
asymmetry, between left and
    right 212–13
Atlas Economic Research
    Foundation (later Atlas
    Network) 18
Attlee, Clement 52
Austen-Smith, David 113n
austerity measures 92, 145
Australia 105, 173n
Austria 39n, 99
authoritarian state 48, 175

babies, free baby market 60–5,
    186
Bader, Lawson 22

Badiou, Alain 99
*Bailey v. Patterson* (1962) 217
Bakunin 101
Bank of America 139
Bankamericard 139
Banks, Jeffrey 13n
Bantam (Java) 174
Barahona, Pablo 26
Bardi and Peruzzi, Florentin
    bankers 137
Barkan, Joanne 74n, 76n, 85n
Barlett, Bruce 39n
Barry, Brian 199
Barthes, Roland 94, 95, 97, 99,
    100, 226
Bartlett, Bruce 39n
Bastille, prison (Paris) 7
Batista, Fulgencio vii
Baum, Sandy 140n
beachheads 44–8, 219
Becker, Gary 23, 33n, 35n, 56, 61,
    86n, 89, 114, 190, 197, 208,
    246, 253
    behaviourism of 170
    circular thought of 118, 199
    economic theory of crime
        54–5, 90
    Kipling of economic empire
        38, 54, 206
    Rotten Kid theorem 200–1
Beethoven, Ludwig van 197,
    210
Begin Menachem 238
Belarus 173n
benchmarking 105, 107–8, 114,
    147, 155–6
benevolence, tyranny of
    76–87

Benedict XVI, pope *see*
　Ratzinger, Joseph
Benjamin, Walter, *Capitalism
　As Religion* 248
Bentham, Jeremy 128
Berkshire Hathaway 150
Berlin Jewish Museum 82
Bernanke, Ben 109
best practices 107–8, 155–6
Beveridge, William 52
Bilderberg group, conspiracy
　theory 48n
Big Bang theory 202
Bill of Rights Institute 12
billionaires, collective wealth of
　11n
biology 202–3
biopolitics 29n
birth rates, decline in 172
black people 43, 97, 99–100
Black Rock 150
Blackwater, mercenaries' firm 72
Blair, Tony 91
Bloch, Ernst 248
Blokhin, Andriy 198n
Bloom, Allan 45–6, 49
　*The Closing of the American
　Mind* 46
Boeing 15
　marquis of 110
Bohr, Niels 169
*Bolsa Família* (Brazil) 69–70
Bolsonaro, Jair 133, 235
Bombay (Mumbai) 183
Bonaparte, Napoleon 230
Bonney, Richard 17n
'born again' 252–3
Bourdieu, Pierre 93, 225n

bourgeoise 137, 161
　ex-nominated class 94–5,
　226
Bouvard and Pécuchet 214–15
Bow Group 18
Boxer, Charles Ralph 174n
Boyer, Paul 240n
Bradley family 8, 9, 243
Bradley Foundation 9, 43, 44,
　46, 48, 216
Bradley, Harry 9, 243
brain, privatization of the 120–5
Brazil 118, 184
　healthcare spending 98
　judicial coup 133
　opposition to *Bolsa Família*
　　by capitalists 69–70
Brecht, Bertolt 99
Bremer Orders (2004) 174–5
Bremer, Paul 174
Britain 52
　debt level 140n
　healthcare spending 98
　homicides rate 99
　rating 148n
　think tanks 18
　university fees 186
Brookings Institute 19
*Brown v. Board of Education*
　(1954) 217
Brown, Wendy viii, 92, 96n,
　103, 105–8, 117, 123–4, 146,
　155–6, 174n, 235, 245
Brunei 173n
Brzezinski, Zbigniew 47–8n
Bukharin, Nikolai Ivanovich
　230
Buddha 209

Buffett, Warren viii–ix, 87, 150, 229, 231
Bundesbank 101
Burkina Faso 148n
Bush, George W. 44
  and Christian conservatives 235, 245, 252–3
  tax cuts 40
business ontology 100–11
Butt, Craig 167n

California 74, 221
Calvinism 248
Cambodia 173n
Camp, Robert 108
Canada 105, 173n
  debt level 140n
Canfora, Luciano 104n
capital 88–111
  acquiring the attributes of a divinity 96
  ambivalence of term 96
  ex-nomination of 94
  invasion of all our social relationships 95–6
  power of 126
  relationship between Christianity and big 242
  unspeakable nature of and reasons 94, 95–6
capitalism/capitalists 31–2, 153, 160, 164–5
  conception of as a system of unlimited expansion 165
  end of x
  internalization of dominion of 93–4
  passage from industry-

dominated to financially dominated 158
  relationship with the future 170–1
  religious and Christian dimension of 239–42, 247–8
  role of public debt in 136–7
  and space 165–6
  surveillance 130–2
  vanishing of term 93–4, 95
capitalist realism 100–1, 120
Caribbean 221
Carnegie, Andrew 79, 80, 85, 90, 241
  The Gospel of Wealth 78
Carnegie Foundation 78
Carte Bleue (France) 139
Carter, Jimmy 23–4, 48, 90–1
Carthage 20
  fall of 9
  Foundation 9, 21
Carthage Foundation 9
Casanova, Carlos Eugenio Vides 238
Casey, William 19
Castle Rock Foundation 10
Catalans, autonomists 74
Catholics 36–7
Cato Institute 20, 169n
Cato, Marcus Porcius 20
Catullus, Gaius Valerius 210
Centres for Disease Control and Prevention 83
CEPS (Centre for European Political Studies) Task Force Report 107n
Centre for Policy Studies 18

CETA (Comprehensive Economic and Trade Agreement) 173n
Chamber of Commerce 4, 7, 209
Chaplin, Charlie 158
Charles I, King vii
charter schools 72
Chase Manhattan Bank 15
Chavez, Linda, *Out of the Barrio* 43
Cheney, Richard 59
Chevron (Oil) 15
Chicago 139n, 249
Chicago School/Boys 23, 24, 25, 26, 27, 37, 38, 62, 69, 70, 86, 101, 194, 197
    University of 23, 26, 43, 44, 45, 48, 51, 52, 58, 187
Chile 28, 69, 157, 175
    coup led by Pinochet (1973) 25–6
    economic programme laid out in *El Ladrillo* 25–6
China 129, 154
    state capitalism 171
Chinese model, and neoliberals 171, 175
Christ, Jesus 52, 208, 209, 210, 215, 240
Christian Broadcasting Network (CBN) 244
Christian Coalition 245
Christianity, conservative
    *Acres of Diamonds* sermon 240–1
    attacks against Arabs 245
    and capitalism 239–43
    and neoliberalism 234–9

relationship between big capital and 242
    Scofield Reference Bible 239–40
    spreading of message through television 244–5
citizen activist groups 13, 14
Citizens for a Sound Economy Foundation 12n
*Citizen Kane* (film) 149
*Citizens United v. Federal Election Commission* (2010) 22, 116–17
Civil Rights Act (1964) 21
civil rights movement
    struggles (1960s) 217
    victories won 217
civilization, inequality and process of 90
Clarke, Conor 229n
class struggle 216, 219–20
class warfare viii–ix
classical economic theory 30
    neo- 165, 170
classical liberalism 28, 29, 103, 127
Cleopatra, nose of 96
Clinton, Bill 91, 168
Clinton, Hillary 238
Clio, muse of history 187
cliometrics, historic discipline 187, 189, 206
Cloward, Richard A. 116n
Coase, Ronald 30, 52–3, 169, 196–7, 198
    'Letter to the Gentiles' 53–4
    'The Problem of Social Cost' 53–4, 56

Coca-Cola 160, 162, 180
Coen, Jan Pieterszoon 174,
 193
Cola di Renzo 123
Colbert, Jean-Baptiste 174
Colcom Foundation 8
Cold War 243
collectivism, ants/termites
 metaphor for 177, 178–9
Collège de France 29, 103n
Colorado 8, 10, 80–1, 84
Columbus, Christopher 131
Comisión Rettig National de
 Verdad y Reconciliación
 (Chile) 25n
Comisión Valech Nacional
 sobre Prisión y Tortura
 (Chile) 25n
Compass Lexecon 60
common law 57, 218
'compassionate conservatism'
 44, 226
competition 90, 193, 194, 215,
 246
 and Freiburg School 246
 and inequality 90
 and neoliberalism 30
 and war 193
conditional cash transfers
 (CCTs) 69
Condor, Plan 25
Congo see Democratic
 Republic of Congo
Congress of the United States
 17, 44, 80, 84, 101n, 199,
 217, 218, 238
consequences, unintended
 172–82

conservative Christianity see
 Christianity, conservative
Constant, Benjamin 230–1
contiguous disciplines 199
Convention of the National
 Association of
 Manufacturers (1940) 242
Conwell, Russell Herman 240–1
Coors Adolph foundation 10
 family 8, 10, 158, 213, 224, 243
Coors, Joe 10, 14
Copernicus, Nicolaus 37
Coppin, Clayton 216n
Cornell, Ezra 44
Cornell University 3, 44, 61, 182
corporate governance 106
corporate law, revolution in 56
corruption 117–18
 and Lippmann's article 119
 as a politics 119–20
 and Tammany Hall 119
counter-insurgency 3
counterintelligentsia 1–22, 6–7,
 216
 coining of phrase 6
 and Olin foundation 3–4, 6
 and political power 6–7
 and Powell's memorandum
  (1971) 4–5, 117
 protagonists and wealthy
  families involved 7–11
 think tanks 14–22
 three stages of reconquest
  11–14
coups 25, 132, 230
 constitutional 21
 from above 132
 judicial 132–3

Covid-19 pandemic 102, 108,
    109, 129, 134
Cox, Harvey, *Market as God*
    249–51, 252
*coyotes* 32
Craig, Freedman 197n
credit 151
credit card, history 139
Crédit Suisse 27
credit system, universities 104–5
credit/debt relationship 154
creditor/debtor relationship
    251–2
creditors' right to cruelty 251
crime 118
    and 'optimum pollution'
        concept 54–6
Critical Legal Studies 58
Crozier, Michel 47
Cuba vii
Cuccia, Enrico 213
Cupertino (California) 159

Damascus (Syria), road to 61,
    161
D'Angelo, Gore 245n
dark profit 115
Dartmouth University 48
Darwinism 203
Davis, Mike 162n
Debord, Guy 134
debt 136–58, 252
    conditions imposed by the
        Troika 147
    and credit card 139
    and developing countries 144,
        145–6
    environmental damage seen

as a debt to pay off in the
    future 171–2
as essential tool of geopolitics
    143–4
financing of rich countries by
    poor countries 145–6
household/family 139–40
Marx on public 136–8
as a mode of domination
    150–3
and mortgages 138–9
with 'nature' 171
and neoliberalism 143–4
and ratings agencies 147–50
'rescue plans' and austerity
    measures 144–5
role in capitalism 136–7
student 140–3
used as a tool for political
    control 138–9
in United States 153–4
use of as tool to restrain
    entire populations 146–7
debt crisis (1982) 144–6
debt mentality, and relation to
    the future 171–2
deforestation 164
Deleuze, Gilles 110, 143
Deloitte 94
democracy 50
    crisis of 47–8
Democratic Republic of Congo
    rating 148
    taxes 99
Demsetz, Harold 61
Denmark 39n, 63
Deparle, Jason 52n, 192n
department stores 55

D'Eramo, Marco 139n, 203n, 218n
deregulation 49, 59, 62, 73, 147
desertification 163
developing countries
    debts 144, 145–6
    dumping toxic waste proposal 168–9
    lending to 144
DeVos, Betsy 72
DeVos family 8, 72
'dialectics of Enlightenment' 162
Dias, Elizabeth 238n
Diners Club, credit card 139
Director, Aaron 52, 61
disciplinary power 127–8, 129, 142, 163
divorce 34–5
DNA 204
    as human capital 33
Dobkin Hall, Peter 77n
dominant
    fighting the 160
    learning from the 222–33
domination 225
    and power 220
dominion 220
Donors Capital Fund 22
Donors Trust 22
Dorset (England) 168
Dostoevsky, Fyodor 54
double truths, theory of 119
Dow Chemical 15
Draghi, Mario 91
D'Souza, Dinesh, *Illiberal Education* 47
Duffy, Michael 17n

Dulles, Allen 9, 243
Dulles, John Foster 22
Durand, Jacques 194n
Dutch East India Company 174, 194

EACU (Eurasian Custom Union) 173n
Earharts 8
economic circuit, circular thought of the 193–211
economics
    and mathematical modelling 195–6
    *see also* Law and Economics
*Economist* 171n, 173
economy
    definition of by Chicago School 37
    of religion 248–9
education 66–7, 184, 229–30
    and parent power 72–5
    and Parent Trigger laws 72, 74–5
    privatization of 66–7, 70–2
    public 70–1, 229–30
    and vouchers 66–7, 71, 72, 184
Edward III, King 136
Eisenhower, Dwight D. 9, 47, 243
Ekaterinburg vii
electoral campaigns
    financial contributions to 22
    spending on 112
electronic money 129
El Salvador 148n
Emanuel, Rahm ix, 110

empire 20, 38, 60, 83n, 87, 104,
    162, 172, 220, 227
  US ix, 60, 154, 161, 226–7
Engels, Friedrich 137n, 216
Engerman, Stanley L. 188n,
    190n, 219n
Enron 148
enterprises 30–1
entrepreneurship/entrepreneur
    203–11
  ideological 208–11, 219
  musician as 210
  and neoliberalism 203–4, 206
environmental market 167
environmental problems 163–4
  relationship between market
    economy and 166–9
  seen as a debt to pay off in the
    future 171–2
epistemological imperialism
    206–7
Erhard, Ludwig 177
Eros Centers (Germany) 185
Ethiopia 148n
eugenics 62–3
euphemisms, fight against 225–9
European Central Bank 48n, 91,
    147, 159
European Union 39n, 44, 92,
    147, 173n
Evangelical Foreign Missions
    Association 243
Extinction, sixth mass 164
Exxon 15, 57, 117

Facebook 110, 130, 131, 132, 179,
    194
facial recognition software 129

Fagan, Patrick 237n
Fairfax (Virginia) 56
Falwell, Jerry 245
Fama, Eugene 23
family 246
'Family, The' 238
Federal Housing Administration
    (FHA) 73
Federal Reserve 16n, 39, 48n,
    109
Federalist Papers 26
Federalist Society 58–9, 117
feedback 172–3
Fellowship Foundation 238
feudalism 227, 231
Fifield Jr, James W. 242
finance 154–8
financial crisis (2008) 102, 108–9
Fink, Richard 209–10
  accumulation of titles and
    positions 12n
  *The Structure of the Social
    Change* 12–13, 14
Fink, Roger 36
firearms 43–4, 99
Fisher, Anthony 18, 19
Fisher, Mark 100–1, 120n, 143n
  *Capitalism Realism* x
Fitch, rating agency 148, 149
Flaubert, Gustave 214–15
Florida 57, 238
Fogel, Robert William 187–8,
    206, 219, 289–90
Forbes 11n, 39n, 46, 82, 216,
    229n
Ford Foundation 213–14
Ford II, Henry, resignation letter
    213–14

*Foreign Policy* magazine 185
Foucault, Michel 29, 33–4, 39,
    40–1, 59, 60, 88, 101, 103n,
    110–11, 127, 143, 193, 194,
    204, 220
Fouché, Joseph 230
Foundation Center 76n, 84n
foundations 4, 8–10, 13
    anti-democratic nature of
        84–5
    attacks on the state 42
    criticism of 80–1, 85–6
    denial of global warming
        166–7
    donations to think tanks 22
    financing of privatization of
        education 71–2
    financing of universities 44–9,
        58
    imbalance between far right
        and left 212–14
    increase in numbers of in the
        US and wealth of 84
    and Law and Economics
        216–17
    non-accountability of and
        not subject to competition
        rules 85–6
    and process of euphemization
        227–8
    strategy of 11–12
    as tax exempt 76–8, 87
    tyranny of benevolence 76–87
    using of state's own money in
        order to demolish it 76–7
    *see also* individual names
Fox Kids Worldwide 244
Fox Piven, Frances 116n

France 11n, 122, 136, 137n, 139,
    150, 220, 224n
    debt level 140n
    colonial empire172–3
    healthcare spending 98
    homicides rate 99
Frankfurt (Germany) 159, 177n
free baby market 60–5, 186
free enterprise 38, 102, 110–11
free market 27, 52, 191, 226
    as a real faith 247
free trade 173
freedom 180–1
freedom of movement 181
Freedom Partners 16–17
Freiburg School 246
French Revolution 230
Friedman, Milton 23, 27–8, 30,
    66–7, 68, 69, 109
Friedman, Rose 28
'frugal state' 39, 40
Fukuyama, Francis 47
fundamentalism 240, 247
    market 29
    religious 189
futility 42, 99, 100, 125
future 170–1
    erasure of due to being
        mortgaged by past debt 172

Gagarin, Yuri 166n
Galbraith, John Kenneth x
Galilei, Galileo 169
'game is rigged' 212–21
game theory 196
Gandhi, Indian political dynasty
    245
gated communities 183

Gates, Bill 85, 87
  Bill & Melinda Foundation
    20, 71
Geddes, Barbara 200n
General Electric 242
General Motors 15, 242
genetics, and human capital
    33–4
geopolitics, debt as essential tool
    of 143–4
George Mason University
    School of Law (GMUSL) 57
George Mason University
    (Washington) 49
Georgetown University 48, 58
George, Susan 145
Georgia 129, 218
Germany 122, 123, 150, 185
  debt level 140n
  healthcare spending 98
  homicides rate 99
  German ordo-liberals 28,
    176–7, 178, 246
gift economy 136
Gingrich, Newt 8, 44
Giscard d'Estaing, Valéry 67
global warming 163, 183, 193
  denial of 49, 82, 166–7
globalization 102, 247
God, market as 249, 252
God Bless America 244
Goldwasser, Michael 21
Goldwater, Barry 8, 21, 27,
    243–4
Gompers, Samuel 81
Google 130–1, 132, 157, 179, 194
  maps 135
  prince of 110, 130

Gore, Al 21
governance 106–7
Graeber, David 126–7, 159, 182
Graham, Billy 243
Graham, Carol 26n
Graham, Franklin 245
Gramsci, Antonio 46, 214, 216
Great Depression 73, 242
Greb, G. Allen 181n
Greece 157, 252
  debt crisis 147
Greeks, ancient 135
green economy 167n
Greenpeace 82
Greenspan, Alan 39, 48n
*Griggs v. Duke Power Co.* (1971)
    217
*Guardian* 15n, 63n, 76n, 83n,
    131n, 168n
Guattari, Félix 110
guilt 97, 152, 158, 172, 248
Gulf (Oil) 8
*Gulliver's Travels* 46, 63
gunpowder, invention of 135
guns 43–4, 99

Haggard, Stephan 26n
Haiti vii
Hall, Peter Dobkin 77n
Hannibal 9
Hansen, Peter 23
Harper's Magazine 10n, 238n,
    253n
Harvard University 47, 48, 49,
    58, 168
  John M. Olin Center for Law,
    Economics and Business 58
Harwick, Cameron 77n

Hawkins, Helen S. 181n
Hayek, Friedrich von 13, 23, 30,
    44, 88–90, 222–3
  on meaningless of social
    justice 27, 52, 88–9, 90, 100
  production model 13–14
  *The Road to Serfdom* 26–7, 41
Haynes Holmes, Rev. John 81
healthcare, public 20, 43, 69, 91,
    92, 98, 100, 104, 104, 123,
    149, 226
  spending 98
Hearst Communications 149
Hearst, William Randolph 149,
    209, 243
Hegel, Georg Wilhelm Friedrich
    201
hegemony 216
Heinlein, Robert
  *Methuselah's Children* 178
  *Starship Troopers* 177–8
Herberger, Arnold 26
Herbert, Frank, *Green Brain*
    177n
Heritage Foundation 14–15, 16,
    17, 19, 38–9
  *Mandate for Leadership* 17
  *The Nation Under Attack* 15
  and Reagan 17
  and Trump 15–16
  *Why Religion Matters* 237
Herodotus 209
Herrera, Genaro Arriagada 26n
Herrnstein, Richard 43
Hirschman, Albert 42, 99, 175
Hobbes, Thomas 184
Hofstadter, Douglas R., 'Aunty
  Hillary' dialogue 178

holocausts, late Victorian 162
Holmes, John Haynes 81
Homestead (Pennsylvania), steel
    plant 80
*homo oeconomicus* 215, 228
Hoover, Herbert 20
Hoover Institution 17, 20–1, 23
Horkheimer, Max 162
Hudson Institute 19
human capital 31–4, 94, 96, 143,
    190, 247
  and divorce 34–5
  and genetics 33–4
  reading of all aspects of
    human life through 34–6
  and slavery 190–1
  and surveillance capitalism
    130–1
human organs, selling of 186–7
'humanitarian wars' 226
Hume, David 121, 122
Humphrey, Hubert 61
Huntington, Samuel 47–8, 185
  'Clash of Civilizations' 48
  *The Crisis of Democracy*
    47–8
  *The Soldier and the State* 47
Huszar, George B. 222n

Iceland 98
ideas
  production and sale of 12–14
  as weapons 6, 23–49, 222
ideological entrepreneur 208–11,
    219
ideological psychic capital 211
ideology(ies) 1–3, 216, 222–3,
    225

ideology(ies) (*cont.*)
  importance of in economic
    analysis 219
  intellectual entrepreneurs of
    208
  and narrative 2
  neoliberals and importance of
    219
  role of 125
  role in shaping human history
    207–8
  and US Army/Marine Corps
    Counterinsurgency Field
    Manual 1–2
Illinois 3
imperialism, epistemological
  206–7
income, psychic 199
India 162, 172–3, 183
indifference 155, 156
  radical 156–7
individualism, as bridge between
  Gospel and capitalism 243
Indonesia 173n
industrial revolution 154–5, 160,
  161, 164
industry 154–5
inequality 90, 221
  and competition 90
  growth of 220
  and process of civilization 90
inheritance 231
insects 176–9
Institute of Economic Affairs
  (IEA) 18
intellect, optimism of 214–15
intellectuals 222–3, 224
International Family

Entertainment Inc. 244
International Monetary Fund
  (IMF) 145
'invisible hand' 166
Iraq 174
  and Bremer Orders 174–5
Iron lady, *see* Thatcher,
  Margaret
irreversibility, problem of
  169–70
Islam 245
'isolated together' 134–5
Israel kingdom 152
Italian Communist Party 91, 161
Italy 74, 105, 154, 161
  healthcare spending 98
  homicides rate 99
  and public debt 150–1
  rating 148n

Jack Miller Center 12n
Jackson, Kenneth T. 73n
Jacob, François 202–3
Jakarta 174n
Japan 140n, 150, 173n, 250
  debt of 146n
jeopardy 42–3, 44
Jews 97
JM Foundation 8
Jobs, Steve posthumous
  apotheosis 206
John Birch Society 9, 10, 48n,
  218, 243–4
John Lackland, king 109
John Paul II, Pope 161
Johnson, Chalmers 226n
Johnson, Jay 169n
Johnson, Lyndon 21, 40

Johnston, David Cay 231n
Johnstown (Pennsylvania)
    flooding 79–80
Jones, Campbell 210n
*Jones v. H. Mayer Co.* (1971) 217,
    218
*Journal of Law and Economics*
    52, 56
Joyce, Michael 46, 216
judicial coups 132–3
judiciary, importance of to
    neoliberals 216–19
justice 49, 50–65, 117, 235
    defence of weak against
        the strong or vice versa
        question 50
    importance of to neoliberals
        59
    and Law and Economics
        53–60
    Von Hayek on meaningless
        of social 27, 52, 88–9, 90,
        100
justice market 50–65

Kafka, Joseph 151
Kaiser, Robert 113n
Kansas 8, 10, 239, 243
Kant, Immanuel 45
Karachi 183
Karaian, Jason 147n
Karolinska Institutet 24
Kazakhstan 173n
Keats, John 210
Kennedy, Antony 116n, 117
Kennedy, Bob 4
Kennedy, John 144
Key Largo (Florida) 57

Keynesianism 23
Khan, Jibran 24n
Khomeini, Ruhollah 208, 209
King, Martin Luther 4
Kipling, Rudyard 38, 54, 206
Kitch, Edmund 53n
Koch, Charles 11, 12, 14, 16, 20,
    22, 39, 49, 82, 101, 216
Koch, David 11, 16, 20, 49, 82,
    216
Koch family 10–11, 243
Koch, Fred 243
Kolbert, Elizabeth 80n
Koinonia (Georgia) 218
Kolbert, Elizabeth 80n
Korea, war of 47
    South 140n, 146, 173n
Kristol, Irving 40, 47
Krugman, Paul 148–9
Kruse, Kevin M. 242n
Kuhn, Thomas 196
Kyrgyzstan 173n

La Boétie, Étienne de 121–2
labour-intensive technologies
    135
*Ladrillo (El)* 25–6
Laffer's curve 40
LaHaye, Tim, *Left Behind* novels
    244
Laika, canine astronaut 166n
Lambe, Claude R. 12n
Landes, Elisabeth 56
Landes, Elisabeth and Posner,
    Richard, 'The Economics of
    the Baby Shortage' 61–3
Laos 173n
Lapham, Lewis H. 253

Latin America 145, 162, 234
  annihilating of Left in 25
  judicial coups 132–3
  Pentecostalism in 37, 239
*Lau v. Nichols* (1974) 217
Laumonier, Alexandre 247n,
  249n
Lavinas, Lena 69n
Law and Economics 51–60, 90,
  116, 117, 196, 233
  and Coase's 'Letter to the
    Gentiles' 53–4
  and corporate law 56–7
  definitions 51
  and Federalist Society 58–9
  and foundations 216–17
  and free baby market 60–5
  impact of on our world 60
  and Olin Foundation 56–7, 58
  and 'optimum pollution'
    concept 53–6
  research corpus 56
  summer schools organized by
    the LEC 57
  and universities 58
Law and Economics Centre
  (LEC) 56, 57
Lazzarato, Maurizio 141–3,
  151–2, 155
Lazarsfield, Paul 223n
Lee, Stuart 63n
left x
  annihilating of in Latin
    America 25
  attack of the ruling class on
    ideas of 7n
  and capitalism 213
  electoral base of the 223–4

ideological war against the 3,
  17
and intellectuals 222–3, 224
view of neoliberalism 29
Lenin, Vladimir 200, 216
Leopardi, Giacomo 161n
Levellers 7
liberalism
  classical 28, 29, 103, 127
  rupture between
    neoliberalism and 29–30
libertines 220, 236–9
life expectancy 184
Lippmann, Walter 27, 118–19
  *An Inquiry into the Principles
    of the Good Society* 118
  *Vanity Fair* article (1930) 118,
    119
lobbying/lobbyists 112–13, 118
London 7
  Stock Exchange 245
Lott, John, *More Guns, Less
    Crime* 43–4
Louis XVI, King vii
Louisiana 74
*Loving v. Virginia* (1967) 217
Lucas, Robert 23
Ludlow mine (Colorado) 80–1
Lula da Silva, Inácio 69, 70, 118,
  133
Lyon, massacre of *canuts* (1831)
  160

MacArthur, General Douglas 47
Machiavelli, Niccolò 228, 232–3,
  236, 239
McCloskey, Deirdre 38, 54,
  170n, 195

Macpherson, C.B. 89n
McGann, James G. 18n
McKenna Foundation 8
McKinnon, Andrew M. 249n
McNamara, Robert 144
Madison, James 113
Magna Carta (1215) 109
Malaysia 173n
managerial perspective 12–13
Mancunian school 171n
Mandeville, Bernard de 228
Manhattan Institute 19–20, 42, 43
Manne, Henry 56, 57, 194
Mansfield, Harvey 49
Mansfield Program on Constitutional Government 49
market economy, relationship between environmental problems and 166–9
market equilibrium 165
market(s)
   bull and bear 250n
   and classical economic theory 30
   environmental 167
   as God 249, 252
   infallibility of 166–7
   and neoliberalism 30, 166
   passivity of during crises 108–9
   politics as a 112, 116, 118, 120
   and religion 248–52
   and the state 103–4
marriage, neoliberal economics of 34–5
Marshall Plan 145

Martínez, Gustavo Álvarez 238
Marx, Groucho 215
Marx, Karl 90, 202, 228, 247–8
   Fragment on Machines 180
   on public debt 136–8
   rationalism of 202
Marxist materialism 228–9
Masaniello, revolt in Naples (1647) 123
Mastercard 139
Master Change 139
mathematical metaphor 197
mathematics/mathematical modelling 195–6
Mattis, James 21
Maxwell's equations 97
Mayer, Jane 14n, 39n, 46n, 48n, 52n, 216n
Mayer, John 48n, 52n
Mayflower, ship 234
mechanics, as metaphor 169–70
Medema, Steven G. 197n
Meese, Edwin 58
Meir, Rabbi 209
Mellon, Andrew 79
Mellon Scaife family 8, 15
Mellon Scaife Foundation 8, 79
Mellon Scaife, Richard 8–9
Mercantile Exchange (Chicago) 249
Mercatus Center 22, 49, 167, 209, 211
merchants 160
Mercurio (El) 27
mergers 56
metaphors 210–11
Metropolitan Museum of Art (New York) 82

Mexico 173n
  debt crisis 144–5
Miami (Florida) 56
Michael, Robert T. 33n
Michéa, Jean-Claude 185–6
Michelin, guide 191
Michigan 8
Midwest 7–11, 14
  billionaires from 20, 38, 46,
    88, 126
migration/migrants 32–3
Milan (Italy), massacre in (1898)
    160
military 47
military bases 226–7
Miller, John 6n, 42, 45n, 46n,
    52n, 214n
Mises, Ludwig von 26, 27, 44,
    49, 89n, 118n
  Institute 253, 346n
Mississippi 74
Missouri 3, 8
MIT (Massachusetts Institute of
    Technology) 48, 82
Mobil Oil 15
Modern Times (film) 158
Moncada, barracks (Cuba) 7
Mont Pelerin Society 27, 89n,
    118
Montaigne, Michel de 121
Montini, Giovanni Battista see
    Paul VI
Moody's 148, 150
Moore, Stephen 16n
Moral Majority 245
morality 235
Morgan, Enid Cassandra 187
mortgages 138–9, 140

Moshakis, Alex 168n
mother-child relationship 35
motor vehicles, billions of 164
Mozambique 148n
Müntzer, Thomas revolt of
    (1525) 123
Murgia, Madhumita 129n
Murray, Charles 191–2
  The Bell Curve 43
  Losing Ground 42, 43, 91
musician as entrepreneur 210
Mutual Life, insurance 242
Myanmar 173n
Myrdal, Gunnar 23, 24–5, 189
myth 100
  function of 97

Nader, Ralph 5
NAFTA (North America Free
    Trade Agreement) 173n
narrative 2
National Association of
    Manufacturers 242
National Prayer Breakfast 238
National Review, The 24n, 45,
    70n
natural law 97, 100
Naughton, John 131n
Nazism 229
negative tax 67–9
neoliberalism/neoliberals 25–31,
    101, 161
  and Chile 26
  and Chinese model 171, 175
  and classical liberalism 127
  coining of phrase 118
  and competition 30
  and debt 143–4

and enterprises 30–1
and entrepreneurship 203–4,
 206
features of 28–9
and Friedman 27–8
goal of 101–2
and human capital 31–4
ideal work relationship for
 163
importance of ideology to 219
importance of judiciary to
 216–19
importance of justice to 59
individuals seen as their own
 manager 31
legitimization by Nobel prize
 for economics 25
and markets 30, 166
and new technological
 panorama 130–5
power of discourse and non-
 challenging of 193
and religion 234–6, 247
roots of US-Chicago 26–7
rupture between liberalism
 and 29–30
and slavery 191
and the state 28, 101–6, 173,
 175
suppression of privacy 175–6
understanding of politics 120
Netherland 140n
New Deal 40, 41, 68, 73, 138–9,
 242
New Democrats 91
New Labour 91
newspeak 225
Newton, Isaac 97, 169

New York City
 attack on Twin Towers 48,
  109, 160
 Puerto Rican *barrio* 43
New York state 44, 80
*New York Times* viii, ix, 16–17,
 27, 51, 52n, 148n, 149n, 212,
 231n
New York University 44
*New Yorker* 80n, 83n
New Zealand 173n
NGOs 41
Niagara Falls, mercury into 82
Nicholas II, Tsar vii
Nietzsche, Friedrich, *Genealogy
 of Morals* 251, 252
Nirvana, entry into 209
Nixon, Richard 5, 6, 8, 61, 243
Nobel, Alfred 24
Nobel prize for economics 23,
 24, 25
North Carolina 8
North, Douglass 206–9, 210,
 219
No Vax campaign 75
Nozick, Robert 20, 39, 101, 184,
 186
Numa Pompilius 236
numbers 194–5
 fascinating power of 194

Obama, Barack 17, 245
Occupy Wall Street 247
Ocean Reef Club 57
October Revolution 230
Odessa (Ukraine) 187
OECD 99, 106, 146
Ohio 74

Olasky, Marvin, *The Tragedy of American Compassion* 44
oligarchies viii
oligopolies 130, 194
Olin Center for Inquiry into the Theory and Practice of Democracy 46
Olin Corporation 44
Olin Foundation 3–4, 6, 28, 44–6, 47, 56
  beachhead strategy 45–7
  financing of universities 58
  and Law and Economics 56–7, 58
Olin Institute for Strategic Studies (Harvard) 48
Olin, John Merrill 3–4, 61, 81
Omaha (Nebraska) 150
optimal/optimum pollution 54–6, 169, 229
optimism of intellect 214–15
ordo-liberals 28, 176–7, 178, 246
Orwell, George 180
  *1984* 225
*Outer Space Treaty* 166
Oxford University 83–4
OxyContin 82–3
ozone hole 163

PACS (Political action committees) 116–17
Paine, Thomas, *Common Sense* 101
Pakistan
  income tax 99, 184
  rating 148n
Palme, Olof 24
Panopticon 128

parent power 72–5
Parent Trigger laws 72, 74–5
Paris 7
  Agreement on Climate (2015) 17
  neolib meeting (1938) 118
'Paris Club' 144
*Partido dos Trabalhadores* (Brazil) 133
patriarchy 93
Paul of Tarsus 52
Paul VI, Pope 37n
Pavlov, Ivan 179
Pecquet, Gary 169n
Pentecostalism 37, 253
  in Latin America 239
Pepsi Cola 180, 212
perversity 42, 43–4, 47, 175
pessimism of the intellect 61
Peterloo Massacre (1819) 160
Petraeus, General 1, 225
Pfizer, corporation 15, 57
Philadelphia 240
philanthropy 44, 226
Philip Morris 5, 15
Philippines 173n
Phillips-Fein, Kim, *Invisible Hands* 11
Piereson, James 44, 45n, 46, 51–2
Piketty, Thomas 221, 224
Pinkerton, detective agency 80
Pinochet, Augusto 25, 27, 28, 69, 90, 175
Pittsburgh 8, 80
Piven, Frances Fox 116n
Planck, Max 169
plastic, production of 164

Plato 50n
plebs 119, 121, 185, 224, 229
    roman 123 232, 236
    tribunes of 123 224
Plehwe, Dieter 27n
pluralism, political 175
Poe, Edgar Allan 210
Poland 161
Polanyi, Karl 118n
Polanyi, Michael 118n
political economy 30, 32
political liberalism 29–30
political power 6–7
politics 112–25
    aim of 112
    and corruption 119–20
    as a market 112, 116, 118, 120
    neoliberal understanding of
        120
    and the privatization of the
        brain 120–5
    and rational choice theory
        113–16
pollution 183
    air 167
    and Olin's factories 81–2
    optimum/optimal 53–6, 169,
        229
Polybius 236
Pongide, Cobol 165n
Pontificia Universidad Católica
    de Chile 26
Pope, Art 12n
Popper, Karl 27
population, increase in 164
pornography, social *see* social
    pornography
positive tax 67

Posner, Richard 60, 63, 85–6,
    187, 191
    *Economic Analysis of Law* 57
    'The Regulation of the Market
        in Adoptions' 63–5
poverty/poor 42, 43
    absolute 68
    and negative tax 67–8
    relative 68
Powell Jr, Lewis F., *Attack on
    American Free Enterprise
    System* memo (1971) 4–5,
    6–7
Powell, Lewis 215–16
Powell Memorandum (1971)
    4–7, 117
power 159
    difference between dominion
        and 220
    disciplinary 127–8, 129, 142,
        163
    and domination 220
    euphemism as technology of
        225
    political 6–7
    remote-controlling 128–9
    technology of 127
    transformation of sovereign
        power to disciplinary 127–8
Prince, Eric 72
privacy, suppression of by
        neoliberals 175–6
privatization
    of the brain 120–5
    of education 66–7, 70–2
    of our lives 150
    of social security 17, 20
Procter & Gamble 15

production model (von Hayek)
    13–14
profit 115, 156, 185, 189
progress 161–3
    crimes carried out in the
        name of 162
proletariat 32
prostitution 185–6
psychic income 199
psychoanalysis, and
    utilitarianism 201–2
Public Choice Center 12n
Purdue Pharma 82–3

quantitative easing 108–9
quantitative studies 196
quantum physics 202
QZone, social medium 194

Rabin, Yitzhak 245
racial segregation 218
racism
    and free baby market
        proposal 64–5
    and housing 73
    monetary component of US
        73
    and Parent Power campaign
        73
Radden Keefe, Patrick 83n
radical indifference 156–7
Rapture 240
ratings agencies 147–50
rational choice 113, 199–200,
    202, 248
rationalism 201–2
Ratzinger, Joseph (Pope
    Benedict XVI) 61

reactionary discourse, rhetorical
    devices as foundational to
    42–4
Reagan, Ronald 15, 41, 244, 245
RECEP (Regional
    Comprehensive Economic
    Partnership) 173n
Red Army 230
Redford, Robert 244
reform, seen as a threat today
    226
Regent University 244
Reich, Robert 76n, 81n, 84n, 85n,
    113, 118
relative poverty 68
religion(s) 36–7, 189, 235–53
    beneficial effects 237
    and capitalism 239–42, 247–8
    drop in Catholic vocations
        after Second Vatican
        Council 36–7
    economy of 248–9
    as a governance tool 236
    libertine use of 236–8
    and market 248–52
    National Prayer Breakfast 238
    and neoliberalism 234–6, 247
    and Romans 236
    as a start-up 36
remote-control society 126–35
remote working 134
revisionists 230–1
revolution(s) vii–viii, 122–3,
    230–1, 232
Rice, Condoleezza 21
Richardson, Randolph 10
Ridley, Frank 177
Riker, William H. 113n, 114, 115n

Rivière, Pierre 34
*robber barons* 78, 80
Roberts, John 117
Roberts, Keith 177
Robertson, Dennis H. 30–1
Robertson, Pat 244
Robespierre, Maximilien 230
Robinson, Joan 198
Rockefeller, David 47n
Rockefeller
   family 44, 241
   Foundation 4, 77, 78
Rockefeller, John 80–1, 160, 243
Rockwell, industries 9
*Roe v. Wade* (1973) 64, 217
Rolland, Romain 214
Romano, Roberta 56n
Romans, ancient 227, 236n
   and religion 236
Roncaglia, Alessandro 28n
Roosevelt, Franklin Delano
   138–9, 242
Roosevelt, Theodor 80
Röpke, Wilhelm 176, 178–9,
   246n
Rotten Kid Theorem 200–1
Rougier, Louis 118n
Rousseau, Jean-Jacques xi, 70–1,
   78, 90, 185, 229
Royal College of Art (London)
   82
Royal Opera House (London)
   82
Rueff, Jacques 118n
Rushmore, Mount (Dakota) 15
Russell Sage Foundation 78
Russia 105, 122, 194, 221
Rüstow, Alexander 118

Sackler family 82–4
sacrifice, act of egoism 36, 114,
   115, 199
Sadat, Anwar el 238
Sade, Donatien-Alphonse-
   François, Marquis de 210
Sage, Russell Foundation 78
Saint-Just, Louis Antoine 230
Saint Peter, basilic (Rome) 160
Saint Petersburg 7
SALT (Strategic Arms Talks)
   245
Saltville (Virginia) 82
*sans-culottes* vii
Sarah Scaife Foundation 8, 9
Sargent, Greg ix
Sassen, Saskia 110
Satan, communist 243
Savage, John 9n
Scaife-Mellon family 8, 15, 224
   Foundation, 8–9, 11, 19, 21, 22,
   28, 58, 77, 79
   industries 157
Scalia, Antonin 21, 49, 102, 130
Scherer, Michael 17n
school vouchers 66–7, 71, 72,
   184
Schor, Juliet B. 140n
Schrödinger, Erwin 202
*Schuld see* guilty, debt
Schultz, Theodore W. 23, 31n
Schumpeter, Joseph A. 205–6
Schweizerische Kreditanstalt 27
Scofield, Cyrus Ingerson 239–40
Scofield Reference Bible 239–40
sea level rise 163
Searle, pharmaceutical company
   15

Sears and Roebuck 15, 242

Second Vatican Council 36–7

Senate, US 39, 84, 112

September 11 (2001) 48, 109, 160

Sharlet, Jeff 238n

Shell, corporation 57

*Shelley v. Kraemer* (1948) 217

Shultz, George 21

Shylock 97

Sicily 221

Siddharta *see* Buddha

Sieyès, Abbot Emmanuel Joseph 330

Simon, William 6, 28, 161, 222
  *Time for Truth* 28

Singapore 48, 173n

Sjaastad, Larry A. 32n

Skype 133

Slater, Alice 227n

slavery 186–90, 231
  economic advantages of 187, 189
  and human capital 190–1
  neoliberals' fascination with 191

smart working 134

Smith, Adam 86, 166, 190, 228
  *The Wealth of Nations* 30

SmithKline Beecham 15

Smith Richardson family 8, 9–10, 15, 157

Smith Richardson Foundation 9, 19, 21, 40, 42, 48

Snowden, Edward 130

social Darwinism 203

social justice 27, 52, 88–9, 90, 100

social media 194

social pornography 183–92, 215

social security 41
  privatization of 17, 20

society 101
  crusade against 89

Solo, Robert A. 67n

Sombart, Werner 205–6

South Dakota 15

South Fork Fishing and Hunting Club 79–80

Southern Baptist Convention 245

'Southern Strategy' 73–4

sovereign power 127

Soviet Union 182
  collapse of 29, 146, 151, 182

space exploration 165–6

Spain 32, 74
  debt level 140n
  homicide rate 99

Spicer, André 210n

Spinoza, Baruch 95, 96

Stalin, Joseph 161, 230

Standard & Poor 148, 149–50

Standard Oil 242

Stanford University 82, 196

Stark, Rodney 36, 37

start-up religions 36

'starve the beast' 39

state
  attacks on and dismantling campaign against 28, 38–44, 76, 90–1, 101
  and crises 108–10
  extending the business model to all sectors of society 104–5
  and free enterprise 111

'frugal' 39, 40, 172
functioning like a private
    company 105–6
and globalization process 102
liberal view of 103
and markets 103–4
and multinational companies
    103, 110
and neoliberalism 28, 101–6,
    173, 175
religion and maintaining
    cohesion of 237
'state phobia' 40
State Farm, insurance 57
State Street Global Advisors
    (Ssga) 150
statistical thermodynamics
    169–70
steam toys in the antiquity 135
Stein, Rob 212
Steiner, Jürg 114n
Stigler, George 23, 27, 38n, 61,
    89, 170, 187, 189, 197, 208
    'Economics – The Imperial
    Science?' 37–8
    'The Optimum Enforcement
    of Laws' 55
stock exchanges 249
Stoléru, Lionel 67–8
Storr, Virgil Henry 209n
Strauss, Leo 49
student debt 140–3
student loans 142–3
Suharto, Indonesian dictator 238
Summers, Larry 168–9
supply-side economics 40
surveillance 128–9, 176
    digital 180

and facial recognition 129
surveillance capitalism 130–2
Sweden 24, 98
Swedish Central Bank 24
Swift, Jonathan, Modest
    Proposal 63
symbolic violence 93, 152
Szilárd, Gertrud Weiss 181n
Szilárd, Leó 181

Taft, President 80
Tammany Hall 119
Tate Gallery (London) 82
tautologies 198–203
tax havens 103, 229
taxes/taxation 39–40, 184
    cuts in 39, 40
    foundations and exemption
    from 76–8, 87
    myth of beneficial effects of
    reducing 99
    negative 67–9
    and war in feudal times 109
Taylor, Leon 169n
Tea Party movement 11
technology(ies)
    of control 129, 159
    neoliberal ideologies and new
    130–5
    nomadic nature of new 133
    of power 127
Tel Aviv, University 82
'teleschool' 74
Teles, Steven M. 57n, 60n, 61n,
    233n
televangelists 244–5
Temple University 240n
Tennessee 239

Terror (French revolution) 230
*Termitenstaat* 176–7, 178–80
termites 176–7, 178–80
Texas 74, 217
Thailand 173n
Thatcher, Margaret x, 18, 27, 41,
    100
theoretical pornography 191–2
'There Is No Alternative'
    ideology 126
Thermidorians 230
Thessaloniki (Greece) 150
think tanks 13, 14–22, 40, 167,
    210, 216, 253
  aim of 19
  attack on the state 42
  and Britain 18
  financing of by billionaire
    families 21, 22
  influence on Trump and
    Reagan 15–17
  worldwide numbers 18
  *see also* Heritage Foundation
Third World 162
Thomas, Clarence 117
Thrasymachus 50
'three imposters' 236–7
Tietmeyer, Hans 104
tracking devices 129
trade unions 241
trade wars 173–4, 175
Traub, James 185n
treaties, commercial 173
Trichet, Jean-Claude 48n
Trilateral Commission 47–8n
Troika, financial 147
Trump, Donald ix–x, 15–17, 59,
    72, 173n, 235, 245

and Freedom Partners 16–17
and Heritage Foundation
    15–16
comparison with Reagan
    15–17
TTIP (Transatlantic Trade and
    Investment Partnership)
    173n
Tunisia 148n
Turkey, coups 132
Twin Towers *see* New York
'two-step flow' theory 223n

Uber drivers 163, 187
UK *see* Britain
Ultra-High Net Worth
    Individuals (UHNWI)
    94–5
underclass 220
Union Carbide 15
Union Pacific 15
United Nations 9
United Nations Office on Drugs
    and Crime 99n
United States 41, 71, 81, 85, 92,
    95n, 113, 123, 144, 173n
  Christian conservatives in the
    235, 239, 240, 252
  constitution 26
  empire imposed on the world
    8–9, 54n, 226–7
  healthcare spending 98
  homicides rate 99
  power and bases 226–7
  number of think tanks 18
  public deficit 40
  status of debt 153–4
  tax cuts 40

universities 6, 7, 13
  campus as battlefield for the
    war on ideas 44–9
  and conservative beachhead
    strategy 44–6
  credit system 104–5
  fees for British 186
  financing of by foundations
    44–9, 58
  and Law and Economics 58
  tuition fees 141
University of Chicago 23, 44,
    52–3
  conservative beachhead
    strategy 45–6
Urban Missionary Conferences
    243
US Army/Marine Corps
    Counterinsurgency Field
    Manual 1–2
US Senate, average cost of
    winning a seat 112
US Supreme Court 116
Utica (New York) 80
utilitarianism 201
utility 194, 198–9, 201
utility function 194, 202

vaccinations, campaign against
    compulsory 75
Vague, Richard 154n
Valencia (Spain) 150
Vanguard Group 149–50
Vanity Fair 118, 119
Vegetti, Matteo 102
Vicks VapoRub 9, 157
Vietnam 4, 144, 145
Vines, Jerry 245

violence, symbolic 93, 152
Virginia 5, 8, 56, 82, 217
Visa 139
VKontakte, social medium 194
Vogel, Kenneth P. 238n
Volcker Foundation 44, 52
Volcker, Paul 48n
Voltaire 126
vouchers, education 66–7, 71,
    72

Wall Street 247, 249
Wall Street Journal 8, 10n, 91
'wallet on the right, heart on the
    left' 215
Walsh, Frank 81
Walton family 8, 11, 71–2
Wanniski, Jude, The Way the
    World Works 40
war, and competition 193
Washington Consensus 157
Washington D.C. 113, 153, 253
Washington Post ix, 59n
Watanuki, Joji 47
wealth gap 221
Weber, Max 239
Weber, William 210n
Weiss Szilárd, Gertrude 181n
welfare state 20, 68
  attack on 23, 41, 43, 44
  negative tax as first step
    towards abolition of 70
Welles, Orson 149
Wells, H.G. 177
WhatsApp 133
'White Terror' 230
Wilson, Edward Osborne 115
Winchester gun factory 44

Wisconsin 8, 9, 243
Winter Palace (Saint
    Petersburg) 7, 159
Wojtyla, Karol *see* John Paul II
Woolf, Virginia 210
work, changing of relationship
    with through perpetual
    reachability 133−4
workers' movement 241−2
World Bank 145
    rise in loans 144

World Trade Center (New
    York) 160

Yahweh 96
Yale University 48, 58
Yang, Yuan 129n

Zia-ul-Haq, Muhammad 245
Zinn, Howard 81n
Zuboff, Shoshana 130, 131n, 132,
    134, 156−7, 179